Northern Ireland in Crisis

Northern Ireland in Crisis

Reporting the Ulster Troubles

SIMON WINCHESTER

Holmes & Meier Publishers Inc.

Published in the USA in 1975 by
Holmes & Meier Publishers, Inc.
101 Fifth Avenue, New York. N.Y. 10003
Printed in Great Britain by
Butler and Tanner Limited, Frome and London

Copyright © 1974 by Simon Winchester

941. 6
Wi

Library of Congress Cataloging in Publication Data

Winchester, Simon
  Northern Ireland in crisis; reporting the Ulster troubles

  1. *Northern Ireland—History—1969*   I. *Title*
DA990.U46W54   *941.609*   *74–84649*

ISBN 0-8419-0180-5

This book is published in the U.K.

under the title *In Holy Terror*

To Jan Morris

Acts of injustice done
Between the setting and the rising sun
In history lie like bones, each one.

W. H. AUDEN

Contents

Maps

Preface

Acre for acre, Ireland has probably suffered more books than any other country on earth. Thus I hesitated long before offering yet another. The eventual excuse I made to myself when I took the final plunge was that what I would be writing about as much concerned the life of a working reporter as it did the twists and turns of Irish politics. The book that results, then, is no attempt to analyse or to solve the tortuous mysteries of Ireland, North or South. It is merely a highly subjective account of thirty months that were always exciting and on occasion fairly uncomfortable and which, so far as I am concerned, will never be forgotten.

It is quite impossible, as any other newspaper scribbler knows, to please everybody. Northern Ireland is almost unique in being a country where it is reasonably easy to please nobody. While I was there reporting for the *Guardian*—and my experiences have been mirrored time and again by other and more experienced reporters—I managed to survive threatened executions by the IRA and promised 'romper room' excursions with the militant Loyalists; I displeased by turns the army, the RUC, the Stormont Government, the Stormont Opposition, the Protestants, the Catholics, the moderates, the extremists; and angered readers and non-readers in Manchester, Milwaukee, Moneymore and Magherafelt and many other places besides. So I am moderately fearful that in this innocent chronicle I shall displease them all once again; my only hope is that they are not angered by any gross inaccuracies for which, of course, I am solely responsible.

Any reporter in a situation like the Northern Irish troubles comes to rely enormously on the inevitable camaraderie of his colleagues; and while most of those colleagues have now departed, as I have, to outposts of supposed significance, the help they gave me during my time in Belfast remains invaluable still.

First, of course, must come my own dear colleagues on the *Guardian*. Simon Hoggart, who spent some five years in Ulster, compared to my paltry two and a half, gave me the huge benefits of his experience, his understanding and his interpretation. To him my debt is vast. Derek Brown's memory for the minutiae was near legendary; and Gill Linscott's tireless energies still amaze those who followed in her trails.

I must thank in particular the staff of the *Irish Times* office in Belfast—from the days of Fergus Pyle in early 1970, through the hard-nosed times of Henry Kelly to the easy competence of Renagh Holohan and Martin Cowley. No other single group could offer more advice and help than did those four eternally friendly and unforgettable chums.

Others deserve my thanks for their help and advice. Robert Fisk of the London *Times* remains a model of enthusiasm. Alf Macreary and Barry White on the *Belfast Telegraph* were always helpful. The staff of the Linen Hall Library in Belfast, surely one of the most comfortable and congenial repositories of scholarship left, filled in all the gaps that endless conversations with newspaper friends could not.

In my subsequent labours, the army has been of unique assistance. Not all who offered their help and advice would wish to be identified: but of those who allow their names to be published, Lt-Colonel Tony Yarnold and Colin Wallace must head the list of suppliers of the myriad of facts and figures and other information. Their advice and suggestions had a value that cannot be overstated. The RUC press officers have been, as always, genially helpful.

At Stormont Castle, two figures stand out, as they did during the reporting days for me and almost every other newsman— Tom Roberts and David Gilliland. Their perpetual kindness in providing tireless explanations of their points of view, and in ferreting out the most recondite of facts, places a hundred reporters in their eternal debt.

The *Guardian* has shown superb tolerance and understanding. I must thank Harry Whewell and George Hawthorne of the Northern News Desk for first sending me to Belfast—and then for having enough faith to send me back, again and again. The present staff of the Foreign Desk have shown great forbearance during the inevitable diversions this writing has caused from

Watergate reporting. And the Editor, Alastair Hetherington, is to be thanked for providing both encouragement and the necessary permission to quote extensively from the paper's news and features columns.

And lastly to those who helped in the final preparations. Mary Wade, who took valuable time off from a pressing job to complete a lengthy chunk of typing; to Nigel Wade (no relation) who read and criticised some of the manuscript; and my wife Judy who, by virtue of much self-discipline and many cups of coffee, managed to have the entire manuscript typed, numbered and boxed for the mails precisely on time. Without her, as the saying so adeptly puts it, this book could never have been written.

Washington, June, 1974.

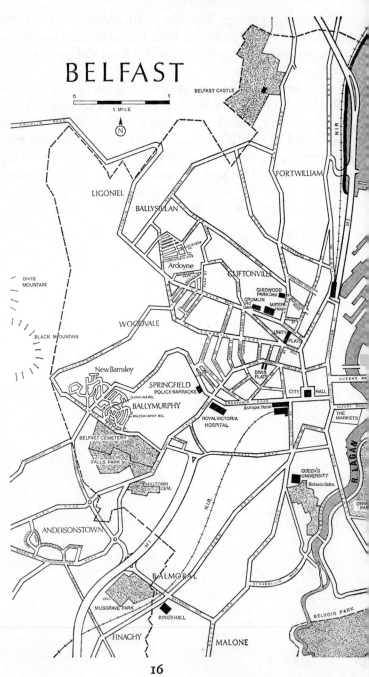

BELFAST

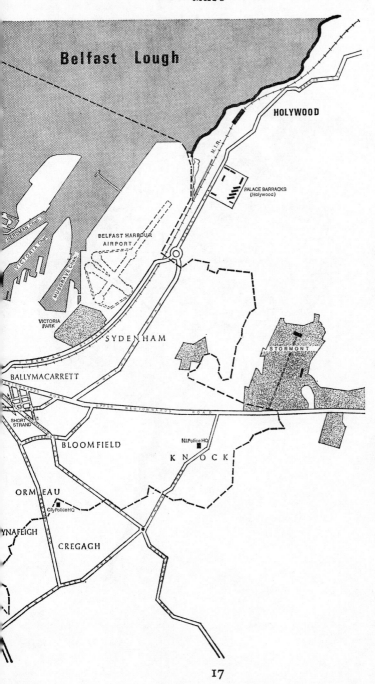

Belfast Lough

HOLYWOOD

N.I.R.

PALACE BARRACKS
(Holywood)

BELFAST HARBOUR
AIRPORT

HARLAND CH'N'L

VICTORIA Ch'n'l

MUSGRAVE Ch'n'l

VICTORIA
PARK

SYDENHAM

STORMONT

BALLYMACARRETT

UPPER NEWTOWNARDS ROAD

SHORT
STRAND

BLOOMFIELD

N.I.Police HQ

KNOCK

ORMEAU

City Police HQ

YNAFEIGH

CREGAGH

17

ULSTER

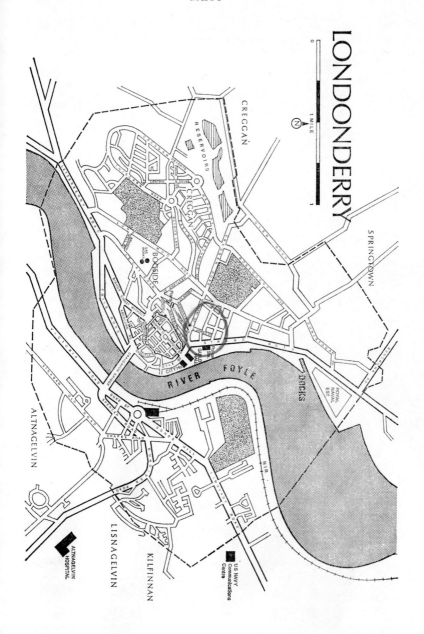

I

Introduction

My marching orders arrived with just the measure of courtesy, tact and lovable lack of organisation that one comes to expect of a newspaper like the *Guardian*. 'I say, old chap,' the Deputy News Editor pleaded down the telephone. 'I know it's frightfully inconvenient, what with your house and everything, but the fact is, our only other man is off sick. Do you think you could possibly slip over to Belfast for a couple of days for us? It would be such a help.'

I was in a phone booth in the Five Bridges Hotel in Gateshead. It was just after midday on Friday, April 17, 1970, and I was just about to write what I fondly thought was going to be the best story of my life. It was going to be about that morning's visit of our then Prime Minister, Harold Wilson, to a chilly and rather lifeless housing estate perched on the banks of the Tyne above the old coaling staithes at Dunston. I had even spoken to Mr. Wilson —easily the grandest thing accomplished in the six weeks I had been working as the *Guardian*'s North-East England correspondent. And not only did I have an interview—I had colour, wit, any number of interesting and informative snippets of news from the assembled burghers of Gateshead town council: it was going to be a vintage Northern yarn, and the news desk was bound to be keen. So, eagerly anticipating the welcoming tones of the Desk, I rang Manchester.

The reception was a little less than rapturous. 'Drop whatever it is you're doing, lad,' said George Hawthorne, the genial little Mancunian who manned the desk on alternate Fridays. He apologised graciously for what he had to do, told me to get off to Ulster and added that I would find all the tickets, and some money, at the airline desk at Newcastle Airport. Four hours later I was on my way.

The journey from Tyneside to Laganside, on the ancient and shuddery Viscounts which North-East Airlines operated between the two shipbuilding capitals, was one I would soon come to know as well as the trip to the local. We would take off over the flat coal country of East Northumberland, head westwards along Hadrian's Wall, over the Pennines at Hexham and Haydon Bridge and Haltwhistle, pass over Carlisle and the Eden Valley and leave the English coast at Workington. Flying over the Solway Firth and the Irish Sea there would be the low hills of Galloway and the snowy peaks of Argyll on the right, the nose of Snaefell and the sandy beaches of the Isle of Man to the left. One hour exactly and we would begin to wind downwards, crossing Ireland at Donaghadee, passing down the Lough streaming with coasters and tankers and ferries and pilot boats, circling over the grime and dust of Belfast herself before flattening out over the plateau above and to the north-west of the capital city and landing with a bump and a screech on the tarmac at Aldergrove.

Back in 1970 the planes were filled with businessmen and girlfriends, students, holidaymakers, boilermakers on exchange trips, Americans hunting their forefathers, scientists off to seminars at Queen's or farmers off to look at a new bull. Reporters were a rarity; soldiers could always be spotted because of their short hair and white necks; but there were few of them.

By next summer one could rarely travel on the planes to Belfast without seeing a reporter with his typewriter, a soldier with his forty-eight-hour pass or a grim-faced father or aunt or cousin of another Belfast victim. But in 1970, and especially on the day I first flew across the Solway Firth, the plane was filled like a normal plane and there was nothing much to indicate we were anything other than perfectly normal people going from one to another perfectly normal country.

Not that my neighbour on that first flight was totally unremarkable. His name was Michael Curran—M. J. M. Curran, his card read, and it was a week or two before I learned his first name—and he was a reasonably prominent member of the Ulster establishment. His father, I learned later, was a High Court judge in Belfast; and the family had been bound up in a curious little tragedy some years before when his sister was found murdered. It was the first murder in Ulster for many years, and it created a major sensation. So here I was, accepting whiskies, cigarettes—and, it turned out, a lift in a snappy little sports car—from a man whose family had been the victims of one of the most notorious and mysterious crimes perpetrated in Northern Ireland. Perhaps the plane wasn't so full of normal folk, after all: perhaps, looking back on it, meeting Michael Curran was an omen of sorts.

The first journey down across the hills to the city was an enthralling adventure—the green of the fields around Aldergrove airport, the small whitewashed cottages and the immense feeling of Irishness—one couldn't call it anything else—washed over me as surely as if I had landed in Killashandra or Waterford or Skibbereen. Sure enough the road signs were the same H.M. Prisons manufacture and the telephones had the STD codes for London and Edinburgh and Moreton-in-Marsh; and the telephone boxes were red, not green, and the language was all English— but still, I thought to myself, as the little red Spitfire purred its way eastwards and to the edge of the escarpment, this is Ireland, not Britain any more.

The old airport road becomes the Crumlin Road without warning about five miles from the city centre. I had heard of the Crumlin, of course; and I was to hear of it again many, many times. Back in 1970 it was probably most famous for its gaol, one of the oldest in the country, a rival to Kilmainham and the Bridewell and the old Curragh camp for its potent political associations. Crumlin Road was famous, too, for the burnings and killings of the previous August, and names of Hooker Street and Disraeli Street somehow stuck in my mind as having erupted at least once during the weeks before.

Our first sight of Belfast came half an hour before sunset. The car swept around one of the wider curves on the upper reaches of the Crumlin Road, the BBC transmitting aerial, its flashing ribbon of red lights just turned on for the evening, appeared on the black and green hillside to the right; and then suddenly, the hillside fell away and we were running along the edge of a veritable cliff. Curran stood on his brakes and with a scrunch of gravel and a curse and a blast from an overloaded cattle lorry behind us, we swerved into a lay-by. The city that would be home for the next three years lay unrolled and glinting in the evening sunshine eight hundred feet below.

Like the views of Wallsend and Byker from the lower reaches of the Tyne, it's the houses that make the first impression. From up on the high hills you don't notice the suburbs and the supermarkets and the hotels; the elegant arcades and the wharves and the parks are details you might pick out with a telescope; but what you do see, and what strikes so very hard when looking at Belfast, are the row upon row of grimy, uninteresting, sorry and forgotten rows of workers' houses.

Long slated roofs gleamed purple in the slanting sun; the parallels and the concentric curves and the congruent intersections of the hundreds and hundreds of exactly similar roofs made the city look like a calming sea of reddened dust, with ripples and swirls of perfect geometricity ruffling an otherwise homogeneous surface. True, there were mounds of occasional interest peering out of the housing sea: there was the bright yellow Krupp crane in the shipyards, known as, and looking like, Goliath, a vast two-legged Panjandrum. There were the two spires of St. Peter's church in the Lower Falls and the ugly great grey monolith of the Divis Flats; there was a crane-encumbered transparent construction down beside where the railway lines merged into the city centre: it was later to become one of the world's most notorious hotels, the Belfast Europa.

There were the vivid blue patterns of dockland—the hammered steel curves of the Lagan widening out to the ship-crowded channels of Herdman and Pollock and Abercorn and Musgrave; there were grand buildings and near-castles and a marble birthday cake surrounded by more slab offices way, way over on the far horizon—Stormont, I would find out a good deal later. There were university spires and donkey cranes and smoking mill chimneys and corrugated-roofed factories and clattering railway bridges and the beginnings of a motorway on either side of the city that sprawled in the dying light.

But that first sight summed it all up: Belfast was a city of ter-

raced streets, miserable houses, outside privies and—I knew it
from eight hundred feet up—dehumanised, exploited, callous-
handed men and women—craftsmen, lace makers, hammer
handlers, crane drivers, welders, postmen, red lead experts,
cobblers, corner store owners, social workers, nurses, taxi
drivers, bus conductors, amateur bird fanciers, coughing old age
pensioners, tarty young shopgirls, couples whose wedding rings
had come from Woolworth's and who still lived upstairs with the
folks, women who wore bedroom slippers to the shops and who
took home a single piece of bacon and a pint of sterilised milk,
who read the *People* or the *Sunday Companion* and kept cats and
budgerigars and did the pools and smoked Weights and Park
Drive and drank beer from glasses.

That was Belfast from eight hundred feet: a city of so obviously
poor, hardworking and probably intensely proud and lovable
people, forced to live in damp, cramped, rotten, rat-ridden, dirty
and dying houses: houses they would adorn with all the glitter
and the tribal gaiety possible to stop the creeping doom of
community despair. I remember saying to Michael Curran,
before we got back into the car and zoomed downwards to street
level, that it wasn't too surprising the folks here rioted from time
to time—from up in the hills there seemed precious little else to do.

What brought reporters to Ireland in those terrible first days of
nascent civil war, had begun in the tiny village of Caledon, deep
in the untrodden green byways of County Tyrone. Few in
England had heard of Tyrone or Fermanagh, in much the same
way they were ignorant of Offaly and Roscommon and Laois. But,
given the pathological ignorance of the average Briton about the
average Irishman, there was less of an excuse never to have heard
of Tyrone—it was, after all, the home of Churchill's 'drear
steeples' that were forever to reappear to dog the English conscience: and it was, after all, superficially British. And it was more
than appropriate that Caledon, which is near-wholly Protestant,
but which has a drear steeple all of its own, should provide the
spark that lit the everdry tinder of the six-county countryside.

The Caledon incident, as it began in April and May of 1968, was a typical symptom of the moment. In a small housing estate on the outskirts of the little village was a small row of semi-detached houses called Kinnard Park. Since early spring, when the box-like homes were completed, a Catholic family named McKenna had been squatting in Number 9, and a Catholic family named Good-fellow had been squatting in Number 11. The families were there with the tacit encouragement of their Catholic MP, and were seen locally as symbols of the protest at the unfair practices of the local, Unionist-controlled, rural council—which traditionally denied houses to 'the rebels'.

It took some time for the slow-moving councils of the country to do anything about the little demonstration; but eventually, in early June, the McKennas were told to go and Number 9 was allocated, as the local council properly decided, to a Protestant. And not just any old Protestant: the council allocated the house to an unmarried 19-year-old secretary who, by her own good fortune and the McKennas'—and Ulster's—poor luck, worked for the man who was lawyer for the local Unionist councillor, and who himself was a parliamentary candidate in Armagh. Miss Emily Beattie, a girl whose role in history was to be minimal but crucial, was thus at the focus of a complicated spider's web of Loyalism: in the view of a Unionist council of the day she, unmarried, Protestant, secretary to a Protestant politician and a lawyer to boot, could scarcely have missed being given a house. Small wonder the Catholics, and especially those who, in spite of overflowing families, had been turned down again and again with ritualist contempt when they came to beg for a house—small wonder they felt bitter at Miss Beattie's fortune.

The case began to bring the television film crews down from Belfast. And on June 18, there was a minor drama when, in front of a throng of reporters and cameras, the Goodfellows were unceremoniously tossed out into the street. The first pictures of crisis began to appear on the nightly news.

The next day the local MP, the young, bright, talented, impetuous, wiry and enthusiastic Austin Currie, joined battle up at Stormont. The debate, which began at 2.41 p.m. on June 19, was essential reading for anyone coming to cover Ulster's troubles: it had all history there in one hour and one minute of bruising debate.

Currie raised the matter of the 'disgusting scene of yesterday' when the Goodfellow family were, as he put it, 'treated like pigs'. He had, he said, used all the traditional methods of protesting the unfairness of the case where an unmarried Protestant girl can get a house while an overburdened Catholic family cannot. 'I have come to the end of the road,' he said heavily.

Argument, some of the most heated in a Stormont debate for many years, started within moments of Currie sitting down. John Taylor, who was later to become a minister in government, told Currie he was 'wasting the time of this House' by arguing the issue. In the end, Currie was thrown out of Parliament for telling a Unionist member that his explanation of the allocation of Number 9 was 'a damned lie'. He went straight down from Stormont to Caledon, and down to Miss Beattie's house. Having survived an eviction from Stormont, he surmised, he could survive another from Kinnard Park.

Heading to a worthy cause like a bee to a honey pot, Austin Currie, with an accurate eye for the BBC copy-taster's sense of judgement and taste, arranged to occupy the girl's house, and for the event to be covered on television film. He sat in the house and waited: was told that what he was doing was illegal, waited, was served documents by officials and tea and soda bread by neighbours until, at last, in full view of the camera lenses, he was picked up by a policeman—Miss Beattie's brother in fact—and tossed out into the street. No policeman could have done a more senseless thing. That single act was to produce a watershed like none in Ireland before. Public feeling about Caledon, while not a roaring furnace in distant Belfast or Londonderry, and not noticed or cared about by the even more distant people in London and Liverpool, grew by the hour: meetings in pubs turned into masses on street corners and masses in churches. And masses in churches, with the priests and the politicians joining hands on a single issue, proved the necessary potency: a march was organised—a small affair that August, from Coalisland, a grim little pottery town which had probably supplied the bricks to build the Caledon houses, to Dungannon, where the civil rights group had its birth and its headquarters. It was a Saturday afternoon, it rained and yet 2,500 Tyrone and Fermanagh and Derry Catholics and a sprinkling of sympathetic Protestants and a handful of students of no relevant religious persuasion came and walked through the warm, wet, heavy Irish countryside, to sing 'We shall overcome'. Caledon had started something.

The obvious success of the first march prompted the organisers to try something grander still, and in the city where old grievances and generations of bigotry and hardened feeling had grown like a callous in the soft countryside—Londonderry on the river Foyle.

The march was planned for October 5, 1968; it was banned by the Minister of Home Affairs, Bill Craig; it went ahead, and there was terrible, terrible trouble. For the first time the men and women in England who watched the news that misty Saturday night with the day's football over and the teapot or the tankard dry, saw something they could never forget. They saw grim-faced policemen battering student girls to the ground—the constables with long batons, the officers with gnarled, shiny sticks known as blackthorns. They saw water cannons trundling through the streets firing volley after volley of cold water to smash through a crowd not very different from the crowds who gathered almost every weekend in Trafalgar Square or at Hyde Park. They saw that the policemen carried guns—long-muzzled revolvers on shiny leather belts with brass buckles—few can have known that any British policemen were armed. They saw a Westminster MP—or a man who was identified as such—named Gerry Fitt, being led away with blood streaming from a cut in his head, inflicted after a policeman had cut down on his skull with a heavy truncheon. They saw recognisable British MPs, who had gone across to Londonderry to observe a march whose origins they did not know and of whose repercussions they had no idea, seething with anger at the 'brutality' of the Royal Ulster Constabulary, as these police were named. And they saw notices with curiously African and Asian requests, like 'One Man—One Vote', a request they were sure had not been recently denied in the British Isles.

So Derry brought it all home to the British with a bang; and for the following years Ireland, and in particular the turbulent six north-eastern counties, rarely left them alone. From Derry in 1968 Ireland proceeded via O'Neill's downfall and Burntollet and Chichester-Clark's assumption of an uneasy power at Stormont to the horror and the killing of Derry and Belfast in August 1969—the events that finally brought the British soldiery back into Ulster in strength. But even this did not still the turmoil. The first policeman was shot dead, by Protestants, in October, shortly after the infamous order was given, on the recommendation of the ill-advised Everest mountaineer, Lord Hunt, to disarm the police and abandon that last line of Protestant defence, the 'B' Specials.

The first weeks of 1970, by the standards of the last weeks of 1969, were placid enough. For Northern Ireland, the spring seemed to be time for the regrouping of political factions, time for elections and electioneering, for the introduction to Ulster *realpolitik* of Ian Paisley and William Beattie, for the reaffirmation of public faith in Bernadette Devlin, as she then was, and for the birth of a small, ignored and then largely irrelevant-looking middle-of-the-road party known as Alliance. For those spring months were a time when, in the relative absence of bottles, bricks and bullets, the men and women on both sides of the abyss were becoming more vocal, winning more support for crisis politics. The birth of Alliance, a body of middle-class, middle-minded, middle-brow Ulstermen, seemed to run strangely counter to the political undercurrents, a sadly hopeless but game attempt to restore a touch of sanity to a rapidly worsening political situation.

As the men of words were regrouping and rethinking during those first weeks, so the men of the gun and the petrol bomb were also preparing themselves. The Provisionals, the most potent of all forces in the conflict, were beginning to creep out of Ulster's woodwork and into the bloodstream of the Catholic ghettos. Their appearance on the scene had been imminent for months, even years: the spark that brought them out and into action happened at the very beginning of April when, for the first time, Catholics and soldiers fought hand-to-hand: it was an unsettling moment for Ulster, and one which needs to be examined.

If the bitter guerilla war can be said to have its moment of violent birth at any one specific place, it was on a street corner on the Ballymurphy housing estate, a spider's web arrangement of concentric street circles jammed in between the slopes of Black Hill and the Belfast cemetery to the west of the city centre.

Ballymurphy is an almost wholly Catholic housing estate; it was built shortly after the end of the war and had been described by one student of the suburbs as 'the worst housing estate in the British Isles'. That was something of an exaggeration: Bally-murphy had its good aspects—one of them being the closeness of its people. There are estates in southern England, and some in Glasgow too, that enjoy more placid times, but where neighbours do not know each other and the children have nowhere to play and the wind howls along empty, grey concrete streets. One test of a housing estate's success is its suicide rate: Ballymurphy scarcely knew the meaning of the word, and might thus be termed, in sociological terms, among the best.

But, best or worst, it was to see the birth of the anti-English war that has characterised Ulster ever since. It began there on Easter Tuesday, April 1, 1970.

One of the traditions of the day after Easter Bank Holiday Monday in Northern Ireland is that the children of grown Orangemen have a day of marching and drumming and skirling all of their own: a sort of kindergarten Twelfth of July, a practice for the days ahead when as adult defenders of the glory of Ulster Protestantism, they would be asked to march for the hallowed memory of King William.

Easter Tuesday 1970 was the day the Junior Orangemen set off for Bangor, a brash, candyfloss and stale beer resort ten miles to the east of the city, on polluted but pleasant Belfast Lough. The marchers were in an unusually defiant mood that day, and spent a good two hours walking and counter-walking—for some reason marches here are known as walks, when they are anything but—along the upper part of the Springfield Road, the wide street that separates the Catholics of Ballymurphy from the Protestants of New Barnsley. The Ballymurphy people, who should have become accustomed by then to early morning drumming and piping from a Protestant crowd, began to get restive; and the army commander on the spot realised, rightly enough, that he ought to put a few infantrymen there for the evening once the Juniors returned to their homes. Some seventy battledressed men of the Scots Guards were accordingly dispatched to Ballymurphy to await developments.

They were certainly needed. Protestant bands coming home up the western arteries of Belfast were stoned and bottled and spat upon by angry Catholics who lined almost every foot of their progress. And in Ballymurphy, where Catholic protesters had gathered behind the Guards barricades, the stones flew thick and fast: for two hours there was a full-scale riot, between the two warring sides. The half company of Guardsmen could do little to prevent it starting, and were not given the necessary orders to bring it to an end.

But the next night was different. A full battalion was deployed in the Ballymurphy estate; a squadron of four-wheeled Humber one-ton armoured cars, with barbed wire coils mounted on their girder bumpers, appeared in support. And every infantryman was carrying, as well as his SLR and his riot shield and his baton, a small supply of gas cartridges, a stubby black Greener gun and, for close support work, a pocket full of CS gas grenades.

The show of force produced its own reaction: the Catholics in Ballymurphy tended to forget the New Barnsley marchers of the evening before; they concentrated simply on the soldiers. They pelted them with stones and bottles and lumps of paving and cast-iron gratings and drainpipes and stair-rods. Some soldiers fell back hurt; a few baton charges were tried, and failed. And then, late in the evening, the order to use gas was delivered from headquarters at Lisburn.

The one-and-a-half-inch cartridges were set in the breeches of a dozen guns, the guns were snapped shut, the barrels were aimed and in an instant, a dozen triggers were pulled. The gas billowed out through the Catholic mob; and what had been a tenuously bonded Catholic group, a mob of hooligans and housewives out for excitement on a spring evening of poor television, became, within moments, a choking, screaming, radicalised and almost totally solid political group.

CS gas has an unparalleled effect on its victims. Its physical effects are well enough known, and rarely forgotten. But its enormous power to weld a crowd together in common sympathy and common hatred for the men who gassed them, has never been measured or accurately evaluated. It was a questionable decision to use gas that April night. It was a decision that half-united the Ballymurphy people against the army. It was a decision that ultimately brought the gunmen of the IRA to act as the 'defenders' of the people. It was a decision that rendered the army no longer a peace-keeping force, but, in thousands upon thousands of Catholic eyes, an Army of Occupation.

One other ingredient was sprinkled into the Ulster stew in those early spring days—the Reverend Ian Richard Kyle Paisley and his Protestant Unionist Party.

Ian Paisley, variously called a bigoted demagogue and a brilliant potential saviour of all Ireland had been lurking on the fringes of Northern Irish politics for a decade: he had caused a riot in the Falls Road in 1964, he had pelted Terence O'Neill's car with snowballs once when the Stormont prime minister had displayed the monstrous cheek of actually talking with the premier of the 'Free State'. Paisley had been at the forefront of all those movements that sought to suppress the rising tide of Nationalism in the days both before and after the Coalisland march—and, regrettably, he had often tended to turn his forgivable political rhetoric into unforgivable religious insults. His repeated reference to the Pope as 'Old Red Socks' and his hair-tossing, head-jerking, screaming derision of the Papists, the Romish plots and the Rebels made him the country's most celebrated bigot long before he was recognised for the talents he undoubtedly possessed.

Ulster was to get its first taste of the brilliance of Paisley shortly after a pair of Stormont by-elections in April. Together with his stodgy lieutenant, William Beattie, Ian Paisley was to transform his Protestant Unionist Party from a church-pew joke into a force of unquestionable potency. As a study of a political development and the effects of political maturity, Paisley's progress in the Northern Irish tragedy is quite fascinating: his attainment of full bloom was to predate by many months, if not many years, the maturity of Northern Ireland as a whole.

While Belfast burned in August 1969, I was sitting on the summit of Sgurr Alasdair, the highest peak of the Cuillins of Skye. When the Shankill Road exploded in October I was back in Newcastle, reporting fires and car crashes for the morning daily, the *Newcastle Journal*. When I joined the *Guardian* in February, Ulster was enjoying its last few moments of peace: as I drove down the Divis Mountain that day in April the time bomb that had been lit in Caledon 22 months before was about to explode —the Catholics had turned against the army, the Protestant extremists were gaining power.

When I checked into the Royal Avenue Hotel that Friday night and as I trekked about the sidestreets and the hillsides and the Orange halls and the churches and the Irish clubs in the city that weekend, I cannot honestly say I realised that everyone in Ireland was coming to the brink of hell. The sub-editors in Manchester were wiser men, though discreet in their forecasts. Over the limp five hundred words I phoned from my hotel room on Sunday night, and which appeared as my first Ulster story in the paper that next Monday morning, they had written the startling prophetic headline: 'Week of storms ahead for Ulster politicians'. It was many years of storms, and for Irish and English politicians and, more important, for Irish and English men and women and soldiers and girlfriends and cripples and businessmen and diners and dishwashers, many years of utter hell. There were storms ahead, and the subs were perfectly right to say so.

2

Election Fevers

At first the routine was fairly simple, and for those of us who had been asked to come and live in Northern Ireland life was, if not exactly an idyll, then at least reasonably placid and pleasant. For Ulstermen, the spring of 1970 was, aside from a couple of lapses, a time of words, not war. The gunmen were in the background, oiling their weapons for the summer ahead, but giving little trouble during late April, most of May and the early days of June. For the reporters it was a time to try to absorb some of the atmosphere of this curious little corner of the world, to drink in its history and its mystery, and to delve into the reasons that lay behind its tragic passions.

Most of us lived out that spring in rooms at the Royal Avenue Hotel, an ornate—if a little fusty—Edwardian structure that enjoyed most of the conveniences and suffered from most of the inadequacies of being deep in the centre of the old city.

It had been bought, a decade or so ago, by a couple of one-time RAF men who had pooled their service savings to transform a tiny, little-used hostelry sandwiched between a druggist's and a haberdasher's, into a large, popular and fairly standard modern business hotel. To sit in the lounge, in one of the memorably back-wrenching purple armchairs, and drink glasses of Harp and listen to the low hum of conversation was an education in itself: one could learn in an hour the recipe that made Northern Ireland tick.

The talk was at first a confused muddle of thick accents. Through it, eventually, however, one began to divine the subjects that brought business to the country. There would be talk of jet engines and linen handkerchiefs and rubber tyres and missiles and perfumes and ships and shoes and bread and cakes and shirts— always shirts, the staple of the Ulster community, which provided vestments for the chests of men from Aberdeen to Accra and Atlanta to Afghanistan—fifteen-shilling creations made by the second in Omagh, which sold at Woolworths to workmen in Scotland, and ten-guinea versions in the finest of Irish lawns that could be bought only on Piccadilly or at exclusive import shops in Fifth Avenue and the Rue de la Paix. Shirts, ships and small aeroplanes formed the distillate on which Ulster seemed to flourish then. The men who came to the Royal Avenue to peddle their wares, or have wares peddled to them, didn't find it all that strange that their usual chairs were being taken up, more and more, by scruffy reporters from London newspapers. They would talk to us from time to time about their faith in the province, and they would mention their earnest hopes that we would write nothing that might disturb the peaceful equilibrium of the past decade. But on the whole they seemed to expect that, sooner or later, reporters would provide the bread-and-butter for Ulster hoteliers, and the businessmen would go into temporary retreat. Perhaps they could sense the coming storms.

The best way for a new reporter to absorb some of the mysteries of Northern Ireland was to read its newspapers. Each morning, along with the thick bundle of the London and Manchester dailies, brought over in the night by steamer and by plane, came two other Belfast journals—the *Irish News*, and the *Belfast NewsLetter*. The three Dublin papers—the *Press*, the *Independent* and the delightful old *Irish Times*—would often not arrive until after breakfast. They were usually left until coffee time: breakfast was the hour for wrestling with the Belfast press.

The *Irish News* and the *NewsLetter* were the pepper and salt of Ulster journalism: they reported each day's events with about the co-ordination and agreement one might expect of the *Wall Street Journal* and the *Morning Star*: they left any reader devoted enough, or stupid enough, to read both, with a spinning mind.

The *News* was the Catholic paper, read by 50,000 families—who bought what was then the cheapest paper in the British Isles—from Andersonstown to Ballymurphy to the Bogside and very few places in between. Its six pages were dotted with sacred mottoes and supplications; its news pages were crammed with accounts of confirmation ceremonies and fleadhs; its sports pages, perhaps the best in the kingdom, told of such recondite activities as camogie, hurling and Gaelic football. It was a paper heavy with the flavour of Ireland—and perhaps because of its nooks and its crannies, it became quite a pleasure to study and to read. The same could scarcely be said, however, of the *Belfast NewsLetter*.

The *NewsLetter* was read by the Unionist people—the Protestant people, the Loyalist community. Though shops could be found on the Falls that stocked it, the *Irish News* was rarely to be found on the Shankill; this was *NewsLetter* territory, and both the people and the paper knew that fact well. Its headlines were blacker than any others and must often have added to the fears of the Unionist people. For what it said was, more often than not, translated into the local patois in the Shankill bars and instilled into the inflammatory rhetoric of the barroom politicians of the day. The papers between them painted an eerie picture of the country: the *News* illustrating the pathos, the mute and colourful tragedy of the Irish scene, the *NewsLetter* echoing, or sounding, the language of those who, on both sides of the fence, were gaining so much headway in the land. Colour, pathos, misery —all was to be found in a single square mile of Belfast, and all was to be found in a single breakfast time with the two papers. Thankfully Lord Thomson provided the more reasonable of men with an evening paper, the *Belfast Telegraph*, which amply made up for the shortcomings of the two morning journals. But the *Telegraph* tended to read like any other evening paper anywhere in Britain: the morning press gave an unpalatable but decidedly realistic portrait of the country it served.

Reading the papers, going to briefings, haunting the local libraries, riffling through the files—this was how we all seemed to spend our time as the days lengthened and warmed into what looked like a fine, long summer. The first reporting job of any note came when we each got a brief telephone call from a former *Sunday Times* reporter then known to be back doing some political work with his former friends. Would we all care to come up to an hotel in East Belfast, he asked us, and witness the formation of a new political party—the only hope that Ulster had, the only way out of impending disaster. It was to be called the Alliance Party, he said—and having no pressing need to be down in the city, all of us, from Manchester to Milwaukee, thronged up to the small hotel to hear what it was all about.

Alliance was the first of many parties to be hammered out by the eruption of a new violence. It sounded too good to be true when its founders spoke about its aims from their hotel table that April day. The group would be non-sectarian, moderate, reasonable. It would contest 45 of the 52 seats at the next Stormont election (though they were not to know that there never would be another election for Stormont, as it was then) and, given the basic non-sectarianism and moderation and reasonableness of the Ulster people, they should romp home to an easy victory and to the formation of a government properly suited to the province.

They had the confidence of evangelists, the naïveté of the middle classes, the charm of the educated. One Catholic, one member of the Church of Ireland, two Presbyterians, sweet with the manner of the manse and the golf club, but brave and wholly sincere, were pledging the world that they could end Northern Ireland's troubles at a stroke. But they were sadly wrong. Ulster people were sectarian in their most fundamental views; they were not a moderate people; and they could be very unreasonable indeed. It was symptomatic of those days that it took even Ulstermen to misjudge the Ulster mood. Alliance, pie-in-the-sky, cloud-cuckoo-land politicians with profound hopes for a better future but no fingers on the pulse of the slums, was three years ahead of its time. It was a brave and an honest attempt to halt the sickening slide into insanity; but as we filed silently out of the hotel room that afternoon to write our stories, our feelings were much the same. It wouldn't work—or at least, it wouldn't work right then. And for the next year or more, perhaps quite wrongly, the press in Ulster treated Alliance like the failure we smelt it to be. Perhaps had we thought otherwise . . .

More of the reality of Ulster politics was to be seen about the same time, when Ian Paisley and his dour colleague, William Beattie, came up to Stormont to consummate their election victories of the weeks before, and assure extremist views a louder voice in the corridors of Ireland's power houses. The occasion of the swearing-in ceremony was the first time I went up to the Parliament, to taste its mock dignities and watch its proud pursuits.

The tall, round-chested doctor looked unusually meek and bashful as he waited outside the Chamber until Question Time was officially over, and protocol was satisfied. Just after 3 p.m., the Speaker announced that questions were over, and motioned to the wizened and ancient Serjeant-at-Arms to escort the supplicant pair inside.

They came through the oaken doors and waited, looking a little nervous, behind the thick blue line of woollen carpet that marked the boundaries of privilege and Parliamentary protection. Who, we all wondered from the press benches above the Speaker's head, would act as sponsors for the turbulent priests?

Desmond Boal, the foxy little barrister from the Shankill Road finally rose to ask that, on this occasion, no one need act as sponsor. The bewigged major who laid down the law of the House ruled that the two did indeed need to be ushered to their seats, and sulkily, Boal sat down again, muttering that he had best abide by the ruling of the Parliament in the 'other place', as Westminster was known in the Stormont language. Finally it was left to Bill Craig, the chubby, right-wing rebel—the man whose order banned the original 1968 Civil Rights march in Derry—to second Boal's reluctant sponsorship, and Paisley and Beattie were permitted to lumber in, sign their registers, pledge their oaths and take their seats at the very back of the Government back benches. There they stayed, beaming and looking suitably intense by turns, until the Minister of Commerce stood to present the latest details of a measure stirringly entitled the Industrial Investment (Amendment) Bill. At this the two members of the new Protestant Unionist Party respectfully detached themselves from the nuts and bolts of running Ulster and left for tea in the lounge. They strolled later in the rain with about a hundred of the faithful from Ballymena who waved flags depicting the Red Hand of Ulster and a few tatty-looking Union Jacks. Paisley and Beattie were amidst the trappings of political power; Boal and Craig had become servants to their majesty and their charisma. It was a union that would flourish and die, flourish and die as it took and released by turns the hands of those who later came to be known by the portmanteau description of Protestant Extremists.

We were to see more of Paisley in his old element—the street meetings and the band marches—within only a few weeks. For in late May Harold Wilson announced the dissolution of the British Parliament at Westminster and the holding, on June 18, of a general election in the United Kingdom. For Ireland the event had become known over the years, with reason, as the Imperial election, and was still called as such in the British North. So while the IRA were planning and regrouping in the South, and while the Protestant extremists were organising under a powerful political umbrella in the North, and while riots broke out sporadically and persistently in the streets, Ulster prepared for another round of an excitement of an Imperial poll. Ian Paisley declared himself a candidate for a Westminster seat; and so, returning to cement her mid-term victory of two years before, did little Bernadette Devlin, the energetic, intelligent and highly articulate girl from the green depths of County Tyrone.

I fell prey to her at our first meeting, and I have been genuinely fond of her ever since. Her style of campaigning, like that of Ian Paisley to the east, was an essential pointer to the mood and the manners of the Ulster people. Both wanted watching in detail.

Mid-Ulster, where Bernadette campaigned, was an almost wholly rural constituency which took in parts of Tyrone and County Londonderry—from the western fringes of Lough Neagh to the islets and marshes of Lough Erne. It was typical, west-of-the-Bann farming country, harsh, poor, small-crofting land where the typical man owned fewer than a dozen cows and where the average income was sickly small.

The principal town of the region is Omagh, which rises out of the famed Black Bog of Tyrone and towers over the flatlands like a lighthouse. The one-street town, with an army barracks and a bus station and a market at its feet, clings squarely to the only hill for miles: its only industry of note is the manufacture of shirts and detachable collars to be worn by City gentlemen who would, until the Troubles, have never heard of Omagh, much less the neighbouring villages of Sixmilecross and Carrickmore and Castlederg.

Omagh was where Bernadette kept her headquarters—a smoky little tap-room at the back of the Diamond Bar beside the Forester's Hall and across from the magnificent Roman Catholic church whose two spires could be seen from twenty miles around. The mixture of beer, holy water and the arcane rumblings from the Foresters next door, the sweat and the swearing and the smoke were a part of the Devlin myth, to be savoured by every visitor, and taken home as a fond memory of Ulster electioneering.

Her message was always the same in those heady election days: she would start out on her daily round of the towns and hamlets of Mid-Ulster bent on converting her constituents from rural indolence to active socialism. Rarely did the Mid-Ulster farmers and shopkeepers and shirt-collar pressers look on Bernadette as a socialist: they only saw her as a brave little Irish girl, and that was enough to bring her the cheers and the tears of the Catholics of the country, and the black looks and the threats from the diehard Unionists.

One rally I went to in the hamlet of Tobermore was typical, both of her and of the people. She had marked it down as a danger spot because when she had spoken there the year before a man with a black beard had waved a shotgun at her, and there were reports this year the British army had come to keep order if she appeared.

Two green Land-Rovers were there with some friendly troopers from the Royal Horse Artillery—were they there to keep the peace, we asked? 'Like 'eck,' one lance corporal said, waving his *Daily Mirror*, 'we're here to see what she's like.'

She wore a trim blue suit that day, more respectably dressed than usual in a serious attempt to show the voters of Tobermore she was a serious candidate and not the whirlwind she had seemed from the London newspaper coverage. Her crowd—about thirty girls who had piled out of a local pipework factory and a few curious lorry drivers and a farmer or two—were gathered on a small gravel mound outside a cement works, and they jeered amiably when Bernadette's muddy old car wheezed up to them. There was no nonsense about this rally—no introductions, no votes of thanks from the local party (Bernadette was fighting as an Independent, and her only organisation was a half-dozen keen youngsters in Omagh, including one former army deserter who ended up working as a waiter in one of Belfast's more celebrated hotels, and another who ended up interned in Long Kesh). She simply got out of the car, swore loudly as she snagged her only pair of tights on a sharp edge of rusty chrome, and then launched into her speech: 'People of Mid-Ulster,' she would begin as ever, 'people of Tobermore . . .' and, standing high on tiptoe her plaintive, singsong voice would chirrup through the tenets of early Marxism for fifteen energetic minutes while her audience peered intently at the gaps in her teeth or at her knees or at her sheer frailty, and wondered how on earth such a person could ever have so much to say about something they had never thought of in all their days in the Mid-Ulster backwaters.

But it all tended to flow off the audience: her appeals for more work and her derisory poke at an English advertisement which extolled the benefits of an Ulster 'where labour is cheap' didn't quite hit home: her repeated contention that somehow the poor people of the country were no more than the tools of the capitalists who sat in cosy London boardrooms didn't quite make sense. They gave her a good enough send-off when she was finished though; their votes could be counted on, even though they didn't have the courage to ask a single question, she muttered as we left.

Generally, Bernadette was hopeful that the Mid-Ulster electorate would choose for political, and not religious grounds. I remember that after the Tobermore 'rally' we went off to a local hotel for sandwiches and a glass or two of hot whiskey, and a moderately prosperous-looking woman who was sitting in the corner of the lounge came up to Bernadette and asked how she thought she had done at the village. Bernadette replied that all had gone rather well, and she feigned mock relief. 'Ah, well,' the woman replied, 'the fact is they're too damn thick down there to cause you much trouble.' The little girl turned on her sharply. 'They're not thick, you fool, they're good working people down there!' and then she remembered how a candidate had a duty to be amiable to every potential vote. 'D'you think she heard?' she asked later, looking worried. 'I suppose that's one vote gone.'

Ian Paisley, who was fighting for the first time in the constituency of North Antrim, was the only other candidate worth watching. He had chosen his battleground wisely—North Antrim was good Loyalist land that stretched from just north of Belfast out to the Glens of Antrim, the marvellous coastland around Cushendun and Cushendall and Ballycastle and west to the river Bann. It enfolded the very Stormont constituency he had won a month before: it also enveloped Larne, the Protestant docking town where Bill Craig, one of his two sponsors, had been returned for many undisputed years. It was all good east-of-the-Bann country—big, rich farms, prosperous tourist resorts, a couple of large and modern towns and, apart from a coastal strip, it was mainly Protestant.

The doctor's campaigning style was altogether more professional than was Bernadette's. He took bands and marchers and girls in kilts along with him: he arranged for the local Orange lodges to greet him and the Lambeg drummers to serenade him in any town in which he planned to canvass. Bernadette was hard to find; her cars had a habit of breaking down; she often missed a village at the last moment, leaving fifty people in the rain because she hadn't the time. But Ian Paisley was always prompt, always well-publicised beforehand, always happy to see the local reporters (though he disliked most of us from England, and Martin Bell, the excellent BBC-Tv reporter, always seemed to manage to annoy someone at a Paisley rally just by standing innocently by).

I first saw him one early summer evening in his old home town of Ballymena: the Shankill Young Conquerors were the band of the day, and their music, their baton-twirling and the steady marching through the drizzle of ten dozen black-bowler'd elders from the local Orange lodge gave the event a kind of late Victorian style and dignity that was bound to bring out the crowds. And when the crowds did turn out, so Paisley gave them promises, polemics and practical advice rather than the doctrines of an irrelevant eastern regime. He ranted and he raved; he cursed drink, the devil and the Irish rebels in the same breath: but he gave an appearance of real concern for his possible constituency members—and it was concern that shone through and eclipsed what he denounced as the hollow dogmas of the absentee-land-lord figure, Henry Clark, who had hoped to win the Antrim seat once more for the official Unionists.

Clark's campaign was hopeless, and he knew it. The party knew it too, and cruelly its organisers decided, one day in mid-June, to send their leader and Ulster's prime minister, James Chichester-Clark, to speak on the incumbent's behalf.

Paisley wasn't in Ballymena that day, but a good dozen of his most red-necked supporters were, and they packed into the front row of Clark's rally. Like Paisley, they waved Xerox copies of Hansard, showing that Clark had spoken for a mere 11 minutes in the Commons that year—at a computed pay rate of some £20,000 an hour: it was unfair, but an easy charge to make. Clark was not, indeed, one of the luminaries of Ulster politics. But at that rally the real jeers were meant not for Henry Clark, but for Chichester-Clark, and when they came, the exhibition seemed an indication of the hopelessness and the sadly sterile times ahead. Chichester-Clark, a weak but essentially decent former soldier, an aristocrat who could hold a candle to the clubbable peers of London and Edinburgh, had survived a terrible phase in Ulster's recent traumas: to see him suffer as he did his party duty before a dozen or more jeering, screaming, ranting bigots, whose political desires were wholly destructive and whose intentions were no more than those of vandals, was a terrible affair. One almost wept to see him shamble his way through his prepared speech, smiling gamely at the insults as they poured and poured over him. He

43

must have been a wounded, tired man; he never displayed any bitterness—not then at least. We could see in his old eyes a deep desire to get out of this nightmare while he still had his health and wealth secure: I always wondered, after watching him that night in Ballymena, why he stayed on so long. Duty, one is led to believe. Pressure, I suspect.

The rule of thumb in an Ulster election is 'vote early, and vote often'. Brian MacRoberts, the dumpy little gauleiter who was trying to win West Belfast for the Unionist Party told me what he expected to see if he ever went down to the headquarters of his opponent, Gerry Fitt, on polling day. 'You go into their hall,' he whispered, 'and you'll see entire changes of clothing hanging up waiting for people to put them on and go back down to the polling booths to vote. You'll see nuns' vestments, too—they make a great disguise. Wait outside on the day and you'll see men and women scuttling in and out in all sorts of different clothes. These people have got the graveyards all sewn up—they know everyone who just died and they'll slip into their identity like it was second nature. It's very ghoulish.' Brian MacRoberts said he had posted a loyal Ulsterman outside every polling booth. 'They're all trained in this sort of thing—they can recognise an impersonator a mile off—we'll stop Fitt getting in by resurrecting half the dead population like he usually does.'

But whether by invoking the spirits of the dead—as MacRoberts suggested—or playing on the fears of the living, Gerry Fitt got in at West Belfast. Bernadette got in at Mid-Ulster and Ian Paisley at North Antrim. Robin Chichester-Clark—the Tory brother of James—won South Londonderry; men with peculiar names and even more peculiar minds got in: men like Rafton Pounder and Stratton Mills and Stanley MacMaster and James Kilfedder for the Unionist Party, and Frank MacManus for a Nationalist body known as Independent Unity.

The election results were declared on the night of 18 June. Only Ian Paisley's vote was late, because the polls from Rathlin Island were delayed by heavy seas in the sound; Bernadette's vote was a

little late too because a television helicopter had blown away
hundreds of the polling slips while they were being counted;
but these minor dramas mattered little compared to what was
happening 'over the water', as they say in Northern Ireland—in
other words, in Britain.

The result that was being forged in the towns from Thurso
to Penzance was to have immensely more immediate impact on
Ulster than the elections of any Paisleys or Devlins, Fitts or
Pounders. The fact of the matter was that by early morning the
next day Harold Wilson was out of office: James Callaghan, who
had seen Ulster through some of her worst troubles six months
before was no longer Home Secretary. A new team was in
Whitehall, led by an unknown and untested Edward Heath, a
man with no apparent knowledge of, or policy on, Northern
Ireland. In Belfast there was some jubilation from the Unionist
side; some apprehension from the Paisley locker room; and some
real fear from the Catholic quarters. 'Jesus, Mary and Joseph' one
woman in Andersonstown murmured to me as the results came
up on her television screen, 'this sounds bad for us.' Whether the
effect was direct or not, will not be possible to tell for some years
to come: but the fact remains that the change of government in
the middle of June was to coincide with a deep, profound and
terrible change in Northern Ireland; we were to know that only
ten days after the election had been held, lost and won.

Between times I managed to get in a trip to Dublin, my first
as a reporter. It was a delightful weekend, and it was to leave me
with a deep and lasting affection for the city. The story had
nothing to do with the troubles: it was a good, standard *Guardian*
story about an elegant house that was about to be knocked down
and in which a group of students had barricaded themselves to
prevent the demolition teams moving in. It was a good way to
fill a quiet weekend. It taught me something, too, of the Southern
attitudes towards the bleak North.

The best way to get from one capital to another is by train—
the four-times-daily Enterprise Express which, hauled alternately
by brown and cream locomotives belonging to Northern Ireland
railways, or the jazzy red and white engines owned by Coras

Iompair Eireann, did the trip in three hours even. The southern Irish trains were best of all, because catering was parcelled out to an independent firm, and one could buy something rather more exciting than ham sandwiches and a bottle of Harp, which is standard Northern railway food; to sit back in the lounge car speeding past the fields and the salt grass meadows and the harbours at Dundalk and Drogheda and the villages of Balbriggan and Swords and Skerries was to go through a lazy spiritual relief, as though all the black troubles of the North were being lifted away by a skilful masseur. Many travellers noticed the feeling of relief passing through a road customs post on the way to a story, or a weekend in the Republic; one didn't get quite the feeling on a train, since the customs inspection was in Dublin and not en route—one never quite knew where the border had been crossed—but there was relief all the same. And stepping out of O'Connell Station into the sunshine and the total peace of the fair city was always like the beginning of a holiday. There was even a smell, redolent of warm beach sand and railway smoke and fish quays that made Dublin seem like the start of a summer holiday.

St. Stephen's Green, where the condemned house lay, is one of the architectural marvels of the British Isles. It is the focal point of a square mile of skilfully preserved Georgian terraces, all polished brass door knockers and foot scrapers and worn granite steps and softened brickwork arches and terraces and splendidly curved swansneck lamp posts; cherry and mimosa trees were in heavy bloom, the streets were filled with yellow and pink and white blossom and the sky was a cool, light blue: Dublin looked her very best that weekend, and one could sympathise with the students who had encamped in the skewered innards of Number 45.

One of the leaders of the students in their vain mission (they were eventually evicted one Sunday dawn) was a young girl named Deirdre McMahon, who lived in a wild shambles of a basement on Fitzwilliam Street with a rabbit who scampered about and ate half her books. I was there to ask her questions about the house she had chosen to defend; all she wanted to know about was Ulster—what was happening up there, were things any better, what did Belfast look like? To these people, as to many, many Dubliners, Belfast was as foreign a town as Bogota or Bombay. Southerners come North to shop for clothes or contraceptives, once in a while, but generally Belfast was far away from the touring route of most Dublin people, and anyone, like me, who had come down for a weekend, was good value at dinner for all the news he could bring.

There had been just one serious riot in Belfast in the days immediately before the Imperial election: John Clare the resident *Times* man and I had been caught in the thick of it on the night of June 3.

It had begun when an Orange band had marched the length of the Crumlin Road to unfurl a lodge banner as a part of the six-month-long preliminaries to the Twelfth of July celebrations. Crumlin Road in those days was what the army called an 'inter-face'—once it had shaken itself free of the city centre and was past the gaol and the heavily Protestant parts of the Old Park and the Bone, it became a narrow dividing line between a small and powerful Catholic community—the Ardoyne, to the north—and a large and powerful loyalist community whose homes stretched in a solid, squalid half mile all the way south to the Shankill Road itself.

The police expected trouble that night, and had told the march organisers they would not be allowed past Flax Street, the edge of Ardoyne. The marchers and the bandsmen and the dancers scarcely believed what they saw when they finally reached the mill.

A hundred RUC men, arms linked, three deep, were ranged across the Crumlin Road from the entrance of Flax Street on the Ardoyne side to Leopold Street on the loyalist quarter. The crowd went wild. Some of the more reasonable men in the procession tried to argue with the senior officers about the indignity of halting the march—a traditional parade, it was said, held every year for the past two centuries; but then bandsmen and young louts and angry Orange harridans started yelling and pushing and spitting at the thin blue line.

Three grey riot tenders revved up behind the police, black diesel smoke billowing into the mob; an army lorry behind the police Land-Rovers rolled slowly down the hill, and a platoon of infantrymen spilled out onto the roadway and formed up. The arguments, the pushing and shoving went on: a few of us got through—Clare and I, waving press cards, got up with the soldiers and were able to watch, from a safe distance, the growing disturbance. And then suddenly, the tactical flaw which threw an uneasy situation into a full scale local emergency could be seen: the police, for all their zeal in blocking the Crumlin, had failed to block the loyalist side streets to the south, and within moments the entire Orange procession had vanished down Cambrai Street, had gathered five hundred supporters, and poured out of Disraeli Street, fifty yards up hill from the soldiers, and right opposite the main street into Ardoyne, Hooker Street.

The Catholics were ready for them: for close on three hours the upper Crumlin Road looked like the Falls and the Springfield Road had looked ten months before. Soldiers chased vast mobs down into the alleys and side streets, firing cartridge after cartridge at the stoning, spitting, screaming crowds. An off-license was set ablaze, and young Loyalists could be seen tearing barrels and boxes out of the flames. Army Land-Rovers were lured into Chief Street and Ohio Street and bombarded with unbelievably thick clouds of rubble; snatch squads belaboured stumbling rioters with their batons, dragging a few hapless men off to the arrest tenders; and all the while a jeering troublesome Catholic crowd surged down Hooker Street and Butler Street and Kerrera Street to get a view of the brouhaha.

For this was a Protestant riot. A hangover from the anger of October, aggrievement that the fears of the Ardoyne rebels had stopped their precious march, the 'insulting' behaviour of 'their' policemen—all this contributed to a sudden unplanned wave of loyalist anger. Troops who six months before had battled in these same streets with the same men were engaging in what was probably the worst riot of the year thus far: it was shorter, but more destructive, than Ballymurphy in April: it was, however, more easily understandable.

General Sir Ian Freeland, who still had command of the 7000 soldiers then based in Ulster, was probably right to think of it as no more than a result of left-over anger. But then he probably mused with some apprehension over the fact that three weeks on the Orangemen had scheduled another, bigger and infinitely more precious series of marches and processions. The date, June 27, 1970, was marked in the Lisburn calendar as a possibly tricky time.

It was, as it turned out, the first marching weekend after Ted Heath's election success: it was also the start of the most violent, deadly weekend Northern Ireland had known. It was the prelude to the single biggest blunder the army ever made in Ulster. And it was the weekend that first saw the Provisional IRA in street action. June 27 was going to be a critical date for Irish history-makers, and those of us who crouched in the doorways of the Crumlin Road that night of June 3 only anticipated the half of it.

3

Provisionals at Battle

The terrible events of the June 27 weekend, which left 6 Belfast-men dead, 58 men and women in hospital with the scars of gun-fire, and 218 others wounded by razor-edged bottles and heavy chunks of rough masonry and pieces of rusty ironmongery, were fathered by two decisions, both, it turned out, misjudgements.

One decision was that to arrest Bernadette Devlin on a Friday night on an old and out-dated charge of incitement to riot—as General Freeland later said, 'a ridiculous piece of timing'. The second was Whitehall's agreement to let the Orange marches of the same weekend go ahead as usual—this, in the words of the resident senior British civil servant in Belfast was 'the greatest single miscalculation I have ever seen in the course of my whole life'. For both decisions Mr. Heath's six-day-old government must take the responsibility, if not the blame: they were costly mistakes to make, as Heath would find out in the months to come.

Bernadette Devlin had been tussling with the law for the previous ten months. After the Londonderry riots of August 1969 she was arrested and charged on three counts of riotous behaviour and one of incitement. The Londonderry magistrates found the doughty little girl guilty, and sentenced her to six months' prison on each count, mercifully for her, to run concurrently. She was given leave to appeal.

The resulting court battle in the Belfast High Court was long and expensive. Sir Dingle Foot, the eminent QC of the eminent family, came across to defend Miss Devlin: he submitted that in her Bogside activities of the previous August she had thrown petrol bombs and organised the throwing of stones at the invading police and Protestants simply because she, and her thousands of Catholic colleagues of the day, were genuinely fearful for their safety, and had to organise their defence. As a legal submission it seemed a good and brave one, and for a time in May and June those of us who clustered in the smoky halls of the High Court to drink coffee with Bernadette and her tow-headed crop of admirers (and to watch the loyalist rabble from the bottom end of Sandy Row come down to scream at her on every appearance) really imagined she might get off with just a ticking-off or suspended sentence. No such luck: on June 22, four days after she had been returned for her Westminster constituency, the Lord Chief Justice, Lord MacDermott—a grim-faced jurist who had an uneasy record with students during his time as a Pro-Chancellor of Queen's—ruled out her appeal. 'Anyone who organises the throwing of petrol bombs,' he growled down at her, 'could not fairly complain at a six-month prison sentence.' He sounded as though he wished she was going away for six years.

Sir Dingle was on his feet in seconds, spluttering out his ritual request for an appeal to the House of Lords—even though Bernadette should have gagged at making any such request of an aristocracy she supposedly detested. But an appeal, she thought, would buy time: and Lord MacDermott told her to be back in court on the following Friday when he would consider whether or not the point of law at stake was sufficiently grave to require a definitive ruling by the Law Lords. The date he set for the hearing was Friday, June 26—the eve of the loyalist marches.

Who should rightly bear the blame for that decision bears a terrible responsibility—but who exactly to blame is probably only a matter of subjective judgement. Clearly Bernadette and Sir Dingle could have restrained their hopes, taken their medicine and have given up at that point: Miss Devlin could have given herself up to the Royal Ulster Constabulary and have been driven to gaol on a Wednesday afternoon. Equally, the Lord Chief Justice—who was far from ignorant of the storm clouds gathering outside his leaded windows—could have postponed the hearing for the Lords appeal until after the weekend. Or he could—though this is a challenge to his legal wisdom—have allowed the appeal on the grounds that it would have defused a dangerous and potentially deadly situation.

But Bernadette did not want to take her medicine: Lord MacDermott, for some curious reason, did want the case closed by the weekend; and when he convened his court at ten the following Friday morning, his decision was precisely as expected. Sitting with the other two appeal judges—Lord Justice Curran (father of Michael, with whom I made that first flight to Belfast) and Lord Justice McVeigh—MacDermott listened patiently while Sir Dingle raised no less than fourteen fine legal points which, he contended, made a referral to the London Lords essential. Sir Dingle finished his submission. Lord MacDermott turned to his two sage colleagues and announced a ten-minute adjournment while the fourteen matters were considered—at the rate of one point 'of great public importance' every 43 seconds.

While the triumvirate was out, the tension rose to an unbearable pitch: no one—Bernadette least of all—really minded if the girl went to gaol. They did mind, however, what her mercurial supporters in the Falls and the Bogside might do if the decision went against her.

Then the three bewigged and gowned judges were back, their faces expressionless. The court hushed; Bernadette uncrossed her legs and listened:

'Having considered the application,' Lord MacDermott intoned, 'we are of the opinion that the points raised are not points that should be certified and that the case remains one of incitement to riot and riotous behaviour. . . .' Miss Devlin was guilty, and she would have to go to prison.

At one of those impromptu press conferences to which Miss Devlin was prone, she was as jaunty as ever, repeating she had done no wrong in Derry in August last and asking to meet Reginald Maudling, the newly appointed Conservative Home Secretary, when he arrived in Belfast for his first visit in the middle of the following week. And what, one reporter asked her, would her supporters think of the arrest? Her answer has got lost in the other news of the day, but I remember it approximately, because it later struck me as suited to the occasion. She grinned wickedly, I recall, and then said, with what I can only describe as a sardonic smile: 'I urge them to keep calm.' She sounded more than a little like a cross between a Pompadour and a Defarge—she knew what would happen just as soon as the RUC got hold of her and took her away.

They got her just about two miles outside Londonderry, to where she was headed for refuge. She was travelling in a small convoy, Eamonn McCann, Mary Holland of the *Observer*, Loudon Seth, her former agent, and a gaggle of helpers and hangers-on. It was due to be a victorious return to the barricades of Bogside, and a well-publicised arrest at the Victoria Barracks afterwards.

'But the police must have tapped our 'phones,' McCann said later on. No one knew what our travel plans were, and yet they managed to get her before we ever got to Derry, and there was no publicity at all.' The convoy was stopped at the village of Drumahoe, just a mile or so east of the river Foyle and well out of the way of any of the hundreds of Bogsiders who were gathering in the long shadows to greet their heroine. A police and army road block halted the white Ford Consul carrying Miss Holland, Mr. McCann and Miss Devlin, and a senior police officer reached in with an arrest warrant. Bernadette got out with no apparent fuss, was handed over to a bulky pair of policewomen and driven off at high speed to the A wing of Armagh gaol. Eamonn McCann had to go to the Bogside empty-handed, and the rioting began within minutes. Derry was to have its first bad night for weeks. Belfast, by coincidence, was to have even worse.

The Belfast rioting of that Friday began in the same place, and in the same fashion, as it had three weeks before. Another flag-raising ceremony had been called by the Orange lodge of West Belfast. The necessary 'traditional' march had to pass along the Crumlin Road, and it had to pass in front of the Catholic lane-entrances outside the cramped Ardoyne. It had been anticipated; the trouble had been forecast; but nothing had been done to change in any minor way the inflammatory and downright dangerous route the Loyalists had chosen.

And so it was quite predictable that as the straggling marchers walked and strutted across Hooker Street, the bottles and the stones would begin to fly. I will always remember one boy, a small, pudgy and not too attractive youth of about eleven, who detached himself from one of the marching bands just to stand and yell and scream the vilest of abuse towards the Catholic houses. I cannot still, after two years of seeing the most degrading sights and hearing the most unpleasant of screams, recall any single act that depressed me more: here was a little lad who should have been out—it must have been around seven at night on a warm June evening—kicking a football around or hanging about outside a cinema or round the back of the pub.

Instead he chose to stand a hundred feet from a community of which he can have known little but rumour and a community in which children just like him would have been living and playing and watching television: and to scream over and over again 'You bloody bastards, you bloody bastards!' with a face suffused with purple and contorted with inexplicable rage. It was a grim education for those of us who watched that boy: it tended to convince the pessimists among us that, for all the good that Ulster undoubtedly held, and for all the people we loved and cherished and placed faith and hope in, there was this boy, and a thousand like him, who were totally dedicated to a manner of hatred stronger than we could even begin to fathom. It was a depressing sight and for me tended to overshadow the rioting and the wrecking that went on in Belfast, and in Derry, for much of the night.

Saturday morning dawned warm and sunny, and there was unusual excitement in the air. In West Belfast, and in particular in the streets around the Ardoyne and the Disraeli Street loyalist stronghold, the houseproud Belfast women, all curlers, carpet slippers and lip-dangling cigarettes, were out with their sweeping brushes, pushing pounds of broken glassware and masonry into the gutters.

Cleaning-up the morning after a riot was almost a cliché situation in Belfast. The grey-faced soldiers would be pacing up and down the street watching for the slightest sign of remaining exuberance; the Land-Rovers, their windscreen shields still up, their inmates hunched behind scratched Perspex shields, would roll softly past the hushed terraces, their wheels scrunching and grinding on the debris of the night. And then, around seven, housewives would emerge, the strains of Tony Blackburn drifting out of a score of doorways, as they worked in near-unison, brushing the sea of ammunition into the gutterways, even where the very kerb-stones had been torn out the night before. Occasionally they would find something—a souvenir from the night that they could sell or keep, like a gas cartridge case or a damp army beret or a potato with a razor blade buried inside that had failed to burst and cut when it hit its target. By breakfast time the roadway would have been clear, the soldiers would be stopping by (in the loyalist areas—never in the Ardoyne) for cups of tea and slices of soda bread. The green Land-Rovers would have dispensed, by then, with the eye-straining shields, and the poor infantrymen would be sleeping sound in the back and the wheels would swish soundlessly over the clean tarmacadam. Belfast would look as close to normal as any city of military occupation can look; but one always knew it was merely the formal stage-setting for the next night's riot, and normality was only a very transient phenomenon.

This, then, was how Belfast looked on the morning of Saturday, June 27. The sun was playing on the red roofs of slumland, the smoke from ten thousand morning fires was curling into the still air, the housewives were sweeping the rubbish of another riotous night away, and in the far distance the tremulous wail of bagpipes and brass instruments could be heard, tuning and scaling for the day ahead. For this was to be a big and colourful Orange day, and in the Shankill and the Bone and Cliftonville and the Oldpark and the Ormeau Road the lodges were gathering for an anniversary march that was to spark off a dreadful, unforgettable night.

They started massing in the Shankill around two in the afternoon: there must have been five thousand of them, many old and proud, many young and lathered for trouble. They assembled in serried ranks behind old men who carried polished silver swords and bucklers and teenagers who threw great staves twirling into the air and a band of kilted pipers or mini-skirted girls with

Orange sashes and jaunty caps and cornets, bent and battered from generations of exuberant playing.

The main march was destined to go from the Shankill onto the Springfield Road, past the charred shell of Bombay Street, burned to the ground at the end of the previous summer.

Bombay Street lies on the fiercely Republican quarter known as the Clonard, a cluster of terraces which lie in the shadow of the Clonard monastery and which fronts on to the Falls Road itself: to march Orangemen past the Clonard was madness in the extreme: the British and the Northern Irish authorities knew this well and the British made a lukewarm attempt to have this one most sensitive encounter ironed out of the Orangemen's itinerary. That they failed, in the face of pressure from an obstinate Chichester-Clark, who feared—rightly—he would be kicked from office were he to agree to a route change, was probably one of the worst mistakes the government was to make in Ireland during that phase of the troubles.

Of course the Tory government was less than a week old; and their agent in Ulster, Ronald Burroughs, despite being charged with such an awesome responsibility, was not always listened to in London as closely as he wanted. But Reginald Maudling, who had just then taken over as Home Secretary and who could, at the end of the day, order the march to be diverted, vacillated in secret and then did nothing. In any case, five thousand Orangemen marched by the Clonard that day, and the spark that ignited there started a massive, uncontrollable inferno.

The Orangemen were prepared for trouble: one could say with some fairness that they initiated it. I remember standing at the corner of Lawnbrook Avenue and Cupar Street, my back to the Clonard and my face to the stream of marchers, watching the huge accumulation of personal weaponry passing before my eyes. Some of the bandsmen had bricks stuffed into their outer coat pockets; marchers who carried their brown paper sash bags in their left hands were brandishing empty milk bottles in their right; one man, five foot of wrinkled hatred, staggered past, perfectly in step, with no fewer than six housebricks held in his two hands. I turned to a policeman, one of a pair watching with me, and pointed to the man with the potential wall in his fists. 'Look at that!' I yelled at him, in naïve astonishment. 'Aren't you going to haul him out and run him in?' The policeman, an amiable soul I was to see again and again in troublesome moments up the Shankill, turned to me and grinned broadly. 'You know,' he said, winking hard, 'I never saw a thing. Not a single thing.'

At first I thought it was a flock of birds, flying low. A small cloud of black objects whistled overhead from the front of the Orange marchers, They were stones—heavy black chunks of road metal picked up from a nearby building site. And they were aimed deep into the Protestant crowd by Catholics standing behind the barbed wire and the policemen who had been put there to prevent what was known in the trade as 'sectarian violence'. A few of them hit home, sending Protestants reeling back with cut faces and skinned shoulders: most just smashed onto the ground—my policeman kicked one out of the way and turned to me again, still winking.

Like the bandsmen on the *Titanic*, the Orangemen kept on playing and marching to the end. The stones were flying, the men were falling, the police were running into battle order: but the bandsmen kept right on rolling out 'The Sash' and 'The Aghalee Heroes' and 'The Green Grassy Banks of the Boyne' in a combination of defiance, doggedness and plain dumb ignorance. In the end the march spilled out into the Springfield Road ragged and disjointed: those who would stay for the fight hung on: those with instruments and music sheets disappeared off to their homes.

The fighting on the Lower Springfield lasted for about two hours of that sunny afternoon. A petrol bomb, launched by a Catholic from the Clonard, set a bakery ablaze: a telephone box was rocked out of its foundations: a sweet shop was gutted and all the windows in Mackie's Engineering Works were smashed. The reporters stayed in the middle of the riot with the Loyalists up the hill and the Catholics down by the Falls. We were with a company of soldiers and fifty policemen: gas, snatch squads and some very determined baton wielding broke up the mobs by teatime and, but for a couple of ill-aimed but ominous shots from a ·22 rifle, it was a fairly routine afternoon. The shots, though, were worrying.

By late afternoon, as the roughhouse on the Lower Springfield was calming, another riot was brewing at the Upper end, at the Ballymurphy housing estate which had erupted so badly on June 3. Here the confrontation was straightforward—1500 resolute Catholics against two battalions of infantrymen—the entire 2nd and 3rd battalions of the Queen's Regiment: one currently resident in the city, the other shipped up by truck and helicopter at short notice from the barracks at Ballykinler, thirty miles to the south.

In Ballymurphy the rate of petrol-bomb manufacture and tossing that evening was higher, I remember, than at any time I had known. The Queen's fired hundreds and hundreds of gas cartridges: the rioters returned with twisting, floating balls of fire that exploded in a massive sea of flame at the feet of an advancing platoon. The weapon was as spectacular as it was lethal: to watch the ball of fire weaving softly through the late afternoon light, smashing on the ground in front of a soldier who became covered in a mass of liquid gold and sent running and falling back to safe ground, his uniform dropping off his legs in great gobbets of fibred orange, was ample testimony to the strength of the weapon. (And to be behind a barricade and watch a youth touch his cigarette to the crumpled gauze, upend the bottle and make as if to throw—only to have a pint of neat petrol course down his arm and catch fire as it ran, was testimony to its weakness.)

Ballymurphy triggered off a madness. The Lower Springfield turned stormy again; then the Ardoyne, East Belfast, the York Road and the Falls erupted. The city was going beserk before our eyes. And in the Crumlin, as darkness was beginning to fall, someone brought out the guns again, and three people fell dead—the first victims to die since the Protestants shot dead Victor Arbuckle, a policeman, on the Shankill eight months before.

No one knows for sure what happened in the Crumlin, and who fired first. As I recall, a loyalist mob, marching through the

Crumlin divide, set themselves up in Palmer Street, a little loyalist sidestreet that overlooks the Ardoyne. They began to stone the Catholics, with good reason, one supposes, since they clearly knew what the Clonard hooligans had done to their big bannered march earlier in the day. The stoning had been going on for fifty minutes or so when suddenly the guns were out, and firing.

The police remain convinced that the gunfire—they saw it was rifle and machine-gun fire—came from Hooker Street, and that the three Protestants who died at the mouth of Palmer Street and Disraeli Street were victims of an IRA murder gang. Five Ardoyne men went to trial for murder a few weeks later: they were all acquitted. Martin Meehan, the Ardoyne commander of the Provisional IRA, told me then, and has told me since, that the first gunfire came from the loyalist streets, and that his 'boys' merely returned like for like, in their mindless Ulster fashion. I had thought the first firing came from Disraeli Street; a loyalist street. Meehan agrees, for what that is worth. And the police failed to make the murder charges stick on the IRA men. No conclusions of any validity can be drawn from this perhaps; but in that the deaths were the first of an incredibly important and momentous weekend, it would be valuable to have the truth, rather than fall back on the easy assumption that the killing was part of a longlaid IRA plan. It is an important matter to decide if the IRA men in action that weekend were acting defensively or offensively: my own view is that the Provisionals, who were undoubtedly at work in both East and West Belfast, were responding to, rather than initiating, a desperate military situation.

By mid-evening the British troop commanders were admitting to reporters on the streets that they were beginning to be 'very stretched indeed', and with fresh trouble spouting every minute the city was beginning to look like a forest fire, and the supply of water buckets was running alarmingly low. Extra forces were rushed into the city from every available military base. Cooks were told to get their uniforms, drop the soup and run out to help: signals specialists were sent to man barricades, officers went into the front lines: some 3500 men from six different battalions were in action during the night: the air was thick with radio traffic as the brigade commander in Lisburn, ten miles away, tried frantically to police a city that was fast becoming unmanageable. Rioting began again in Ballymurphy: the Loyalists in the Shankill were massing to get revenge for their three dead colleagues; crowds were massing in Ballymacarrett, across on the east side of the river Lagan: the Newtownards Road, a shoplined, wide trunk road that ran from Belfast, via Stormont, to the sea, was becoming the focal point of the night, and soldiers, as many as could be spared—and that was terribly few—were sent in to quell two mobs of roaringly angry, payday drunk and rapidly organising factions.

Shooting broke out in Ballymacarrett just after midnight. For those of us there it was a frightening enough situation: we lay in the glass-strewn gutters of the darkened road—soldiers had blown the lights out to prevent snipers taking aim—as the shots whined overhead, from the Catholic churchyard on the south side of the street to the cramped Protestant terraces fronting onto the ship-yards on the north. We knew that a sniper was up in the belfry of the church—it was called St. Matthew's, and still stands, ringed with barbed wire and corrugated tin like a fortress, not at all a haven of hallowed peace—and he was winging off shot after shot into the darkened side-streets. There was answering fire from the Protestant streets.

I had one extra nasty moment: I was running, half-doubled, from behind one armoured car to another, and having to pass, silhouetted against a distant gas light, by the entrance to Seaforde Street. Another man was loping ahead of me: as he slipped in front of the yellow lamp, a shot cracked out and he pitched forward into the rubble. I did the same, my heart beating like a Lambeg drum and my mouth dry as dust. Was he hit? Was he dead? He moved, finally, and cursed loudly into the night. He had tripped, he said, and had cut his face on some glass. Had he stayed vertical through his run, I reflected, he might have been bleeding a good deal worse.

What had happened in East Belfast was, as in the Ardoyne, of enormous importance: the details were not to emerge until a while later. What transpired that night was the opening of the battle campaign of a little-known organisation known as the Provisional IRA—as we all came to know them, the Provos.

The shots fired by the sniper in St. Matthew's church were the first inexpert fumblings of an army that was to prove as expert in guerilla war as any this century: we didn't know it that night—but they knew, as they have said many times since, that June 27 in the Newtownards Road was the beginning of the end.

Briefly what had really happened was this: as the Orange bands were passing down the Newtownards Road, some clown in the Catholic quarter flew an Irish tricolour from a gable end at the top of Seaforde Street. A few stones were hurled by the Orange-men, a few shots were fired, with neither organisation nor effect; and the parade passed on and an uneasy peace returned. That was about teatime on the Saturday evening.

Shooting broke out again briefly about five hours later for no apparently good reason: the Catholics—only 6000 of them lived there in Short Strand, among 60,000 loyalists, and if any Catholic area was likely to be wiped out by a mass revolt of angry Protest-ants, it was the Short Strand—began to get windy. They felt that tonight might well have been their fateful night—and for the reporters waiting under the lamp posts early in the night with the light wind carrying the distant bangs and screams across the river from the other city troublespots, it seemed a fairly rational sort of fear.

At about 10 p.m. a small loyalist posse tossed a batch of petrol bombs at the Catholic church: it set alight an outbuilding. The Catholics sent a deputation to the Mountpottinger police station nearby to ask for help: the police called in an army company for added protection: with half the city going up in flames, the brigade commander could offer little more.

There were some important men around in the Catholic area that night. Paddy Kennedy, the Stormont MP and the closest of the 'straight' politicians to the views of the Provisional Sinn Fein movement (the political end of the Provisional IRA) headed the party to the RUC. Billy McKee was there, as Brigade Com-mander of the Provisionals. Billy Kelly, who was supposedly

mending his car over the river, came across to help when he got
a warning phone call: Kelly, of a particularly notorious Republican family, was the commander of the Falls Road battalion
of the IRA, the one which, ostensibly, looked after the Short
Strand.

The two IRA men were encamped at the back of the church
when the Protestants' petrol bombing began. They took out their
guns—an M2 carbine, a Thompson and an assortment of undistinguished rifles and handguns, and began blasting away at the
attackers. Kelly led the church party; McKee ignoring the written
rules of the organisation that prohibited him from fighting,
mentally tossed away his brigadier's cap and joined in: he was said
to have been the church tower sniper—he crouched under the
church bell, firing shot after shot into the darkness of the loyalist
streets ahead of him, only the winking of the red aircraft lights on
the Goliath crane and the flicker of starting fires relieving the murk
of the night into which he blithely aimed.

The army was into Newtownards Road from the early morning. The local commanders either could not or would not inter-
pose their men between the Protestants and the IRA—or, as the
army supposed 'between the two rival religious factions', as the
fight was then seen—and so the gunfire went on for five hours,
until the dawn came up over the dockyards to the east and stole
away the only protection a night-time gunman can have. The
shadows slipped away, and with them the riflemen. Three more
men died here; hundreds were scarred and scathed by the bullets
or burned by the flaring petrol.

Across the frightened city hundreds of fires still smouldered or
burned fiercely into the Sunday morning. The fire brigade
estimated that 108 major blazes had been set during the night,
from way up to York Road in the north to the far west at
Whiterock Road and beyond. It was a night that cost the citizens
of Belfast more than half a million pounds, and set them inexorably on the road to full-scale guerilla war.

As we said in the *Guardian* that next day 'The Security Committee met at Stormont shortly after breakfast to discuss the night's
rioting, which was unquestionably the worst Belfast has seen.

The most common phrase was that Northern Ireland had gone back to Square One, and possibly even further than that.' How horribly prophetic that phrase was to become.

On Sunday afternoon Chichester-Clark acted with consummate speed to bring some order back to his shattered land. He issued a set of new orders designed to prevent this sort of thing happening again: he ordered all of Belfast's thousand pubs to close each night at 8 p.m.; he ordered troops to close all the main roads leading into the major disturbed areas at 9 p.m.; he told the Ulster Defence Regiment—an army-controlled local militia which had been designed to replace the old, police-controlled B-specials—to be mobilized immediately, and he announced he would introduce new laws in Stormont to provide mandatory prison sentences of six months and more for anyone found guilty of riot, affray or looting.

General Freeland, commander of an army that had done an impossible job as well as it could, but badly, chipped in with a frightening order to the effect that anyone seen carrying, let alone using, guns, in the troubled areas would be shot without warning.

The establishment was reacting as any guerilla army might have prayed for it to act—by repressing the country to prevent the sins of the few; by introducing laws that were inevitably unjust; and by making military regulations that read like the rule book of a South African or South American dictatorship.

Ronald Burroughs, that genial, ineffectual civil servant who had tried in vain to have the Orangemen re-routed on the Saturday went on to make his remark about Maudling's inability, or his unwillingness to act—it was, he said, 'the greatest single miscalculation I have ever seen'. And Chichester-Clark and Freeland blundered on in turn; their blunders of that weekend were to resound through the length and breadth of Ireland long after the six coffins of the night were safely deep in the thick loam of the Belfast cemeteries.

4

Of Curfews and Carnivals

'Inevitably, harsh cases will arise as a result of this Bill, perhaps even wrong convictions on the basis of mistaken identity.'

The sentence was spoken during the late-night debate, on the Tuesday following the dread weekend, when Stormont politicians grappled with the introduction of a new law that, Chichester-Clark naïvely assumed, would put an end to such displays of public abandon as had been witnessed two days before. But it was not spoken by an Opposition member of Parliament as a criticism of the harshness of the intended measure: it did not even come from an opponent of the new law sitting on the Government benches. It came, in fact, from the author of the Bill and the man whose job it was, ultimately, to ensure its application —the Northern Ireland Attorney-General, a friendly, overweight Orange lawyer, Basil Kelly. Kelly, whose tasks included the supervision of the continuing standards of law in his domain was speaking as he introduced a new law which he was willing to admit might lead to 'wrong convictions' and 'harsh cases'. Something, somewhere, seemed very wrong.

The Criminal Justice (Temporary Provisions) (Northern Ireland) Act 1970, was the first lasting consequence of the June 27 tragedy, and it was to contribute to the eventual undoing of the Stormont parliament. It was an appalling piece of legislation; on hind-sight, Kelly's astonishing admission—made perhaps in a spirit of frankness and honesty, but more, I suspected then, in a spirit of arrogance and contempt for those against whom the new law would be applied—should have struck us all for what it was. Instead, we bought copies of the new Act at the Stationery Office on Linen Hall Street in the middle of the week, and remarked only that it was 'very strict'. Line by line the Act provided for a minimum, mandatory prison sentence for anyone convicted of 'riotous behaviour', 'disorderly behaviour' or 'behaviour likely to cause a breach of the peace'. It mattered not, we realised later, whether the offences had been committed during the height of a battle in Ballymurphy or in a pub fight outside a bar in Bally-nafeigh; no mercy would be shown to a peace-breaker, whether a man of 45 or a girl of 17. The law that had been drafted under the desk lights of Stormont over the weekend was the kind of law Pretoria would have envied (in fact the South African government issued a booklet in 1967 to show to the world that the Suppression of Communism Act and the Terrorism Act were mild compared to some. The Northern Ireland Special Powers Act was held up as an example of the strictest type of law—the Criminal Justice (Temporary Provisions) Act 1970, could well have been another). It had been drafted by the Northern Ireland government: the 'police' who would enforce it was the British army, and the RUC—or at least its commander, pleasant old Sir Arthur Young–was said to be 'appalled'.

The police were appalled simply because they knew just how much the two minor charges—those of disorderly behaviour and breach of the peace—were the standard armoury, in Belfast, as in Glasgow or Liverpool, in the continuing police battle with the late-night pub fight and the excesses of the slumland gangs. There was no other charge that would stick on these dozens of offenders: but now, those who habitually escaped with a fine or a ticking-off would do so no longer. They would go to prison, six months and no less, with no questions asked and no quarter given. The police would have an impossible task; the courts would be jammed to bursting; and the law would be made to look an ass— and all for the British army, at whose behest—it sometimes appears—the Northern Ireland cabinet acted that weekend.

Only Ian Paisley, to his everlasting credit, fought the Bill in parliament as being too ambiguous and too imprecise. He lost, though; and the Bill became an Act, the Act was taken by courier through the winding country roads to the lovely old Georgian house at Hillsborough, and Lord Grey of Naunton, the New Zealand businessman who was given Northern Ireland to govern for the Queen in 1968, appended his signature with a fountain pen. It was July 1, and the law stayed on the books as it was for just five months and seventeen days. The prime minister who introduced it lasted only three months longer.

The Act was the most lasting of the results of the rioting: the pubs were soon open again until the late hours, the UDR was swiftly stood down as soon as the farmers in the regiment began to complain about their neglected acres; and the roads—which in spite of being riot centres were still commuter routes of some consequence—were soon open again, day and night.

Reginald Maudling, the new Home Secretary, came across by RAF transport aircraft later that week to have a look at the province he had inherited. It was not, by all accounts, an over-whelmingly successful visit. He was, according to those who shepherded him about, amiable, confessedly ignorant and not very eager to learn. Soldiers at Lisburn remember his visit well: one officer there recalled how Maudling had seemed 'amazed' at the seriousness of the situation; a politician expressed his own amazement that a senior cabinet member, even of a government less than a fortnight old, could be quite so ignorant of a problem that, in one way or another, had been dogging the various English governments for very nearly a century. And the reports of his last remark, on leaving on the evening of July 1, dogged him until he left the government. 'For God's sake bring me a large Scotch. What a bloody awful country!' he was supposed to have said on the plane back to London. That was the measure of the man, and neither reporters, politicians nor the people of Northern Ireland loved him much for it.

Northern Ireland is not a bloody awful country; that was becoming abundantly clear to those reporters from 'over the water' who were beginning to become tolerably familiar with the land and its people that summer. There still was the undeniable sensation of relief when the bus or the train or the car took one across the border and into the lazy, tranquil sweetness of the South. But Ulster had its other charms; and throughout my stay little vignettes of local colour, or brief respites from the violent tedium of the cities provided a constantly fascinating backdrop of charm, history and character. Few of us who stayed ever left without shedding the odd tear for our leaving: perhaps my feeling for the country began around late June and July, when for a brief day at a time I could slip away and breathe the cool air of a remarkably beautiful little corner of the world.

One such trip I made often in those long summer days was to the wild and wonderful sea coast of North Antrim. The area I discovered week by week lay between the solidly Presbyterian industrial town of Larne and the lush coastal valleys from Cushendun to Carnlough, across to the small Catholic coast resort of Ballycastle and beyond. I make no apologies for noting the religious affiliation of a town if I knew it: one was bound to notice the details that marked the one from the other—the Orange lodge, or the plastered Union Jacks in Larne, or the names— Feeny, O'Hagan, Fegan—on the shopfronts in Ballycastle. But out there, it mattered less than in the cities—back in 1970, at least.

The North Antrim coast was to be my first true taste of the countryside and its people. Years ago they had prepared a grave for Roger Casement down by the shore at Murlough Bay; and I used to take my books there on those warm Saturday afternoons when all the other newspapers had sent their men back home, and the *Guardian* had wisely decided to keep me on. I would lie among the long grass and the bluebells, gazing all the while out past Rathlin Island to the rock of Ailsa Craig and the far coast of Scotland and the blurred, white-topped gneiss hills of Mamore and the far North. Seagulls would wheel and call in the cool air drifts; small lobster boats would putter about on the sea, flat and blue as hammered gunmetal. The old lobstermen would tramp past me in the evening, and might stop for a few friendly words and snippets of local gossip and legend. The peace and quiet, the local tales, the new words and the dialect and the new friends— all this I absorbed and treasured each time I was lucky enough to make the long journey up through the Antrim Glens and out to the sea-coast. I always thought it might stand me in good stead one day: it probably did, if I care to remember precisely when. But it gave me one significant advantage over Reginald Maudling: I was never to have to call Ulster 'a bloody awful country', and I made as many friends on that account as he must have lost.

While the Home Secretary was reporting back to his masters in London, I went home for a brief attempt to tidy up the new house I had bought two weeks before the news editor had asked me to 'fill in' in Belfast in April. I was allowed time off—but as happened, it seems, every time I went away, Belfast blew its lid again and I was phoned in the night and sent right back. My holiday lasted 48 hours. I left on Thursday afternoon: I was back on the plane on Saturday.

What happened on the afternoon on Friday, July 3, threw the last vestiges of hope for Northern Ireland out of the window. It was the start of a weekend now known as the 'Falls Curfew': it was one of the most clearly identifiable steps on the road that led, eventually and inexorably, to the downfall of the Stormont government nearly two years later.

At about 4.30 p.m. on that Friday afternoon, a police car and two army Land-Rovers turned into Balkan Street, a quarter-mile-long alley that runs through the Lower Falls from Bosnia Street to the Long Bar in Leeson Street—long known as the local talking shop for the members of the Official IRA, who still held sway in this small Catholic part of the city. A company of Royal Scots, brought in four three-tonners, brought up the rear, sealing off Balkan Street and leaving the remaining Catholics penned in, and very curious, in the myriads of side streets beyond.

The army was in Balkan Street to get at a small arsenal of guns —Official IRA weapons that had been cached in the house at Number 24. Police knocked on the door: soldiers rushed in, pushing past the terrified occupants of the tiny house: and in a quarter of an hour the guns—15 pistols, a rifle, a Schmeisser sub-machine gun and some ammunition—were found and were being loaded into the back of a Land-Rover. It was, by IRA standards, a small arsenal, and by rights the incident should have been over in no time at all. By 5.30 p.m. the soldiers were ready to go, they radioed that they were preparing to leave and started to get out.

The three Land-Rovers made it, and onto the main Grosvenor Road, which was crowded with rush-hour traffic. But the lorry-loads of Royal Scots were not so fortunate: curious Catholic crowds that had gathered at the ends of Balkan Street, and who had seen the whole affair, jostled the infantrymen as they tried to get back into their lorries and the Humber one-tons. The soldiers began to get angry and use their batons: the crowd began to throw stones: a pig—the local name for the Humber—reversed suddenly into a mob and one man was crushed, badly, on some cast-iron railing spikes. He was to die in hospital later in the night. The scene had been set for confrontation.

Military commanders in Ireland seemed to live, in those days, by the theory that a military presence had a calming effect. They should have known that since their Ballymurphy Easter, this was false. Troops in Catholic areas create as much trouble as they prevent. The Royal Scots commander in the Falls that night probably never realised that, and so, when a shower of stones hit the last of his departing lorries, he slammed on the brakes, jumped out of the cab, and ordered his 'Jocks' out onto the streets once more. It could scarcely have seemed a less prudent move.

The brigade commander in Lisburn heard the news a few minutes later. A company of Scotsmen, he was told, was effectively besieged inside the highly charged rabbit-warren of the Lower Falls; so he compounded the apparent mistake of his subordinate by sending in another company of soldiers to act as a rescue party. These soldiers went in hard—too hard, it turned out, and began to fire gas, clouds and clouds of choking, drifting, alienating, political, radicalising CS smoke. The stones came harder and harder, the gas crashed and banged out of the stubby black guns and out of cup-dispensers fitted into the soldiers' SLRs and from handlobbed grenades. The clouds wafted silently up in Bosnia Street and Raglan Street and Cardigan Street and all the other little hovelled alleys named, as the British always do in the slums with macabre irony, after famous British glories in battle.

The more glorious the old battle, the grimmer the street; and in Belfast, the grimmer the street, the worse the new battle.

And by 6.30 p.m. it really had turned into war: old ladies and young children in the upstairs rooms and the downstairs parlours were crying out for relief from the dreadful, grey-white clouds that seemed to be killing them by painful degrees. The young men, bathing their faces with vinegar-soaked rags, dashed out into the affray to help drive the soldiers away; gelignite bombs were stockpiled and thrown; more soldiers were rushed in from the out-lying areas: the Lower Falls was going noisily and rapidly berserk.

Brigadier Hudson, the commander of 39 Brigade, was called in to watch from a scout helicopter in the early evening. He reasoned, at around 7 p.m., that the only way to bring order back to the area was to pull out all his soldiers: and so, at around 7.15 p.m., he signalled the order to withdraw and regroup around the peripheries: the lorries and the pigs revved up, the soldiers leapt on the screamed instructions of their sergeants, and with a few defiant bursts of gas and stones, the army moved away.

But not far, it turned out, and not for long. Within the hour the Falls Road IRA was organising the youths and younger men of the area to build barricades: lorries were overturned, paving stones were torn up, milk crates and old beds and rusty cars were dragged out to make a dozen or more rickety barricades. Outside them the army gathered and waited: the Royal Scots and the Fusiliers were supplemented by men of the Queen's and the Devon and Dorsets, the King's Own Scottish Borderers and paratroops and the Green Howards. There were to be 3000 soldiers in the Falls that night—two-thirds of all the men in Belfast. A few hundred extra had been hurried in from England after the week-end before: but as it was, the army massing on the flanks of the half square mile of the Lower Falls that night was nearly half of the total force stationed in the troubled province.

At 8.20 p.m. the army, with a squadron of sappers, moved in to tear down the barricades. The Official IRA men, who had rounded up their weaponry for a major defensive battle—and who, in an act of unforgettable chauvinism, had turned down an offer of help from the nearby Provisionals, who themselves seemed spoiling for a fight—began to fire their guns. The gunfire that began around 8.30 p.m. went on and on, and it invited inevitable reply by the army.

To anyone who experienced the battle it was perfectly obvious that hundreds and hundreds of bullets were being fired by both sides—and yet the army had the gall, when asked by reporters later in the weekend, to say that its soldiers had fired only 15 shots in sum. The official figures were to be published later: soldiers in the Falls that weekend fired no less than one thousand, four hundred and fifty-four rounds—17 rounds of ·303, from the telescope-equipped rifles of the company marksmen, 10 rounds of 9 mm. from the Sterling sub-machine gun, and an almost incredible number—when compared with the 'official total'published over the weekend—of 1427 rounds of 7·62 mm. ammunition, the standard, deadly ammunition for the soldiers' SLRs.

Ever since those later figures were quietly published, many reporters found it terribly hard to accept contemporary accounts of a serious disturbance by the army public relations' men, Never, since then, have I found myself able to take the army's explanation about any single incident with any less a pinch of salt than I would take any other explanation. Fourteen rounds, indeed —it was almost as though the army was trying to explain away how it had managed to kill so few people. And certainly, in the knowledge that nearly 1500 army shots had resulted in such a mercifully small number of casualties, one must wonder seriously about the competence of those 'professionals' who were serving under the British flag that weekend.

Gas, too, was fired in unbelievable amounts; 1600 cartridges and canisters, and the huge clouds swirled and billowed through the laneways: no one could escape the terror. Bullets whined around like furious bluebottles; the gas seeped everywhere. The shouts and screams of panic, especially from the children and the older women, were awful. Nothing seemed able to stop the nightmare, as on it went, screeching and crying and whining and belching its terror out into the fast-growing dusk.

And then, from above it all, came what many remembered as a sepulchral doom-laden Eton-accented voice from the skies. A helicopter paddled slowly about above the streets, and from within an amplified English voice was telling everyone to get indoors, to stay off the streets, to disappear under penalty of arrest. No one can be absolutely sure whether the word curfew was ever used by that unknown, public-school voice up in the skies, but that is what it palpably was: the British were declaring a curfew on the Irish down below, and were telling men, women and children they'd be slung in the cells if they so much as showed their faces on the streets.

The curfew lasted from 10 p.m. on that Friday night until mid-morning on Sunday, with a brief shopping break in the middle of Saturday afternoon. It was an unforgettable experience. Huge Saladin six-wheeler armoured cars, their 76 mm. cannon training uselessly from side to side at the little houses, cruised up and down the deserted streets. Soldiers, their faces charcoal-blackened, paced furtively beside the crumbling walls while white-faced women and sneering men watched disgusted from the windows. From hundreds of houses the sound of crashing and wrecking could be heard as soldiers searched and searched for guns—they found more than 100, together with some 20,000 rounds of ammunition and some explosive—and men would be marched away from time to time for either breaking the curfew or being present in a house where weapons had been uncovered. Three hundred men were taken away, for one reason or another.

Saturday was an eerie, still day in the Lower Falls. The army let the press swing through the curfewed zone in an open truck in the mid-afternoon, and there were some good PR snaps of weary soldiers sleeping full length on the glass-strewn pavements to be taken. But it was not until the mid-morning mass on Sunday, when General Freeland ordered the five main army blocks taken down, and the people permitted to go to church, that the suffering and the damage of the two curfewed nights and the searching could be determined. Michael Lake and I wrote that report for the *Guardian* of Monday, July 6, and our account, gleaned from half a day of padding through the saddened community, speaks for itself:

When the curfew was lifted a number of people dressed in their best clothes went straight to Mass. The majority, however, stayed behind to clear up the mess, and to display to squadrons of visiting pressmen the evidence of the alleged army brutality.

In some houses which the army had searched for arms very little of the furniture was left standing, or indeed intact. Gas and water pipes had been torn out, holes smashed in walls with rifle butts, beds upturned and broken, floorboards torn up. It will be several days before people living in the houses will be able to get back to normal. Army spokesmen would not discuss the general complaints.

There was a severe shortage of food in the beleaguered area. Shops had either been looted or, as was more likely, had run short of supplies because delivery vans had been unable to pass the army lines. A welfare centre set up by the Legion of Mary and the Knights of Malta attracted a queue of house-wives which stretched two hundred yards down Sultan Street waiting for milk, bread, tinned meat and cigarettes.

Old people, especially those who were unbale to get their pensions on Saturday because of the restrictions, suffered worst of all. They tend to buy food only for the next day or even the next meal, and consequently had little or nothing in their larders when the day and a half of siege began. One pregnant woman with two infant children said she had no milk from late on Friday until lunchtime on Sunday.

Twice during the day women from outside the Lower Falls marched through the barricades bringing food, newspapers and tobacco to their comrades. In an attempt to quell any possibility of violence all men were banned from the streets down which the liberating armies made their noisy ways. And the soldiers were clearly too tired or too uninterested.

Most of the thousand women and children who had been evacuated on Friday night returned yesterday morning to inspect their houses and property. Often they found that their menfolk had been arrested, and one, Mrs. Pauline McGourn, of Plevna Street, said she had not been able to find her father-in-law, Mr. Thomas McGourn, who had been arrested on Saturday morning.

'His friends say he had been lifted by the army at about 2 a.m., but the police say they cannot tell me where he is now,' Mrs. McGourn said. 'He has heart trouble and I simply have to find him soon.'

As we picked our way through the rubble in the miserable jungle of streets the residents came out of their mean little terraced cottages to invite us in to see the damage, to show us looted pubs, to take us to the priests.

One priest, who refused to give his name, said that if the Catholics were exposed again as they were last August—and there had been no troubles in the Lower Falls since then—he would personally take up a gun. He believed, however, that the bubble had burst. 'There's nothing so stupid as to think you can beat the British army.'

The mood in the streets was angry. The rhetoric flowed ceaselessly. Yet somehow it seemed that the residents were strangely enjoying the new martyred role in which they had been cast—beaten by the English, the old enemy, in an unfair fight. An elderly woman combing her hair said: 'They'll never beat the Irish. They'll never beat us like that.'

But they did beat three people that night, aside from the man crushed by the armoured car. In all three Irish Catholics and a middle-European postman from London named Zbigniew Ugilik died. The night was costly for them and for their families. And the Falls curfew in its wider sense was costly for the British, for the Stormont government, and for peace, sanity and stability in that steadily maddening land. The army proudly took two Stormont ministers, John Brooke (the son of Lord Brookeborough) and William Long (who came from Yorkshire, and joined the Ulster cabinet as its Minister of Education and resident showman) around the subdued Falls on that Saturday afternoon, to display with evident satisfaction how well it was carrying out the orders of Stormont. 'We must supplant these rough, rugheaded kerns,' Stormont had appeared to say; and the 3000 soldiers allotted to the Lower Falls went ahead and supplanted them.

The change in the Falls Road people was striking and memorable: there were many months left in which Catholic people and soldiers would talk together and swap tea and gossip: but the curfew was the beginning of the end for the army, and before very long, any Catholic seen 'fraternising' was in for a head shaving, a smashed kneecap, or a bullet in the brain. And after the curfew, few in the Falls would have minded.

The Falls curfew was over by the Sunday: the following weekend, by contrast, was a time for celebration, not confrontation: the Twelfth of July, Orangemen's Day.

The *Guardian* had two men covering the curfew: like most of Fleet Street, we over-reacted wildly for the Twelfth. Eleven members of staff, almost the biggest *Guardian* team to be mustered anytime, came across for the weekend.

It was a splendidly picturesque day. Dawn broke cool and clear: the tense mood that underlay the occasion was set at first light when some of the 7000 soldiers brought in to keep the peace ordered the various 'peace lines' established in the city between Protestant and Catholic communities to be snapped tight shut: all the gates that had been opened temporarily for the milkmen and the early-morning workers were locked and bolted: soldiers with submachine guns settled themselves into 'sangers'—their sand-bagged boltholes—to watch the two communities disport themselves. Armoured cars rolled softly through the cold morning air, tired soldiers piling out to take up their posts at every conceivable trouble spot. 'It's monstrous,' a member of the Central Citizens Defence Committee complained from his office in the Falls. 'They'll be splitting families up all around the city. We won't be able to move around at all.' And that was how it seemed to the Catholics: the Orangemen, 100,000 of them, would be marching today, and the Catholics would have to stay home and be good boys and girls. Hadn't there been a curfew the previous weekend? And wasn't this much the same?

The Ligoniel True Blues were, as always, the first of the bands to come down from the hills and onto the launching pad just near the Crumlin Road gaol. They would come down the hill from the Divis mountain suburb, picking up four more smaller marching bands at the Orange lodge, and come on down the Crumlin Road, their accordians pumping with all the more zest as they passed the heavily protected grey walls of Ardoyne. One old lady who lived on the Crumlin Road between Hooker Street and Butler Street, and whose telephone we always used during the riots, told me that morning she had been woken up every Twelfth for twenty years in a row by the 'Tin Lizzies' of the Ligoniel True Blues. Like so many of the older generation of Catholics, she had no objection to the Orangemen: they had their day of the year, she reasoned, and the Catholics had theirs when the Hibernians marched, and on St. Patrick's Day as well, so why shouldn't the Protestants? True, they tended to have rather a lot of their 'days', but it was all good fun, and when you came to think of it, did little harm to anyone.

But that particular day (it was actually July 13, a Monday, since you cannot have Orangemen marching en masse on a Sunday) she was up early, just in case the trouble we had all predicted broke out. It didn't: the True Blues and their colleagues from the smaller lodges trudged on down the Crumlin, to be almost totally ignored by the people of the Ardoyne. Some would later ascribe that to contempt, others to terror. But in any case, the peace of the Ardoyne morning was a foretaste of the calm ahead, and the relief of the helmeted troops guarding the side-streets once the band had whistled and thumped its way down the hill and beyond their responsibility, was to be typical of the relief felt at the end of the day by every single soldier, from the corporals manning one of the forty roadblocks on the M.1, to the drivers revving up their great crowd-pushing bulldozers, to the generals and brigadiers who were waiting up in the ops. room at Lisburn and in London.

But the *Guardian* had taken ample precautions. In Belfast, aside from an elaborate photographic team and men whom the union insisted came along to wire the pictures across the Irish Sea, we had three writers. Another reporter went to the tiny County Derry village of Maghera, where James Chichester-Clark was expected to rally to his local Castledawson lodge; and yet another

76

took on the natives in the town of Pomeroy, where there was a possibility of trouble, because the Orangemen were grumpy with being re-routed to avoid a sensitive Catholic area.

King Billy's victory at the Battle of the Boyne was commemorated in nineteen separate places in Northern Ireland that day. Belfast was the natural centre of things; and by 10 a.m. the dispersal area at Carlisle Circus, at the bottom of the Crumlin Road, looked like the main entrance to Wembley Stadium on cup-tie morning: it was an incredible maelstrom of superbly attired men, all colour, noise and Brylcreem, who bustled here and there giving last-minute polishing flourishes to their silver pikes and swords, who tuned up their accordians and bugles and practised the timeless art of baton hurling, and unfolded, with supreme care, their honoured sashes and collarettes that identified each man by his lodge, his rank and his number. You could tell the old boys from the newcomers: old men kept their sashes in crumpled brown paper bags. New boys had theirs encased in polythene sandwich bags. But both, plastic or paper, were folded neatly and put into pockets for the evening once the fringed and metalled sashes had been carefully slipped over the head and settled proudly on a hundred thousand pairs of shoulders, ready for the day ahead.

The purpose of the marching was to get all the men and boys from Carlisle Circus to the Finaghy Field, a small, damp meadow that lies south of the M.1 motorway, a little way from the troublespot of Andersonstown. There had been fears that the field might be mortared or mined: long before the marchers reached the grass, army metal detecting machines had swept the area clean: heavy armoured cars up on the motorway embankment beside the field scanned the Catholic quarters for potential trouble: but at Finaghy, as all across the city, the day was one of perfect peace and sobriety—the latter complemented by the government ban on all drink sales, just in case the enthusiasms of the day got the better of anyone with a stone in his hand.

It took the leading marchers about an hour to bang and shrill their way through the closed and shuttered and flagged centre of the city: behind them a column five miles long, with bands each two hundred yards, and tens of thousands of steadily marching patriots, stretched out, taking a full two hours to pass the spot where we all watched, in the Royal Avenue Hotel's first floor lounge. There were the Temperance Dockers and the Total Abstainers of York Street; the Saracen Defenders of Glasgow and the True Blues Flute Band of Sandy Row: there was one lodge bearing a huge hand-painted placard showing a kindly looking Queen Victoria handing down a Bible to a crouching black man (this was a constantly popular theme on Orange banners, blending as it did the glory of Empire with the benefits of Protestantism; under the picture of Her Majesty's bestowal of the good book to the ignorant native was the phrase 'The secret of England's greatness'); and there were countless others inscribed simply 'Britannia Rules the Waves'. King William himself, usually rearing up on his frisky horse, the river Boyne flowing blue behind him and the Jacobite hordes fleeing away in Papist disorder to his right, appeared on many of the lodge banners—though not as many as one might have thought. And for the first time in years one could see a massive collection of Ulster flags—red and white, with the Red Hand of Ulster firm and stiff in the middle—fluttering in the parade. Over the months this flag, which came to symbolise the independent mind of Ulster men, came to displace the official Union Jack, with its red, white and blue. It started to appear in quantity that Orangemen's Day, though few of us realised the significance in those times.

Down at Finaghy the mood was gay and country-fair like. Strawberries and cream, hot-dogs and soda pop were served by the ton, soda bread and a strange sweet concoction known as 'Yellow Man' were on sale at a dozen small side-stalls. The Orangemen and their sons and young brothers sat and listened to men like the Reverend Martyn Smyth, the Grand Master of the Belfast Lodges, deliver a windy and wordy polemic on the state of the union: there were resolutions of loyalty, welcome, faith and state; there was a divine service of thanksgiving and there were reluctant interviews to be given to a hundred curious newsmen.

'A strange devotion to a long-dead Dutchman', Harold Wilson

had later called the Orange frenzy: few of us there that day could begin to understand what it was that welded these people together in such a gaudy community. They all had a religion in common, of course, and most had a class to share. They all felt a deep suspicion of 'the rebels' in their midst, and they were all beginning to comprehend the stirrings of a deep mistrust of the intentions of the British government. But the reason why so many thousands braved the discomfiture and the rigours of an organisation that was regarded with hostility by their peers in the Catholic community and with contempt and amusement by their peers in England, remained something of a mystery for many months.

Across the land that Monday afternoon the Orange celebrations were marked by relative decorum and total peace. In Maghera, the Prime Minister failed to appear, displaying an ambivalence, almost a scorn, towards his fellow lodge members that was to rankle with the Orange leaders for months to come. One speaker at Finaghy claimed that 'what we need is six more Ian Paisleys' and the assembled crowd refused, somewhat pointedly, to read the traditional oath of loyalty to the incumbent government at Stormont. Perhaps it was simply a rebuff to the rudeness of the amiable premier: more likely it was another sign, as with the Ulster flags and the tone of some of the speeches, that an independent monster was stirring its head, and that some were beginning to feel that true satisfaction of their age-old cause was not to be won through the government sitting up on the hill outside Belfast.

'Ulster has a day to remember', the front-page headline read in the next day's paper; 'N. Ireland had a day of peace' read the rubric on the account on the back page. Whether it was a day of 'peace' with 7000 soldiers, 5000 policemen, all the members of the Ulster Defence Regiment and a thousand tons of barbed wire, barricades and bullets to keep the two sides apart, remains an issue to debate; that it was most certainly not a day to remember is without question. We all took off home—all, that is, except me, who crept up the stairs to my now semi-permanent hidey-hole in the hotel—and the Twelfth, or the Thirteenth, to be correct, was over.

There was one amusing sequel. One of the more imaginative things the army did in Northern Ireland that year was to issue all the press with gas masks a few days before the marches, just in case there was trouble and soldiers, as was their habit, tossed around a good deal of CS smoke. Harry Whewell, our news editor, was over one day to see that the *Guardian* operation was going smoothly; and together with another couple of reporters, we all went out to a restaurant somewhere near Glenarm, on the North Antrim coast. The gas masks, like our notebooks, were buried somewhere in the back of the car.

On our way back into Belfast there was a monumental traffic jam at the end of the M.2 motorway: it was, as we suspected, an army road check, taking every tenth car and going through it with a fine-tooth comb to prevent anyone smuggling weaponry or explosives into the city. As always seemed to be my luck back then, I was one of the tenth cars, and we were waved into a lay-by for the customary inspection process.

At first the soldiers found nothing, as they patiently went through the engine, took out the seats, felt under the wings and tapped the chassis members to test for suspicious hollows. It was obvious that the men, all dour-faced members of the Black Watch who had been called across from a leisurely time in Germany, had found nothing all day, and were feeling pretty brassed off with their luck. But then, as two of the men combed through the boot, there was a warwhoop of delight, and one of the soldiers tore around the end of the car, to the amusement of all the passing motorists, holding two gas masks up in the air—our army-issue gas masks. 'And wheer d'ya get theese, me laddie?' the sergeant, a Mr. Currie, demanded. 'From the army,' I said. 'Don't be funny,' he rejoined. 'No, seriously, they're legitimate,' I protested. 'Another bloody wurrd from you and y'r' all for the glasshoose,' he snarled, and so we shut up, rather smartly. He took the masks away, threw them in the back of the armoured car, took my name and address, told us not to be 'so bloody cheeky' and let us away.

I was showering back at the hotel when the first of the telephone calls came. It was the adjutant of the Black Watch. 'So sorry about your experience, old man, we're sending a chap down with the masks, and he'll explain.' Half an hour later, another call—could I go down to the lobby, there were an awful lot of soldiers, the little girl on the switchboard inquired? I went down: there were, indeed, a lot of soldiers, most of them guarding a nervous looking subaltern who carried a batch of gas masks in his left hand and a stiff envelope in his right. Could he buy me a drink? I said yes—he dispatched his sentries to guard the hotel, and followed me up to the bar where, for a good two hours, he poured drink after compensatory drink down my throat. The envelope contained a note of apology from the Commanding Officer, and a standing offer for dinner in the Mess. That delivered, the gas masks returned, and me well and truly staggered by the whole affair, the subaltern slipped out into the night, his sentries snapped to attention and into the waiting convoy, and he was off. I never saw the Black Watch again that year—but it was a splendid display, we all thought, and worthy of the Tattoo.

And there was one other feature of that July, which had begun so badly but which finished so calmly, that added to the delights of reporting in Ireland. It was when I went out, very early one Sunday morning, to go to sea in search of something that came to be known as the Big Egg Scramble.

There was a dock strike in England and Scotland during July 1970, and the chicken farmer and the pig breeders in Northern Ireland were finding they had no markets for their eggs and their ham and their bacon. And so, shortly after the Orange excitement was over, a team of enterprising fishing-boat owners on the County Down coast decided to go into what was, in effect, the smuggling business. For a fee these buccaneering sailors would take their little boats—their *Prides of Ulster* and their *Golden Orioles* and their *Jenny Wrens*, and sail them out from the little ports of Donaghadee and Carrickfergus and Bangor and over to the nearest port in Scotland, Portpatrick, on the Wigtown-shire peninsula, twenty odd miles away over the current-ridden turbulence of the tiny North Strait.

Henry Kelly, then the number two man on the *Irish Times* team, came down with me to Bangor on Saturday night to talk to a few of these enterprising crewmen. We took one into a small bar and coaxed him gently into promising us a lift the next morning—'Okay,' he said at last, after a great deal of warm Powers had slipped down his throat, 'you be here at five and I'll see what I can do.'

The next day Henry and I were driving out of Belfast through a scudding rainstorm at half-past four in the morning. It had been a quiet night in Belfast, and we felt sorry for the bored-looking soldiers who stood dripping softly under the street lights on the old slums of East Belfast, with nothing to do but wait for the shift to change.

We got to Donaghadee, where Jack Miller had told us to meet him, on the dot of five. The skies to the east were lightening fast by then, and when the clouds lifted one could see a faint grey smudge on the north-eastern horizon that was the Galloway coast: the sea looked rough on the far side of the harbour wall, and, with no breakfast inside, both Henry and I felt less than confident.

But then the egg lorry from Armagh got itself delayed; and Skipper Miller took a phone call saying the eggs could not possibly be on the quayside until eight at least. Henry and I adjourned to a small hotel on the seafront to read the Sunday papers and eat a momumental Ulster breakfast on a white linen table cloth, with gallons of steaming coffee and bowls of thick, hot porridge. We stayed and read and basked in this unexpected luxury for four long hours, before an amused shipmate from the *Golden Oriole* turned up to tell us the eggs had been stacked away, and would we like to come?

There were 300 boxes aboard—108,000 eggs to be sent down to the hungry English markets in Newcastle and Manchester and London. Lorries were already waiting on the Portpatrick quayside, we heard on the BBC news; and such was the need for them over in dock-struck Britain that importers had agreed to pay the *Oriole* crew half-a-crown a box for the trip—£36, plus a bonus, which would go down well on a ship that tried hard to make that much a week fishing the plaice and mackerel grounds off Kintyre.

We only just got away from the quay: just on the stroke of ten a group of angry Belfast dockers, who had pledged solidarity with their brothers in Scotland and England, tore up to the waterside in a battered old car and leapt out, yelling at us about what scabs we were, and how we'd be for it when we got to Scotland. We left them yelling and screeching their rage while we attended to the more serious problem of getting across the strait without losing our balance or our breakfast.

To get to Portpatrick you simply point your bows at the great granite pyramid of Ailsa Craig and, allowing for a tide race of about six knots to the south, buffet across eastwards. We only saw one large ship on our way out—the frigate HMS *Ulster*, which watched us with what we all interpreted as avuncular interest as we passed under the gun turrets—though there was some talk on board of whether we might be arrested for egg running or some similar offence unknown to landlubbers.

It was a rough, whitehorses sort of day once the rain had cleared up, and as the little boat bobbed and corkscrewed around on the rollers there were jokes about the 108,000 egg omelette we'd be delivering, and there was a little, though refreshingly little, talk about the problems of the country that was fading in a greenish mist to our stern.

By late lunchtime the white-painted village of Portpatrick was looming on the hills in front of us, and we all prepared for our arrival. Remembering our fond farewell from Ireland, might there not be a reception committee, we asked ourselves, armed with boathooks and marlin spikes and the like? In the event there was no need to worry; there were just a thousand gawping summer tourists who had come to look at the slightly illicit spectacle, and a dozen lorries with nameplates from towns like Cardiff and Southampton, that had come in search of a sample of our precious cargo.

While the crew unloaded, Henry and I went up the cliffs to the fine old Portpatrick Hotel where, sitting over pots of tea and piles of cucumber sandwiches and sticky cakes, we wrote our copy onto the backs of old doilies and newspapers we found scattered about and phoned the stories over, Henry to Dublin, me to Manchester. The 'Big Egg Scramble' was what the *Guardian* called the episode the next morning.

The next morning, when we were safely back in Belfast, Fleet Street woke up to the story and one paper sent over a sweetly blonde reporter from Manchester to repeat the journey. I took her down to Jack Miller's boat first thing the next day and watched the pitiful sight of her standing on the open deck, clasping a black patent handbag in one hand, the other clenched tight onto a hawser, and the sea lashing round her ankles, as the *Oriole* lurched out into the channel. I didn't see her for six more months, when I bumped into her in a pub in Manchester. She had been violently ill all the way, she said, and the paper hadn't used her piece the next day anyhow.

Back in Belfast, the calm lasted out the month. But then a young, unknown, apprentice electrician named Daniel O'Hagan came up from a week's summer holiday in the South at the end of the month. His return would mark the end of his life, and the beginning of a new round of desperate violence. Ireland had had its breathing space, and it was flexing its muscles again.

5

Bombs and Rubber Bullets

Just after one o'clock on the morning of the last day of July—
a Friday—the Belfast police emergency operator took a 999 call:
a voice told her that an intruder was trying to break his way into
a house on the Antrim Road, just by the entrance to the New
Lodge Road. The caller also said that one of the bars in the New
Lodge was still open and serving drinks, long after hours—perhaps
the constabulary would like to investigate.

While the New Lodge Road, a Catholic sector of North Belfast, had escaped fairly lightly during the previous twelve months,
it was some way from a police officer's idea of paradise on earth.
The houses were old and crumbling. The local bars—and in
particular the Starry Plough down the New Lodge Road itself,
in the shadow of the aptly named Artillery Flats—were recognised
as haunts of some of the wilder republicans. The crime rate was
high. The people were traditionally unfriendly to the forces of
law and order. So the dispatcher that cool morning sent along one
police car, with unarmed patrolmen abroad, and one military
police Land-Rover, with a formidable armoury of gas, riot sticks
and sterling sub-machine guns, just in case.

The dispatcher's caution was well-judged: the phone call
turned out to have been a hoax: and as the two vehicles turned the
corner, they were met by a thunderous hail of stones and bottles.
It was a perfect ambush.

Radio messages crackled into the night as first the RUC, and
then the MPs, called out for help. Within fifteen minutes a
company of the 1st Battalion, King's Own Scottish Borderers,
spilled out of the gates of Girdwood Park Barracks, just across the
road, and what had by now become a familiar set-piece confrontation—though in a somewhat unfamiliar setting—began.

The riot, like the ambush, was well organised. The Provisionals, who had used the previous three weeks to prepare themselves for a weekend of highly co-ordinated disturbances, were clearly behind the initial trouble-making. As the army used to say, 'older, sinister men could be seen in the background . . .' organising the riot and then melting away to let it continue under its own self-generating momentum. The men were rarely 'old' and in truth they were not very sinister either: but they were there in the New Lodge, and once the night had swung well and truly into action, they retired to watch the fun.

But not before they had seen to it that a few dozen extremely well-made and well-thrown petrol bombs had been hurled down at the Scottish soldiers. The army, which logged the bombing as having started almost on the dot of 3 a.m., said that the fire-balls were 'perhaps the most accurate and well organised we have ever seen'. The Borderers, who returned gas by the roomful, took the bombing for ninety long minutes: then, in line with the 'Yellow Card' drill (each soldier carried a small, yellow folding card in his breast pocket telling him when, and in what circumstances, he could fire one of his weapons: as befitted a rapidly changing situation, the card went through a number of significant alterations) the company commander grabbed a megaphone and shouted down one of the blackened side-streets that any further bomb-throwing would be met with rifle fire.

The response from down in the ghetto was predictable. There was an outburst of wild, derisory cheering, a few hearties yelled 'Up the Republic', and with a cry of 'Throw well, throw Shell!' another salvo of the yellow perils was launched into the velvet air.

At 4.40 a.m., the company records show, a private fired three shots at a man he claimed had just thrown a petrol bomb. The private claims he had an excellent sighting of the man: he saw him, according to army reports, with a second bomb in his hand, preparing to throw that. He fired his self-loading rifle, a weapon of unbelievable power and range, ill-suited for urban work and a killer by shock if not by direct hit: a single round of standard NATO 7·62 mm. ammunition hit the young man in the neck and he fell to the ground, at the corner of the New Lodge Road and

Shandon Street. His name, it turned out later, was Daniel O'Hagan, and he was the first civilian to be killed deliberately by British army gunfire during a riot since a Mr. Cuthbertson was shot in Liverpool during the 1921 riots. He died in the Mater Infirmorum, a nearby Catholic hospital, just as dawn was breaking. He was 19 years old.

Daniel O'Hagan, his neighbours pointed out instantly, was an innocent victim of British army brutality. He was out in the streets at 4.40 a.m. for no more sinister a reason than 'running messages'—which in Belfast means going shopping. The fact that few Belfast shops are open at 4.40 a.m. did not diminish the neighbours' account: Danny, they said, had been innocent, had never been in trouble before in his life, wouldn't know one end of a petrol bomb from another, was a quiet, respectable apprentice electrician who wouldn't hurt a fly and had only just come up North from a holiday in the Republic: didn't that prove, they opined, he must have been a murdered innocent.

That tale may well have been apocryphal in part: the reaction to his killing was both immediate and vengeful with the New Lodge locals clearly believing he had either been wrongly killed or that his death warranted an instant reaction. There was violent trouble in Belfast for the next five nights: dozens of soldiers were badly injured: a fragile peace had been shattered once again.

For five bloody days and nights the trouble went on and it started the politicians talking as they had not talked before. Brian Faulkner, the dapper little shirt-maker from County Down who was the premier's second-in-command, issued a strong and important statement of Stormont's new and toughening policy. Rioters, he told a meeting in Downpatrick, were gambling with death. 'Make no mistake, the government and the security forces mean business. Rioters are now literally gambling with their lives.' Privately, government officials were saying that the shooting of O'Hagan, and its expected reaction, might be the excuse necessary to re-introduce some of the clauses of the Special Powers Act. The fifth night of the riots was the night when one first began to hear the cautious use of the dreaded word 'internment': and Stormont officials were brought down to man the police press office during the period, preparing for the very real possibility that something more than simple counterforce might soon be needed to curb the troublemakers. Propaganda, it was realised, would be an important weapon—and the O'Hagan riots provided the propagandists with the opportunity for a dry run.

The army, though, being unwise to these political rumblings, dealt with the troubles as best it could: the deployment of a few more soldiers, the wheeling out, for the first time, of a brace of new Mercedes watercannon, and the introduction of a strange, Alice-in-Wonderland sort of weapon, the rubber bullet.

The KOSB's charming press officer showed the soft and squidgy things to reporters that Saturday morning. Six inches long, one and a half in diameter, and rather obviously phallic ('the girls in Derry will love it' some soldiers used to say) it seemed a bizarre way for a modern army to be going to war. 'I just don't know what they're coming to,' mumbled one reporter from the *Observer* at the press show, 'firing bullets made of rubber. Soon they'll be lobbing grenades full of confetti, and guns that fire rose petals. You can't take this sort of thing seriously at all.'

And in spite of the earnest effort of the KOSB's own PR man, it was difficult to take these strange things very seriously at all. Hong Kong's wooden bullets, from which these were developed, were another matter, but these were very hard to take. The first six were fired on the Saturday night, when rioters in Divis Street bombarded an army patrol with steel-tipped arrows and someone spoke of a crossbow in action from a high-rise flat. Six of the Greener gas guns were used—the bullets were made by the same firm in Kent that made CS cartridges, and neatly fitted the same shell cases and the same guns—and there were six loud cheers from the Fallsmen as the stubby black phalluses bounced and twirled their way into the mob. The next morning reporters were called into bars to be shown the deadly things—and someone, the first of the hustling rioters, tried to sell them for five pounds each. Later in the year they would become a substitute for money in the

Bogside, and mounted on a steel pedestal, worth a good ten guineas from a visiting American reporter.

The riots of that weekend—which, while bad enough, were happily free from deaths—caused me one minor embarrassment in the paper of Monday morning. It was about midnight, just below the Divis Flats. The Catholics had built a number of flimsy barricades across Divis Street and were tossing stones from behind them at the army grouped around the Hasting Street police station, a couple of hundred yards east, on the town centre side. I was with a reporter from the Press Association, the London-based agency which supplies some of the news needs of the local British papers and a little of the reporting of the nationals: he was a busy man, forever having to dash to the phone to add a new line or two to bring his story right up to date. The two of us were just beside one barricade, crouching under a street light, in the middle of the riot but just out of target range of most of the stones. Only if the army fired gas would we be in trouble: and (the Black Watch having so kindly returned it) I had my mask as well, just in case.

But the Royal Regiment of Fusiliers were not in a gas-happy mood: they were not, unlike some battalions of the time, a gas-happy unit: and it was clear they had something else up their sleeve—a clever tactical move designed to clear the street by stealth and surprise. At midnight precisely, the colonel ordered it. From the Hastings Street side of the riot we suddenly heard the whining of a dozen Rolls Royce engines being gunned hard, and within twenty seconds the entire street was filled with dark green pigs and Saracens and Ferret armoured cars rushing rapidly and relentlessly up to the barricade walls.

A Ferret, its lights out, its turret swinging wildly around as its commander searched for snipers, was the first one to hit. There was an almighty crash, the front two wheels of the little machine reared up over the oil drums and the beer kegs and the knife rests, and carried them along the street, screeching and screaming as it went, for fifty yards. Then it detached itself from the mess, with only a long strand of barbed wire trailing between its rear wheels, sparking and sputtering in its wake like a jet flame. It went on into the Falls Road dark, the sparks spewing out from behind: more and more armour piled in after it: and within the quarter hour, Divis Street and the Lower Falls was quiet.

The PA man, who had seen the first onslaught by the Fusiliers, had gone to telephone. And what he phoned was printed in the *Guardian* story under my name on the front page that next morning:

> 'The troops introduced a new weapon—electrified wires trailed behind a Ferret armoured car which would give a 24-volt shock to anyone who touched them.
>
> It is believed to be the first time these weapons have been used in Ulster—although they have been in operation in riots in other parts of the world.'

It took a long time to live that one down, needless to say. And we took a solemn vow that we would only use the PA when all else had failed.

The restless five days came to an end with Danny O'Hagan's funeral. He was not, so far as we ever knew, a member of the IRA: but his funeral was the first of a long long string of IRA ceremonies that proved the Irish supremacy in turning the art of death into one of the great folk industries of the country. In Ireland no death is ever forgotten: it is the stuff of legend, martyrdom and romance: life, in Belfast anyway, has rarely any romance about it and little of legend either. O'Hagan was canonised that Monday afternoon; rather more substantially, one suspects, than his Maker might have decreed.

His coffin was draped in a tricolour: stout, grim-faced men, of whom only some were relatives, carried the wooden box out of the O'Hagan house on Antrim Road, down past the harp-marked spot on Shandon Street where the Scottish bullets found their target. A lone piper walked ahead, blowing a mournful valley dirge that was swept by the wind down the mean streets of the New Lodge: behind the coffin walked six hundred ranks of men— three thousand of the new Republicans who would form the charter members of the new model army forming slowly but steadily under the British and loyalist eyes in the Belfast of those times. Danny O'Hagan's funeral may have been a mawkish, unnecessarily rosy-decked affair: but it presented to those of us who watched —and to the generals and the ministers and the secretaries of state too—an awesome picture of a rising and a risen people. The three thousand who tried to keep in step behind the casket on that day were not just restless Catholics, out for civil rights and for the right to sleep in beds in houses like the one Austin Currie had been tossed from two years before: these were the soldiers of a new army—a great new army that would, in time, bring a state very nearly to its knees and a proud people almost to a state of desperation.

Up to mid-August such violence as had occurred in what the old-timers were now dignifying again with the phrase 'The Troubles', as in the 20's, the 30's and the 50's, had a fairly standard list of weaponry. On the rioters' side was the brick, the bottle, the petrol bomb, the odd half stick of blasting explosive, the rifle, the pistol, the occasional Thomson machine gun. On the side of the forces of law and order there had been, up until that time, the water cannon, the baton, the CS gas cartridge (and its sister the gas grenade), the lead bullets fired from either the SLR or the Sterling sub-machine gun, the ·38 service revolver and, since the beginning of August, the ludicrous rubber bullet. Neither the army nor the opposition had begun to get really inventive: the IRA took the first step in this direction on the night of Saturday, August 8, when it used the first of the car bombs; and its men planted one in a little lane in the border country, near the small but celebrated Northern town of Crossmaglen.

The Lisseraw Road, as the lane was called, half a mile from the town, is a little-used byway that snaked across the granite foothills of Slieve Gullion, a mountain that divides Armagh from County Louth. Some farmers drive their cattle along it to the milking sheds; since early spring the army had been using it as a convenient border patrol route. Generally though, it is a forgotten little lane, coming from nowhere and going nowhere.

So the villagers on their way to mass the following Sabbath morning—the area was heavily Catholic—were more than a little surprised to see a red Ford Cortina parked in the lane, near the entrance to a field. One or two of the more curious churchgoers peered in, and saw a bag of golf clubs in the back and a radio in the front seat. The car was still there on Monday night, and it became something of a talking point in the village bars—of which there were many.

On Tuesday evening Paddy Murphy, who lives in a small white-painted cottage nearby, decided to take his small lad Colm for a short spin to have a look at the now famous red car: Mrs. Murphy had seen a grey police Land-Rover stop and look at the vehicle earlier in the day. Colm and his father clambered all around the car for five or ten minutes, noting its County Down registration number and trying in vain to open the locked driver's door. They could see the passenger window was half open, but the car was wedged hard into the blackthorn hedge. So the two drove away home—and on their way passed a second police Land-Rover from the Crossmaglen station, off presumably to have another, more official inspection.

In the Land-Rover were two young policemen, Bob Millar from Ahoghill in County Antrim, and Sam Donaldson, whose home was in the pretty Mourne-side fishing port of Kilkeel. They had found out at the barracks that the Cortina had in fact been stolen, as the locals were suspecting: it had belonged to a businessman from Warrenpoint, and it had been taken from outside the Newry hotel where he was drinking that Saturday night. So the two policeman drove down to the car to check for fingerprints—it was 8.45 p.m. and still light, and would be for another hour—and perhaps even to take the car back to the station for return to its owner.

At five minutes to nine, Colm and his father, by now almost back home, heard a massive explosion from where the car had been parked. They rushed back to find the scene of what was soon to become a familiar horror.

What was left of the shiny red car was now lying upside down, a smoking, blackened, oily mess of twisted wreckage, barely recognizable: wheels, the radiator grille, huge chunks of red body-work and the smashed golf clubs had been hurled hundreds of feet across the field, some of the metal bent against the small bushes of a hedge that bordered the meadow. And over this hedge, half in and half out of a shallow ditch, were the heaving, moaning bodies of the two policemen, both horribly mangled, bleeding heavily and evidently beyond hope. Paddy Murphy rushed home to call the ambulance and the police: the whole village tore down to look at the wreckage in the fast fading evening; and up in Belfast we heard about the bomb—or whatever it was, around midnight. We had twelve lines in the last editions of the paper, telling how two RUC men had been injured by a 'booby trap', and how they were in hospital in Newry in what the matron described as 'serious' condition.

The forensic people told us next morning that it had been a bomb. Fifteen pounds of gelignite placed under the bonnet of the stolen car had been wired to the courtesy light inside the passenger compartment. What happened, they believed, was that Constable Millar had edged his way around to the locked passenger door, put his arm through the half-opened window, clicked the lock back and pulled the door slowly open. As he inched it free, the micro-switch that would have put on the interior light triggered the detonator and the bomb exploded: Bob Millar's arm remained inside the door, torn off and mangled by the heat and pressure of the gases. He died before dawn next day: Sam Donaldson, who had been on the driver's side of the car, was dead just after midnight.

It is strange to look back at the kinds of reaction the politicians of the time expressed. Brian Faulkner, who was officially Minister of Development, but in reality the most available and most literate and intelligent spokesman for the government, placed the blame for the bomb squarely on the IRA—he called on the Irish prime minister, Jack Lynch, to order a search for the culprits and to send them back for justice; the Northern prime minister said the attack was 'foul and vicious' and 'as cowardly an act as any of those which for too long have stained the pages of our history'. Robert Porter, the ineffectual little lawyer who was

Minister of Home Affairs, and theoretically the man who should have the powers to run the IRA to earth, issued a statement saying the bombers 'had no right to call themselves human beings'. Dutifully we all reported all we heard: those of us who had been to see the mangled remains and who saw the widows and the children of the dead men and who came down to the funerals later in the week would accept all that had been said as true and reasonable responses to a vile, terrible crime.

Sadly, though, this ready acceptance and understanding of the condemnations and the cries of rage was to become less and less evident as the Ulster tragedy magnified. When two policemen became twenty policemen, and when one victim a week became ten victims a weekend, and when the children and the mentally sick and the crippled became as fair game for the murderers as the trained and equipped and fit men who ran the forces, the process of killing in Ulster became little more than a numbers game to many of us. The editors tended to want to know how long it would be before the total dead reached a certain, arbitrary figure, rather than the tragic circumstances of each individual death; funerals that rated a page in 1970 rated less than a couple of lines at the base of page three a year later. And yet, of course, the widows of the men killed in 1971 were no less tragic figures than the families of Sam Donaldson and Bob Millar in 1970. It is one of the tragic inconsistencies of newspaper reporting that sympathy is a mortal commodity, and that a routinely violent death in Northern Ireland rates less now than a traffic accident. Had newspapers always attended as closely to the individual tragedies of Northern Ireland one might have shocked someone into action before their time: as it was, our reactions to the killings of the policemen at Crossmaglen seemed right and proper, and our reactions since often woefully cynical and inhuman.

1970 was a good year for forming a political party. The spring had brought the Alliance Party to premature bloom; the summer saw the emergence of a one-man party with the cumbrous title of the All-Ireland Democratic Party, under the firm hand of the ultra-loyal Major Ronnie Bunting, who had simmered down from his notorious passions of 1969 to revert to his post as a maths teacher at Belfast Technical College; now, come the autumn and the Catholics were in party mood. Ideas for a coalition of the Catholic left had been floating around the island for half a year: and once the floods that disrupted the city in mid-August had subsided, these ideas, like flotsam, began to solidify into something more substantial, and a name, and a policy began to emerge.

It all began with John Hume and an *Irish Times* leader-writer getting together one summer evening over a pint or two, and discussing the disunity of the Stormont 'Opposition'. It certainly was a shambles: ranged against the Loyalists united on and behind the government benches were representatives of the Northern Ireland Labour Party, the Republican Labour Party, the Nationalist Party, and three Independents. Each party had old loyalties and aging visions of its own eventual triumph—the Northern Ireland Labour Party was even viewed by the *Guardian* leader-writer of the day as a possible eventual saviour of the entire calamity. But ranged against the Loyalists, the splinter groups of the left wing had no effect, and Brian Faulkner and Roy Bradford and the other Unionists ministers of the government treated the opposing factions with a contempt for their inadequacy that was to a large extent deserved.

It was a British Labour MP, Maurice Foley, who first came to comment loudly on the inadequacies of the left in Ireland; and he proposed informally, both to John Hume and the Dublin leader-writer, that something might be done to change the old alliances. The editorial that resulted from the ideas led to Radio Telefis Eireann, the Dublin broadcasting network, wheeling in one of the younger and more spirited Nationalists, Austin Currie himself, for a wireless interview. He expressed enthusiasm for the formation of the new party. Things then began to move swiftly. Gerry Fitt, the senior Belfast Catholic politician—who had seats at Stormont, Westminster and on the Belfast City Council as the representative of the Republican Labour Party—rushed back from his holiday cottage at Cushendun as soon as he had heard Currie on the radio (some remember him hitch-hiking back, because he

95

missed a bus and didn't have the money for a taxi) and put the word around he'd like to lead the new group. The Northern Ireland Labour Party, despite its links with Transport House and with Maurice Foley, kicked out one of its members, Paddy Devlin, for associating with the new group: John Hume and Austin Currie pledged their loyalty to Gerry Fitt; and within a week the new party was seven members strong and was given its name, straight from the revolution, the Social, Democratic and Labour Party.

Fitt's Republican Labour colleague, Paddy Kennedy, turned down with scorn the idea of joining the new party. It was, he had heard, to be an offshoot of the British Labour Party 'and I will have no truck with any British-based party here in Ireland,' he declared. As Kennedy went on to become the leading spokesman for the Provisional IRA in the North, his decision to abandon party politics at this juncture was quite probably reasonable.

The vital plank to the SDLP's policy was the first point in a nine-point manifesto that was circulated on beer-soaked paper at a news conference held in the Grand Central Hotel on August 21. 'Our primary aim,' the manifesto read, 'is to promote co-operation, friendship and understanding between North and South with a view to the eventual re-unification of Ireland through the consent of the majority of her people.' A policy with which few reasonable people could honestly disagree. The Alliance Party, issuing one of its few press releases, did sound a somewhat discordant note amid the fanfares of good cheer that rang out for the SDLP that night: the party's formation, Alliance put it somewhat loftily, 'will harden religious divisions'. Harden them or no, the SDLP was due to become a potent force in Northern Irish politics.

In those moments when either the words, or the bricks, had stopped flying, there were some fairly pleasant stories to report on in Belfast. In the late summer of 1970 all the hardened old reporters who covered the night time troubles were forced to double up as William Hickeys for a while as two of the more famous females of the world outside came to visit us. Kathleen Winstanley was first. A lissom young lady from Wigan, Miss Winstanley had won the title of Miss Great Britain just eight days before, and was in Belfast as part of the tour of her realm.

She stayed with us at the Royal Avenue: and for some as yet unexplained reason, collapsed within hours of waking up on her first morning, and had to be carted unceremoniously back across the sea to England. Unkind men who didn't care for the hotel said it was all to do with the breakfasts, and immediately cabled their home offices for food parcels.

The second lady stayed a little longer and created a bigger stir. She was Mrs. Aristotle Onassis, the former Mrs. Jack Kennedy, who had come over to Belfast with her husband (whom the Irish papers named Aristotle O'Nassis) to look at one of the shipyards he owned. Jackie took to the Belfast people like the Queen to the housewives of the East End: she treated them with a mixture of courteous condescension and distant warmth, and the Belfast women, Protestant and Catholic alike, seemed to adore her for it.

She had been booked to open a new social club for Harland and Wolff men down on Queen Street, right down near the entrance to the Lower Falls: the crowds who turned out in their thousands to watch her trip inside for her salmon lunch and for her presentation of an orchid spray were as homogeneous a mix as anyone could find in Liverpool or London or Cardiff. Catholic housewives from the Falls, great burly shipwrights across from the yard, their faces still brushed with the oxyacetylene tan and their overalls smudged with grease and their religions and their loyalties as Protestant as the party they espoused—they all mixed close together to see this tall, handsome, legendary woman wave and smile on her way through. It was a moment of easy unity for ten thousand Belfast people, which would soon be forgotten. It was one of those fleeting city moments that gave some of us faith that perhaps all was not hopelessly lost.

Aristotle himself was a charming if rather morose little man, with a cash register for a mind and a drawing board for an imagination: he looked sadly down into the well of one of the dry-docks at the Harlands yard, while his wife was away to the luncheon back in town, when someone asked him, what did he think of all the troubles? 'What troubles is these?' he asked, in painful English, 'I just don't understand.' Perhaps it was just as well: the

visit of the Onassis family was one of the final normal moments
the province was to know, and it was perhaps only fair that Ari,
whose investments in Belfast totalled millions, had seen it smile
its fairer smile on him and his wife that September Saturday.

The fusion of ideas on the Opposition benches at Stormont,
which had to be reported in detail and interpreted in even more,
was not the only political development of that autumn. For
while the Catholics were coming together, so the Protestants—
the Loyalists—were drifting apart once more. The uneasy peace
which had reigned since the Imperial election was being steadily
ruptured by a further rightward drift of the Unionist Party: and
it was one of our more fascinating jobs that autumn to chart the
loyalist ship of state as it hit every rock, escaped every sand bar,
and launched every lifeboat at the start of its tortuous journey
towards its final stranding 18 months later.

First, little 'Beezer' Porter, the good, honest, respectable, faintly
pompous lawyer who had run the Home Affairs ministry since
William Craig had been kicked out of office and his Yorkshire
replacement had been found wanting, decided it was time to cut
and run. Officially, Porter claimed that he was running short of
money—after all, the salary he received as a Stormont minister
was scarcely comparable to the sums he made from his prosperous
city law practice. Porter resigned that autumn because he had no
taste for the job: within two years he was to leave the party
altogether. But then, although we reported his decision as having
'no special political significance' it was a subtle indication that
the Cabinet Room was becoming too hot a spot for a man of
essentially moderate views.

James Chichester-Clark, the prime minister, took over Porter's
job and delegated the minor responsibilities of the post—traffic,
police pay and parking wardens—to a young and tolerably bright
right-winger called John Taylor. (Taylor and Austin Currie had
gone to Queen's together a decade before, where they were given
the joint sobriquet, the 'heavenly twins'.) Taylor's appointment
was immediately seized on as a concession, albeit a small one, to the

right wing of the party. 'The elevation of Mr. Taylor to this delicate Ministry [delicate because the Ministry, though not Taylor, controlled the police and, more important, took responsibility for the wielding of the high powered weapons of the Special Powers Act] looks to us like a coming-home present for Mr. Paisley and a serious piece of appeasement to Mr. Craig and the lunatic fringe of the party. This proves to us,' the Alliance Party declared, 'that the Prime Minister will not be removed suddenly over night by the hardliners: instead they will take over by a process of slow and steady poisoning.' Mr. Taylor, nevertheless, was given a seat in the Cabinet; and his first decision, which was to prevent a march by the famous 'Black Men' of Belfast—a loyalist group still more awesome and arcane than the Orangemen—did much to still the early fears.

But the rightward drift continued. Early in September one of the more extreme branches of the Unionist Party—a body known as the West Ulster Unionist Council, which was led by the jovial one-time Agriculture minister, Harry West, who looked as though he might be at home with a pig and a pitchfork rather than pen and portfolio—split well away from the mainstream of the party. Harry West's men—who claimed to be fed up with the fact that Chichester-Clark was getting nowhere in his repeated, but supposedly half-hearted, demand to London for more guns for his policemen and for a re-establishment of the B Specials, the old part-time Protestant police—held meeting after meeting in the small towns to the west of the Bann. They eventually came up with a pamphlet openly condemning the Chichester-Clark government and pledging their support for Craig, who, a former Minister of Home Affairs, had been relegated to the back benches in 1968 for his supposed extreme views.

Bickering went on like this all autumn long. We would wait for news of the squabbles day after day, outside the crumbling red pile of buildings in Glengall Street, next to the Belfast bus station and beside a cinema, where the Unionist Party power still lay. With genial loyalist experts like Billy ('Flack-Jacket') Flackes of the BBC and John Wallace of the *Belfast Telegraph* and Henry Kelly, by then the number one man on the *Irish Times*, I used to

stay and drink endless coffees and beers and eat mountains of
sandwiches while waiting for the stars of each particular Unionist
occasion to emerge and say their piece.

The party was more complex than its importance demanded:
it had endless standing committees and councils and executive
bodies, and proceeded with business with the efficiency of a
Women's Union and the keenness of a schoolboy philately club.
Its members either talked (like Harry West and Brian Faulkner,
who often couldn't be stopped) or didn't (like Commander
Anderson of Londonderry who once referred to the *Guardian*
as 'The damnable IRA Times—the one paper I shall never talk
to!'); and one way or another the days spent in the sun outside
the Glengall Street mausoleum were as pleasant a way to report
the more delicate strainings of the Ulster scene as any we had
then discovered.

By late autumn the soldiers were beginning to worry about the
effects the political splits seemed to be having on the streets. The
Unionist divisions at Stormont, and the obvious lack of success
the premier was having in winning any major new concessions
from Mr. Maudling in London, seemed to be taking their toll
on the patience of the Shankill Road.

By the end of September the soldiers of the King's Regiment,
who were based in a disused bakery on Snugville Street, deep in
loyalist country off the Shankill, were getting as rough a deal
as they might expect from the Ardoyne or Ballymurphy. The
trigger was always the same—football crowds, the skinheaded
hooligans who mobbed round the goalmouth of their Linfield
Football Club, and who invariably tried to create a stir on their
way home from the Saturday match. As they streamed past the
small Catholic block of flats—the Unity Flats, they had been
named, in more hopeful times—they would yell abuse, sing
loyalist songs and toss small stones in the Catholics' direction.

It was the duty of the Kingsmen to hurry the Protestants along
and past this flashpoint—'ought to have a bloody turnstile at the
bottom of the Shankill and let the blighters through one at a time'
one sergeant moaned out loud one night—and keep the shouting
to a minimum. But occasionally the Linfield crowd were too

exuberant, and the soldiers went in after them quite as zestfully as into a Catholic mob, and hauled the ringleaders out.

The Shankill Protestants—already suspecting that London was snubbing their leaders at Stormont, and already aware that the real military control of their little province belonged to the Chiefs of Staff in Whitehall and not the Chief Constable of the RUC (who was, in any case, an Englishman at this point) decided, after a few Saturdays of this sort of thing, that to be arrested and roughed up by English soldiers was just not to be tolerated.

And so they rioted: the first serious Protestant riots aimed specifically at British soldiers since those of October 1969 after the 'B' men had been disbanded and the policemen disarmed. The Protestant riots of October 1970 were brief, violent, bloody; they were fewer weapons around then, and the unhealthy cunning of the Catholic rioters—who put razor blades into half-potatoes and who skimmed the broken bottoms of milk bottles and aimed cracked marbles at you with catapults—all this was happily not in the Protestant armoury. The Kingsmen, with a bit of help from outside, managed to put the disturbances down with little fuss: but for Chichester-Clark up at Stormont, who was seeing the anger of the Harry Wests and the Bill Craigs—and even of the young John Taylors—now spelt out in broken glass and broken heads on the Shankill Road—the autumn riots must have been a sobering experience.

And then, the prime minister fell ill. Gaunt, avuncular, easygoing Chichester-Clark succumbed to some minor ear infection and took the opportunity, as we saw it then, to show his distaste for and his lack of interest in the unseemly wanderings of the party of which he was the nominal leader. His illness led some of us to suspect that he might soon leave the corridors of power at Stormont, to make way for a more ambitious, more blunt and more accomplished politician: the piece that follows, though denied all round at the time, indicated fairly well the direction the party was taking and the leader who was likely to emerge:

The standing committee of the Ulster Unionist Council meets this morning [Friday, October 2] and the Prime Minister's absence from it, especially now that his health is reportedly much improved, is both mysterious and uncharacteristic. It is the first time he has been conspicuously absent from any of the graver party meetings and although one accepts the Stormont assurances that he will be back at the Castle on Monday morning, fit and rested, some are beginning to wonder whether weariness and a gentleman's longing for his labradors and his brogues and the peace of the country is beginning to overtake him.

The standing committee meeting has been called primarily to discuss . . . local government reforms. Without a doubt there will be present a substantial proportion of right-wing dissidents who will do their very best to embarrass the architects of reform and who may yet attempt to slow its progress. . . .

The spotlight will thus tend to fall today on the man who has to defend these local government reforms, the Minister of Development, Mr. Brian Faulkner. Whether or not the Prime Minister had been able to attend, Mr. Faulkner would still have been compelled to speak simply because it is his Ministry that has to carry out these specific reforms.

But since Tuesday, when the Prime Minister's illness first became apparent, Mr. Faulkner has also been in temporary charge of the Ministry of Home Affairs, the most sensitive of all political appointments in Northern Ireland, and one that he has held before.

The significance of this is that Mr. Faulkner has now responsibility for defending all of the reform proposals against today's right wing snipers: local government and housing reform under the banner of Development, B Specials and law and order reform under Home Affairs: he is in effect appearing before the standing committee as a party leader on trial, and will have to take the full force of any attack that develops.

It is too early to say if Mr. Chichester-Clark's world weariness is the beginning of his downfall. Clearly an early resignation on the grounds of ill-health would suit West-

minster immensely more than a swift palace revolution.
Mr. Maudling . . . has warned of the dire consequences . . .
of a right wing take over at Stormont.

Following a possible resignation the only obvious successor would seem to be Mr. Faulkner, who can combine an
astute political mind with a reasonable degree of acceptance on both sides of the Irish Sea . . .

His candidature is not yet imminent but, although Mr
Chichester-Clark will probably appear at Stormont this
Monday, there may not be many Mondays left for him. Mr
Faulkner's movements will be watched closely.

And that, give or take a bullet or two and a bottle or three and a
visit from a minister here and there and any number of angry,
kindly, soothing, irritating, Christian, devilish, pleasant, vile,
loving, hating, placatory and bigoted words, was more or less
how Ulster ended 1970. Bernadette Devlin came out of prison,
getting two months off for good behaviour; the Orangemen took
advantage of Remembrance Sunday to march in perfectly legal
defiance of the Stormont ban on parades that had been brought
in after the summer riots; there was a spirited free-for-all in the
streets after the Belfast Corporation announced a rise in bus fares;
and Jerry Rubin, one of the current American high priests of the
coming revolution came across to Ulster from Chicago, only to
be unceremoniously booted out by policemen muttering that
they had enough trouble already, thank you. There were some
minor riots, some troop withdrawals and some unpleasantly
large bombs; there was a massive confrontation between police
and civil rights demonstrators in Enniskillen, which passed off
peacefully enough; and there was the grim news that thus far the
disturbances had cost the British taxpayers no less than £5
millions.

But basically the outlines of the year had emerged. The IRA
had come out to fight. A spray of new parties had blossomed. A
curfew had come and gone and a people had mobilised their
feelings in consequence. The loyalist blood was up. The prime
minister was on his last legs, assailed by his countrymen, plagued

by his inability to act as fiercely as he wanted, constantly wishing for the peace of the countryside and aching to leave the troubles of his province to someone else.

A new chapter was about to be opened in Northern Ireland. Its precise origins probably came with the tossing of a small, deadly, fizzing parcel at a party of Royal Marines in the Crumlin Road in late October. But, in essence, the new chapter was to begin as the Near Year was chimed in over a sober province just two months later; what happened in October was the dress rehearsal for the grimmest period in Ulster history to date.

6

Declarations of War

At the close of 1970 the British army commanders announced they were planning actively to 'loosen their grip' on the wild men of Ireland. A year before, after James Callaghan, the Labour Home Secretary, had reluctantly decided to send the Prince of Wales' Own into Derry and forces had been dispatched to the riots that spread to Belfast, there had been about 3000 soldiers stationed in the province. By late autumn 1970 more than twice this number were billeted throughout the six counties—some of then sleeping well, in solid old barracks like Armagh and Omagh and Ballykelly, others on the top deck of Corporation buses in a depot at the top of Belfast's Springfield Road.

They had seen their fair share of action that year, it was true; a few men had been hurt in the process; a lot had taken their first test in peace-keeping duties after only a couple of days' training on the drill square at Catterick. But by late autumn it was becoming clear to the generals and the brigadiers of the time that a force of 7000 soldiers—many of them needed in Germany, others due to go out for exercises in Malta or Norway and still others needed for the United Nations peace-keeping group in Cyprus—was too large to maintain in what was thought, wrongly, to be a settling situation: and so in early November the orders were given for two battalions to pull out.

The commanding officer of 41 Royal Marine Commando, Major Peter Spurgeon, could not have been one of the keenest supporters of the move, even though his was one of the units destined to leave and to return, in his case, to Plymouth. Two weeks before he left his Commando was involved in the last big riot of the year, in late October, and he held a press conference afterwards to say, memorably: 'This riot ended a month of peace in Belfast, according to the record. But to say there has been a month of peace in Belfast is a misapprehension: Belfast is never truly quiet. The situation can blow up any minute. This is not a peaceful city.'

Major Spurgeon's riot might have passed relatively unnoticed, were it not for the fact that on this occasion the Provisional IRA commander in the Ardoyne, where the trouble had its epicentre, chose the event to try out a new weapon.

It was just after 1 a.m. on a cold, drizzling Friday morning: the Crumlin Road was in turmoil, and with a few wet and miserable reporters I was hanging around waiting for anything to put into our last edition of the night.

A Commando platoon, dressed in full riot gear, had been standing in the dark at the entrance to Kerrera Street for about half an hour. Such reporters as were there so late in the night were standing next to the marines, chztting idly to them, stamping their feet, ducking behind the Perspex shields the marines obligingly yanked up each time a half brick whistled out of the thick blackness ahead. From time to time we would see a flicker of a match in the gloom as a rioter paused for that moment of refreshment before sending another broadside of masonry in our general direction. Usually the bricks were deflected by the shields: once in a while, though, they hit home—and of all possible places, the ankle seemed the most usual and most painful place to be hit; the reporters, having no shields, were hit depressingly often. The marines, their faces blackened and their helmets jammed firmly down over their ears, grinned gently from behind the Perspex each time I winced with pain. It was that sort of night—'easy aggro' as they would say, no points to be scored on either side, no major injuries or concerns.

After about ten more minutes the platoon commander decided that it might be politic to advance into Kerrera Street and try to haul out a few of the riot ringleaders. So after a moment of crackling radio requests and receipts of the necessary orders, the officer barked softly to the sergeant that a slow advance was to begin: the dozen or so men in the front ranks began to edge their way into the pitch-black street.

Without warning, two grey cylinders, each about six inches

long, floated out through the air from some unseen point ahead; they hit the ground about two feet from the gaitered legs of the leading marine and fizzed gently on the tarmac. We all thought they were gas cylinders—Ardoyne men had a favourite trick of stealing CS cartridges and tossing them back at the troops once in a while—and all of us, marines and reporters alike, pulled down our masks.

But there was to be no gas. Instead, there were two enormous bangs that echoed and re-echoed between the little houses. There were screams of pain, clouds of smoke, the crash of windows coming out, and shouted orders of command from the Land-Rovers behind. When the dust cleared, six of the marines were lying immobile on the ground, two of them bleeding badly from their legs, one with a foot half torn off. From down in the Ardoyne there was a burst of wild cheering, yells of 'Up the Republic!' and 'Fuck youse all!' A pair of ambulances shot up to us and took the six men away. Everyone was stunned by what had happened.

The mood changed in an instant. A few moments before the marines were friendly, sportive, enjoying the night as much or as little as the rioters. But after the bombs they were angry and understandably vindictive, aching for a chance to hit back with something stronger than just another dose of gas or a douse from the ancient Humber water-cannon which trundled up and down the road, alternately squirting and refreshing itself from a hydrant, like some senile, half-crazed elephant.

There were three more bombs that night. It was obvious that they were shrapnel devices, and that the shrapnel involved was a collection of sharp nails, for we found dozens of grotesquely twisted six inch nails lying in the roadway or fused into the tar. But what exactly the bombs were, and just why they were being thrown just then was not, as they say, immediately clear.

Martin Meehan, the young, chubby, prematurely bald labourer who had the command of the local battalion of the IRA, explained the bombs a few days later. The lads called them nail bombs, he said. They were just a half-pound stick of blasting explosive, with two dozen six-inch nails arranged around the stick, held tight in the folds of a piece of corrugated cardboard, and the whole lot bound up tightly in black masking tape. The weapon could hardly have been neater or more effective: a grenade that cost less than sixpence to make, and yet one that could lay low a quarter of a platoon of British soldiery. 'You can say it's our weapon of the moment,' he said triumphantly, and tossed a few in the air, like a juggler.

Next day an angry Peter Spurgeon told reporters that 'in future our men are not going to wait and see what's thrown at us before we open fire—we can't take the risk that what we think is a brick may turn out to be a bomb.' Major General Tony Farrar-Hockley, the cheerful and slightly flamboyant Commander of Land Forces in Northern Ireland, and the chief of day-to-day military planning in the province, tried to tone down Spurgeon's remark by pledging that 'We are not prepared to shed innocent blood, even if our innocent blood is shed.' But then he went on to say something far more interesting. It was in response to a nicely timed television interview, broadcast by the local station back at home in Newcastle. Cathal Goulding, the Dublin house painter with the Burt Lancaster looks who ran the Official IRA was the subject, and he told the reporters, while the riots were going on in Belfast, that 'a military campaign is being planned now by the IRA against the British Army. We are going on the offensive.' Farrar-Hockley had seen the transcript of Gouding's remarks. 'I believe what has been said. I think there very probably is a campaign in the making.' But it was not the Officials he worried about—it was the Provisionals; and as Farrar-Hockley rightly believed, they too were to begin an offensive campaign.

Until June, the IRA had been dormant: at the end of that month the Provisionals took on the defence of the Short Strand; in July the Officials, the ball-pen Marxists from whom the militant Provos had split the year before, took on the battle of the Lower Falls. Both these actions, and almost all planned and operated through the rest of 1970, had been essentially defensive operations, both of limited scope and intention. The Provisionals, true, had exploded two big offensive bombs—the one that killed the policemen at Crossmaglen, and another which should have wrecked an electrical sub-station in the Malone Road, but which instead killed the volunteer planting the device. But essentially the work of both wings in 1970 was defensive: the offensive actions which culminated in Martin Meehan's over-arm tossing of the nail bombs in November were no more than practice. The offensive campaign was to begin with the New Year; and by then the two small armies had had all the practice they needed.

Up until the New Year I had been living a nomadic, unsettling sort of life: I was in Belfast for weeks at a time, perhaps getting home to see my family in Newcastle once a month, or less often, for only as long as the news dictated. For most of the year, I had lived in the Royal Avenue Hotel, moving out for a brief while in the late autumn into a flat a mile from the city centre, and bringing my family over for a few precious weeks. But even then, I was technically the *Guardian*'s Newcastle staffman—no one had been appointed to take my place there, and I still received regular invitations sent on to Belfast, by the ever-efficient secretaries, to attend meetings of Northumberland County Council and the Hexham Rotary Club.

At the year end I came home for a while, spent Christmas in Oxford and then—since the news desk had decreed that Belfast was quiet enough to remain covered solely by our able 'stringer' on the *Belfast Telegraph*—took the train up to Manchester to write for a while on the big news stories of the Black Country. It was a prospect I did not cherish, after eight months of sheer excitement, and I longed to take the BEA flight back 'home', even though it meant leaving the family again. I didn't have long to wait—and when I went to Ireland again, after a two-week pause, it was to be as permanent correspondent on a story which the *Guardian* at long last had come to acknowledge simply would not, for the foreseeable future, join most other news sagas and steal away into oblivion.

The year began badly with a rash of minor incidents—including four tarrings-and-featherings inflicted on young Catholic men and women who had found themselves on the wrong side of the Provisional IRA. Intimidation had become a serious problem once again—I came across a number of savage incidents in early January, including a man who was knocked down in a city centre car park and whose legs were driven over again and again by a heavy saloon car until his bones must have shattered to dust; and another youngster who was driven out to Lisburn and his arm smashed with a heavy iron bar; and a pregnant Catholic woman who was beaten hard and had her hair pulled out in fistfuls. And of course many of these same 'offenders' were shot in the kneecaps by men who wanted to make sure they remembered all their life that they should never 'offend' again.

Tarring-and-feathering—a punishment which Richard I first introduced in the twelfth century to cope with an outbreak of pilfering aboard his Crusade-bound warships—seemed a bizarre action to those of us in England who were recovering from the excesses of yet another prosperous Christmas. To hear that a young man had been tied, with barbed wire, to a lamp standard somewhere in the centre of Belfast; and that his hair was thickly matted with varnish by a mob of jeering youths; and that a mattress full of dirty feathers had been emptied over his head; and a notice hung around his neck proclaiming him a traitor—all this seemed a thousand miles removed from the acts of a civilised people. It gave the British another of their periodic feelings of superiority in any relations with the Irish: and it gave all my unknowing and uncaring friends and relatives another excuse to say, as I packed once more for the flight to Ireland, how awful it was 'over there', how 'there just doesn't seem to be any end to it, does there?' and how 'they seem to be no better than animals'.

But I was glad to be back; and waking up on those January mornings to hear the sepulchral tones of the morning newsreader intoning a litany of yet more shootings, an explosion, an act of arson, eight more petrol bombings, a five-hour riot and some more tarring incidents, made me realise that however deliberately most Dubliners tried to ignore the fate of the Northern six counties, the pathological ignorance of the Englishman was unsurpassable. Part of this was our fault, of course—no newspaper published in London had ever made a deliberate attempt to cover the country, before these troubles, with any degree of depth and sympathy. The television coverage was patchy in the extreme; and the radio coverage, while better, was often ruinously super-ficial. It was up to us to try to change British attitudes. Harry Whewell, the Northern news editor and architect of the *Guardian*'s Ulster coverage, said as much when I first telephoned from a Belfast coin-box once I was back. 'I don't care if the readers think it *is* boring. You report it all, every day, and we'll get through to them in time—it's a duty now. We have to see it through.' Some other newspapers began to think the same way—*The Times* and the *Financial Times* especially. Most of the rest, though, were con-tent to proceed as before, taking Ulster as just another horror story.

The IRA campaign was beginning: one could see it out in the open, read it in the dozens of little street newspapers, hear it in the bars and learn it from conversation with the senior soldiers out at Lisburn. It was beginning where the first anti-army riots had started the previous Easter—the Ballymurphy housing estate and the Springfield Road—the home of the 2nd battalion of the Provisionals and of the 2nd battalion, the Royal Anglians. The British troops had their battalion headquarters in the Springfield Road RUC barracks, a short way up from where the Falls and the Springfield Road cross: their forward headquarters was in a converted Presbyterian church hall on the very edges of Bally-murphy and the Protestant quarter, New Barnsley, called the Henry Taggart Memorial Hall. The Anglians in Ballymurphy, led by their stalwart CO, Dick Gerrard-Wright, were the first to meet the IRA campaign head-on. It began for them when, as a low-level effort of intelligence gathering, they opened a small evening discotheque up at Henry Taggart Hall to win some short-lived popularity with the local Catholic girls.

Just after Christmas the Provisionals began a stealthy campaign of propaganda to drive a wedge between these girls and the soldiers, to whom, it was suspected, they were beginning to warm. A small picket was put on the gate of the Henry Taggart Hall: mothers gave graphic accounts of how their girls had been raped or drugged and 'introduced to heavy drink' inside the barbed wire compound that housed the bleak little dance hall.

Girls who continued to go to the dances were spat at and abused as they left for home. Eggs were thrown: girls who had been seen with black soldiers—and the Anglians had a considerable number of men from Africa and the West Indies—were the targets for the nastiest of racial taunts. Gerrard-Wright acted promptly and closed the dance hall down, though kept a cinema open to any girl who wanted to share some of the cheerless night hours with the soldiers. This had a worse effect still, and soon the visits of the girls triggered off a riot.

> More trouble broke out in Ballymurphy last night when a crowd of 50 or 60 youths stoned troops, injuring two of them. Five men were arrested after petrol bombs were thrown. The rioting began early yesterday morning after police Land-Rovers were attacked and one was overturned . . . during Wednesday night's disturbance the 50th petrol bomb of the New Year was thrown . . .

This was how I reported the night of January 14—it was the kind of report I had had to file almost every night since my arrival and which would continue as the *leitmotiv* of the next several months.

It was an important time for the army. Unknown to us, Gerrard-Wright and his subordinates were only then beginning to talk to the men who were then prominent in the Provisional movement—Frankie Card and Liam Hannaway and Paddy Leo Martin (a trio of old-time Clonard IRA men who were controlling and supervising the activities of a growing army of irregulars —1200 or more by early 1971, they estimated) with a view in part to cooling the Ballymurphy situation. Equally though, the joint discussions were begun in an effort to win valuable intelligence about the strength of the burgeoning enemy and to try to divine their tactical plans.

By all accounts the furtive meetings—which were tolerably successful, at first keeping the Ballymurphy troubles at a low level, but which failed in most other respects for the understandable reason that neither side trusted the other—had ended by January 15, the night after that last riot in 'the Murph'. The first, unsuspected tactical plan which Card and Hannaway and Martin and Kelly and McKee and the other IRA men dreamed up was put into operation at 5.50 p.m. that evening: it was, in guerilla terms, something of a masterpiece.

Late in the busy Friday afternoon six small teams of IRA men drove into the centre of Belfast. Each team had one or two small cigarette-packet incendiary devices on hand, and each had been dispatched to lay their little bombs in big and well-known stores in the main shopping streets. By 5 p.m. devices had been set in a department store in the Cornmarket, a drapers in Castle Street, the Old Park Road public library, Boots the chemist, also in the crowded Cornmarket; a furniture store in Donegal Street, and another in Arthur Street. At ten minutes to six the first of the copper wires snapped closed, the first of the sparks ignited the gelatine petrol capsules, and the first of the cigarette packets burst into flame. A thick spiral of black smoke began to spiral first out of the windows of the Cornmarket department store.

Inevitably there was total chaos. As soon as the first of the 999 calls had been placed, and three fire engines had screeched up High Street, scattering shoppers and worsening the traffic jams of the weekend evening, so another call came from a man who spotted another blaze in Arthur Street . . . and another in Donegal Street . . . another in the Old Park, and so on. Within half an hour frightened people were scurrying the hose-ridden streets like crowds of rats; huge columns of smoke towered over the city; fire engine bells and police sirens and ambulance bull horns whined and clanged from every direction. Business men alerted by persistent radio news-flashes hurried back into town to check that nothing had been left in their stores or offices; traffic backed up for miles and miles; people stood unbelieving as firemen battled hopelessly against vast towers of flame which shot up the side of some of the best known buildings in town and as walls crashed down into the roadways, crushing parked cars and smashing ten thousand windows.

By late evening most of the fires were out: insurance assessors were reckoning the damage in hundreds of thousands of pounds—perhaps even millions. Belfast was quiet again, but it was shaken.

Half its centre had been racked by fire, just like the bombing raid days of the Second World War; out in the suburbs rioting had started and was worsening by the hour. Shots were being fired and more petrol bombs were being thrown. Army vehicles were clattering in droves through the charred streets. The IRA had chosen terrorism as its weapon and had struck its first blow with pungent success: Belfast was no longer a city struck by inter-necine strife alone, or rocked by Protestant and Catholic rioting and bitter fighting. It was a city that was now being shaken with terror: and the firebomb campaign of that Friday night was its introduction to a year of terror such as it had never known before.

The firebombs of Friday night led to a weekend of grave and widespread rioting and destruction. The army did its very best to contain the howling mobs, but—with only six battalions in the city ready for duty after the December stand-downs—it was a difficult task: the disturbances, which had come on top of three near-continuous weeks of minor aggravation, led the Unionist Party's right wing to complain bitterly to Chichester-Clark that he was not doing enough, that a 'tougher line' was needed. The prime minster, still not fully fit after his winter ear-troubles, was exasperated and dispirited. He had planned to fly across to America the next week to bring a little business back to the burned factories in Belfast and Derry: but his right wing prevailed on him and on the Monday morning he sped up to the Royal Air Force base at Aldergrove and took a flight out of the chill morning Antrim mists up and across to London. He needed help from London, and he needed it quickly.

What would he bring back, we all wondered, as we tramped our feet in the cold of the city streets, looking at the weekend damage and talking to the locals. The Protestants wanted him to bring back the policy of internment—'We've given in to those bastards across there,' an old man said, nodding his head quickly at the corrugated iron wall that was once the 'peace line', and behind which lived the Catholics. 'We've given everything to them, and now look what they do. They should be run in, no questions asked, and slapped behind bars. We've had internment before—let's have it again.'

All Tommy Roberts and his dragoons of pressmen would tell us from his warm little office at Stormont Castle was that his prime minster had gone to London to see the Home Secretary 'to discuss with him how we may best act in concert to tackle the problem of disorder on a most firm and determined basis.' No word about the nature of what was needed other than a concern 'that the security forces must now take whatever firmer measures are needed'. The prime minister said, before he got on the plane, 'I feel sure this is the view of Her Majesty's government in London.' It sounded to us all as though the Northern Ireland prime minister was going begging—begging for London to understand him and his terrible problems. Only he wasn't sure just which was his real problem—the IRA down in Belfast, or his own right wing up on the Hill. And if he didn't know, London certainly didn't either.

It was a depressed and dejected man who flew in from Northolt aerodrome that evening. London had evidently failed to grasp what it was the old man had wanted; there were no firm promises, he told us at the airport—nothing apart from the assurance of a visit the next week from Lord Carrington, the Defence Secretary and from Richard Sharples, the polite it ineffectual politician who was then Secretary of State at the Home Office.

Stormont reconvened at two the next afternoon, and it was a wild and uncomfortable session. Chichester-Clark, who had left the province in an atmosphere of high drama and who had returned deeply disappointed, was pressed again and again by the bogeymen of the right—Craig, Paisley, Beattie and Boal and other, less well-known men like Joe Burns on the back benches. Why had he come back with so little—would he do this, and that —would the Prime Minister introduce immediately a policy of internment and curfew, internment, internment, internment. . . .

All he could do, like any politician, was promise. 'I can give no firm assurance that we will not introduce a policy of either internment or curfew,' he told a worried Catholic Opposition.

'When the security chiefs advise us to take this course, we will not be slow to act. If the situation requires it, the Government will not shrink from doing its duty.' Chichester-Clark had given his word he would do his duty when the time came. He wanted internment, his officials told us later, but the army wasn't advising it, and London wasn't allowing it. It was an intolerable position for him and one of the saltier old men in the Stormont press gallery commented that night, 'He can't go on peddling these promises for much longer.'

He had to stop peddling the promises precisely a week later when, for the first time in his career, the party called on him to resign. Not all the party of course, just 170 of the 900-odd members of the full Unionist Council—but it was enough to send a shiver up the spines of the sober officials of two governments. The powerful William Craig–Harry West rump of the Unionist Party filed a formal motion of no confidence. 'That this council,' the resolution intoned, 'recognising with increasing anxious concern the abysmal and costly failure of the Government to maintain law and security in this community, calls upon it to resign so that a new administration may urgently attempt to save the country from impending disaster.' Everyone knew Craig and West could not win the 400-odd votes they needed to place the prime minister under an obligation to quit: but the resolution itself was the first sign that the mortar was crumbling away from the edifice of the state, and those of us who lived around the doors of Glengall Street began to watch the struggle with mounting concern.

Lord Carrington came to Belfast for a day, talked to the Ulster Cabinet with something approaching faint contempt, perhaps in an attempt to shock them out of their stone age thinking, and made the brilliant public relations decision to announce the possible introduction of a new weapon 'a weapon that has been especially developed for use in Northern Ireland'. The promise tended to draw attention away from the fact that he had omitted to give Chichester-Clark the military support he claimed he needed to survive. Carrington agreed to increase the establishment of the Ulster Defence Regiment to a new target level of 6000 men: but he would not bring any more regular soldiers over to Belfast right away. They were always on hand, he reminded everyone, if they were needed urgently. But there would be none right now—only that 'new weapon', which never materialised. Now Chichester-Clark really was in trouble.

In its own way the army did little enough to help the ailing leader. The contacts with the Provisionals were still renewed in mid-January. And the Provisionals succeeded in persuading the army to keep the supposedly detested police out of what were rapidly becoming known as the 'no-go' areas. William Craig dropped the bombshell revelation in the Stormont Commons on January 27—when he recounted how two Ulster policemen had been patrolling in the Clonard—where the army's best Provisionals contacts were living—when two IRA men strolled up and calmly told the constables to leave immediately. The policemen, said Mr. Craig, did not argue with the IRA men, but went across to a patrol of Gerrard-Wright's to ask for help. Yet Craig went on to say that the soldiers, after radioing in to their H.Q., confirmed what the IRA had said—the police would find it in their own best interests to keep out. And the army patrol escorted the RUC men to safety and away.

Craig's report of the incident caused a minor sensation. For the army was appearing to be working in some collusion with the IRA. The tough, traditional Ulster approach was being replaced, it appeared, by a soft, conciliatory British approach. And all the while Chichester-Clark was standing idly by, watching his country dying under his nose. But conciliation was about to end. The British army was about to lose its first soldier to an IRA bullet— and it was about to turn its weeks of intelligence-gleaning into substance: the real confrontation was starting.

It began early in the afternoon of Wednesday, February 3. I was up at Stormont when Billy Flackes came up to me in the lobby. 'I hear there's trouble down in the Clonard, Simon,' he whispered in a strangely confidential manner, 'and I heard it's pretty bad.' I called the office, told them the news, and raced down the hill and across the Lagan bridge as far as my battered Hertz car would take me.

By the time I got there the Clonard was a terrible shambles. What had happened, according to sources both in the army and in the Provisionals, was that earlier in the day the police had warned soldiers that the IRA had lists of Special Branch men working in Belfast, complete with the numbers of their cars and their addresses—and from 'information received' it was probable one such list would be found hidden in the home of either Card, or McKee or Liam Hannaway. So the army, in what was at first a quiet and efficient operation, went into a number of houses in Ardoyne and Clonard to look for the lists. One of the houses they entered was that belonging to Liam Hannaway on Cawnpore Street. Once again it was the Royal Anglian Regiment (the *Guardian* once inadvertently called them the Royal Anglican Regiment, a misprint to join 'President Eisenhowever' in the list of all-time greats) who were brought in to do the searching. They finished, reportedly, by about noon; but then, for reasons which have never been properly explained, Gerrard-Wright kept his men on in the area—and, predictably enough, the soldiers became the focal point of an attack. The riot started at noon: the Protestant workers at Mackie's factory over the road came out for lunch a few moments later and, equally predictably, gathered in the roadway to jeer and toss armfuls of 'Belfast confetti'—rivets and bolts and heavy chunks of ironware—into the fray.

The fight developed and subsided in an hour; but the troopers stayed on, and the IRA began to organise itself. Women were brought out to taunt and harass the soldiers—a couple of them were to be knocked over by military Land-Rovers racing up and down the streets in a crude display of force. Then the barricades began to go up. Lorries were hijacked out in the main Falls Road, driven deftly into the rabbit warren of the Clonard, set down sideways on and overturned. Great fires were lit—rubber tyres made the very best blazes, which would lift any CS clouds up and out of effective range. The womenfolk scurried around with buckets of vinegar and bottles of water for the weary youngsters at the barricades: it looked like Derry all over again, with soldiers and police and Protestant workers on the outside, and a tiring, violent, half-crazed mob of people on the inside, hurling paving stones—which children were pounding to pieces in the doorways —out at the men whom they considered their assailants.

That night machine guns were brought out and nail bombs were thrown. The army wheeled out its water cannons once again and the rubber bullet guns were fired all night long. It was the curfew all over again, but with the IRA now fully ready to begin battle.

It was appropriate, perhaps, that General Freeland chose that day to retire. The sleek, grey-haired general had seen his command expand to unprecedented levels, he had done his best to contain a deadly situation, but he had not had a single one of his men killed. His successor would not be so fortunate.

The next day London acted with the consummate swiftness Carrington had promised. A battalion of soldiers was sent across the Irish Sea immediately, he announced. More than 1400 men of the UDR were being put on immediate full-time duty: and the Duke of Kent himself (perhaps he was Carrington's secret weapon, one reporter mused when he heard the news) was coming across with his unit, the Royal Scots Greys. Up at Stormont we heard Chichester-Clark say that 'we are now witnessing a trial of strength between extreme Republican elements and the security forces—the police and the army will defeat this ugly thing which is holding the community to ransom.'

The rioting went on, nevertheless: five hundred men of the 1st Battalion the Royal Regiment of Fusiliers, and the duke's squadron of armour, poured in through the Belfast docks. Buses that had to pass through the 'troubled areas' were cancelled, and huge traffic jams built up in the city during the evenings. Stormont issued formal warning that parents would be held criminally liable for their children allowed out on the streets during a riot. The city was gearing up for a major battle, and everyone, whether he listened frightened to every news bulletin, or cursed his weary way home over the mounds of broken glass and burned-out lorries or stayed in the suburbs listening to the faint thumps of distant trouble, seemed to be involved.

And General Farrar-Hockley, aware that his scheme for 'co-operation' was now out of the bag, and that further contacts between the army and the IRA would be impossible, staged a still-remembered press conference and later went on television to do the unprecedented—to name five men who, he claimed, were prominent officers in the Provisional movement. Purpose-fully, he intoned to the cameras that 'We have searched this area because we have good evidence that it harbours members of the IRA Provisionals—and I can say that among these are Francis Card, William McKee (he stumbled artfully over the English version of the names he knew so well, adding to the sense of drama), William and Kevin Hannaway and Patrick Leo Martin, who parade their Republican persuasions with'—and he finished with a flourish 'some braggadocio!'

His purpose in naming names was, he said later, to show the Stormont politicians what they had scornfully doubted—that he knew who the Provisionals were. And in naming he released them from any further need for confidential contact. It was an act of public relations' defiance that would be met by gunfire less than 24 hours later.

Three men died during the riots on Friday night and Saturday morning: one was a soldier, Gunner Robert Curtis from New-castle upon Tyne, the city I had left nearly a year before. The two other men were Catholics who were shot dead by the army. The death of one of the Catholics, Barney Watt, who lived in Ardoyne, embroiled me in a short, but serious controversy that was to be thrashed out in the House of Commons. The circum-stances were complicated—it was a terrible, confused night—but they deserve some explaining.

The rioting that began on the Friday night was no worse than, but certainly no improvement on, the two nights that had gone before. In fact, so routine had the trouble become, and so much of a similar sort had appeared in the previous two nights' papers that I was even able to get away and play a few games of squash out at the Conway Hotel, three miles out to the west of the city.

We had developed the coverage of some low level rioting to a fine art out at the Conway: if I was playing squash one of the hotel's night-porters was detailed to dash across and let me know if anything serious had come up on the excellent Belfast grapevine. (Most hotel staff were Catholics who lived in the 'riot areas' of the city: the bush telegraph of relatives and friends worked well: and providing one was in one of a few particularly good hotels—like the Conway or the Royal Avenue or the Hamill or the Grand Central—one had a good chance of getting first news of any event considerably more quickly than someone who relied on making hourly check calls to the army and the police.)

That Friday night, though, nothing disturbed the game and my partner and I were able to shower and even have a quick half of Harp before motoring back into the troop-filled city for another survey of the scene. 'Suggest you have a look at the Crumlin,' one of the porters ventured as we left: and so I pointed the car through Andersonstown and Ballymurphy, sped across the Protestant streets of Ballygomartin and Woodvale, and arrived at the corner of the Crumlin and Woodvale Roads at a little after midnight. It was obvious something was up.

The Crumlin Road itself was pitch dark, except for the flickering redness of a fire which had started somewhere down in Kerrera Street. When we got a little closer we could see what it was—a petrol bomb had gone off under a pig, and the armoured car had burst into flames: the popping and banging of exploding ammunition inside the car, the swirling noises down in the ghetto and the fact that the troops—marines and paratroopers— were lying on the ground, their rifles pointed unwaveringly down the Catholic side-streets, gave the scene an air of drama.

Luckily there was a paratroop officer who I had come to know well, and I was able to find out what had happened. 'They've been throwing petrol bombs at us,' he said, 'and we've been shooting back. We saw someone fall down, and his mates dragged him away. The squaddie who fired at him thinks he copped it.'

I raced to a telephone—yes, the Mater Hospital confirmed, a young man had just been brought in, and he was dead. His name was not available just yet—but he was dead, and he had been shot, probably by a rifle.

Within seconds I was on to Manchester and dictated a few paragraphs: the army, I said, shot and wounded a rioter who threw two petrol bombs . . .

That line appeared in the last but one Manchester editions of the paper. In the final, the paper 'topped up' my report on that particular killing by adding, with laudable circumspection, a paragraph from the Press Association that quoted a spokesman for the army as saying that 'an army marksman shot dead one rioter who threw two petrol bombs' and proceeded to name the man as Bernard Watt, a 28-year-old man from Hooker Street. In London, meanwhile, the sub-editors were content to take earlier 'top up' copy from the eternal maw of the PA, and in the last London editions, under my name, appeared the damning, unqualified line: 'An army marksman shot and killed one rioter who threw two petrol bombs at an armoured car in Butler Street, off Crumlin Road, Belfast. The dead man was Bernard Watt.'

It was the following April that the storm broke. Bernadette Devlin, a long-time critic (as was her constant companion Eamonn McCann) of the British press and its treatment of Northern Irish news, publicly accused the *Guardian* of altering my report from Belfast that night—and altering it wilfully for the express purpose of telling the people of London and the Home Counties that a petrol bomber named Watt had been shot dead: when in fact there was no absolute proof that Watt had ever picked up a petrol bomb in his life.

There were, as Bernadette observed on reading the last London edition, 'no ifs, no buts, no hint that it [the suggestion Watt had thrown bombs] is an allegation. You set it down as flat fact. The story was altered, and altered in a way that cannot be explained by the details becoming more available, and to an extent which goes beyond normal sub-editing.

'You casually libelled a Belfast worker a few hours after he had been gunned down by the British army, the effect of the libel being to justify the killing.'

She was terribly right . . and terribly wrong. We had—at least,

some unfortunate, hard-pressed London sub-editor had—
'casually libelled a Belfast worker' by the immense pressure of the
work so early on that Saturday morning. But we had not libelled
him, we had not 'justified his killing' for any reason other than
the purely human reasons of tiredness, carelessness and a reasonable reluctance to try to get hold of me in Belfast as soon as the
PA snap had appeared on the wires. The sub-editor would have
known I was still out at the riots. For Bernadette to suggest, as
she did by implication both in the Commons and in her subsequent letter to the paper, that the sub-editor, in liaison with the
Ministry of Defence, or in deference to a subtle reactionary line on
Ulster that she suspected the *Guardian* to have been developing,
had concocted the report—this merely displayed the poor girl's
naivete, her hysteria and—if one dare use the word in connection with a situation that so often justified it—a kind of paranoia
that tended to devalue too many of her later pronouncements.

But I had not been happy with the army's account of the shooting of Barney Watt that morning. From talking to other soldiers
during the night, and from long conversations in the Ardoyne
the next day, and with reporters who had been closer to the incident than I, it did appear that Mr. Watt—who, while a Republican
sympathiser was never identified as a member of the IRA—may
have been shot down for no good reason. One had, in any case,
to accord Watt the presumption of innocence: and so the following Monday I wrote a long article on the apparent change in
army policy that seemed to accompany Watt's killing.

> The army's action in the Crumlin Road, after an armoured
> car had been set on fire, was the action of a military and not
> a civil force. Whatever may have been said subsequently,
> there is no doubt troops fired deliberately at a group who
> they thought had been responsible for burning out their
> vehicle. There was no suggestion at the time that troops were
> 'returning fire'. No 'enemy' shots had been fired at the time:
> the army shot and killed Barney Watt as they might have
> shot an Arab guerilla—not for what he had done but for what
> he was.

The actions of that Saturday night were not confined simply to the death of Barney Watt and the burning of an armoured car. Another civilian—this time an active and admitted IRA man by the name of James Saunders—was shot dead. He was described later as a 'staff officer' in F Company, 3rd Battalion, Provisional IRA. And he was just 19 years old.

A British soldier, Robert Curtis, was killed as well, the first ever to die in that conflict; he was shot dead while he was patrolling in the Antrim Road at about 2 a.m.: the single rifle shot that killed him came from the New Lodge Road, where Danny O'Hagan had been shot by a KOSB marksman the summer before. It was, as the New Lodge Provisionals might have said, an adequate revenge.

But when we heard the news early that morning, it was more to most of us there than simply another big news story. 'A soldier's been killed' someone shouted down the road to me: and even though I knew it was inevitable, and even though I should have voiced no more and no less regret than when I heard of the deaths of Watt and Saunders in the hours before, I have to confess that I did. There was an indefinable feeling of being in a foreign country in Ireland, North or South—and, it must be admitted, there was some identification, some commonality between the ordinary British squaddie on the street and the ordinary British reporter or photographer or television man who followed him around and wrote about him or took pictures of him or whatever. Often both would moan together about the ills of Ireland; often he would understand you, and equally often you would understand and sympathise with him. Like us, he, the individual soldier was no real part of the trouble; like us, he had been sent out from England to do a job—and the manner of its doing was a source of professional pride to him, even though it was a matter of high politics and high emotion to everyone outside. It was probably for reasons like this—and more visceral feelings beside—that made me and most of the other British reporters who came on the scene to watch the blood pumping out of the dying Curtis feel a dreadful, inexplicable sense of loss and shock.

John Chartres, the delightful man who covered the North for

The Times—a man who had seen plenty of war action and was still a major in the Territorials back in Manchester—probably felt worst of all: and for days after the shooting he was quiet and grim-faced. For my own part, I suspect that as soon as the Curtis funeral was over, and the valedictory rifles had been shot into the air and the coffin sent out of sight, I forgot it completely; it then, and only then, became just another news event, another statistic. My feelings were magnified tenfold by military men like John Chartres and magnified again a thousand times at army head-quarters and at the Ministry in London. As one colonel said bitterly the next morning, once the blood had been washed off the paving stones, and the spent cartridge case found across the street in a gutter: 'My God, we've got a bloodied nose now—and we're not going to let these sods forget it.'

The soldier who died was a 20-year-old married man from back home, from Newcastle upon Tyne. The irony didn't escape us: and my wife, who was in Newcastle at the time, remarked the next night on a double irony—the fact that 'Songs of Praise' on Sunday came from a church in Belfast and while she was watching it Curtis was being flown back to Newcastle to stay for ever. While something good and glorious was coming across the Irish Sea by cable, something tragic and terribly futile was coming across, in the body of a boy killed for no better reason than he was a convenient symbol of a system that half a nation hated.

From a purely military point of view, Robert Curtis' death was all the more pointless. He was no infantryman, but a gunner, a highly skilled technician whose regiment—94th Locating Regiment, Royal Artillery—was normally based in Germany, hard up against the Iron Curtain. His job, to look at it in its widest context, was to protect men like the very sniper who killed him from the supposedly aggressive intents of the soldiers of the Warsaw Pact, and for his pains he was rendered into a street patrolman in Ireland, to be killed, with a single shot, in the middle of a Belfast night. Many of the soldiers who died after him did so for similarly futile reasons: yet somehow, the death of Gunner Curtis seems still to provide us with a classic example of the sheer waste of life that the Irish troubles have brought in their wake. Gunner Curtis and his wife could be considered as making a positive contribution to the European peace. But that counted for nothing with the single pressing of an Irish nationalist's trigger finger. It suddenly seemed—for Watt, for Saunders and for Curtis—an awfully hard world.

Even the funerals that inevitably followed were a peculiar nightmare. When Barney Watt was being carried to his grave the Tuesday following, a Protestant youth dashed up to the cortege and snatched the tricolour from the coffin. Immediately about a dozen men wearing blue trench coats and berets jumped from cars following the cortege and chased after the youth. There was a report that at least one of these men carried a gun, but the young man, whoever he was, escaped with his trophy into the safety of a small loyalist crowd that had gathered to shout and jeer at the passing coffin—the bravest man on the Shankill that night, and a candidate for fifty free pints of Harp.

There were other curious happenings on that day of keening and catafalques: when James Saunders' body was borne out of his little house on Ardilea Street, four men wearing khaki uniforms raised silverplated revolvers to the sky and fired them, one at a time, while British soldiers, hopelessly outnumbered, looked on blankly. And as the procession moved on up the Old Park Road a group of sober-mouthed RUC men on hand to keep some semblance of order became the subject for five minutes of intense abuse from the leaders of the cortege. I remember vividly how one constable, tall and erect and impressive in his long blue raincoat, stood and argued patiently for a long minute with one of the angrier mourners. Finally, the mourner could stand the argument no longer, and raised his hurley stick—a heavy-headed club resembling a hockey stick—over his head and brought it down with a thick thud on the constable's head. The policeman never bent an inch: his body fell backwards, his long raincoat stiff and straight until he hit the ground, cold and quite unconscious with a great purple weal spreading across his forehead. The other RUC men dashed to his aid: the funeral procession moved on: the supine policeman brought undisguised grins to the supposedly sad faces of the cortege followers.

There was a final incident when James Saunders was being taken along the Falls Road up to the IRA grave at the Milltown Cemetery: as the coffin passed the junction of the Falls and the Springfield Road, a British soldier in the turret of a parked Ferret armoured car did what to most onlookers seemed an astonishing thing. He raised his arm to his brow and stood, for half a minute, while TV cameras from a dozen countries trained on him, in full salute.

'Would have saluted Hitler if he had been in the box,' an officer explained later in the day, when the questions began to rattle up to Lisburn. 'One of our chaps was just being a bit wet,' went the later explanation. The Unionists, who saw the pistol firings and the salutes and the graveside orations on television later in the afternoon were purple with fury, and demanded that the troops do something in response: all the army could muster was three young men who had been arrested in Saunders' procession—they were dressed in khaki and wore berets and carried hurley sticks. They were charged, under the Special Powers Act, with wearing a banned uniform and carrying offensive weapons. Their appearance in court three weeks later caused further serious riots and further arrests and further deaths. What had happened in the Clonard on Wednesday set off a chain reaction that was to become a feature of disturbances for all the following year. An arms search provoked a riot; a riot produced a shooting; a shooting produced an IRA funeral; a funeral produced arrests; the arrests led to court appearances; the court appearances led to riots; the riots led to shooting and the shootings led to deaths. It was, in truth, a vicious circle, and one that no one seemed able even to think about breaking.

At the end of February two policemen, Inspector Cecil Patterson and Constable Robert Buckley, were shot dead by Martin Meehan's men in the Ardoyne. Cecil Patterson's loss to the Special Branch was incalculable. His knowledge of IRA operators in the city was more thorough and more accurate and more up-to-date than almost anyone else on the force: he was a man uniquely recognised by both sides as of immense value and he was respected by the men he hunted as the wry, sardonic agent that he was. His killing was a tragedy inevitable to his calling: and it was, coincidentally, the most significant military gesture the Provisionals were to make for many months. Meehan claimed later the policemen had been shot by mistake. 'The luck of the Irish,' he grinned stupidly.

Lieutenant-General Sir Harry Tuzo took command of the British troops in Northern Ireland after the weekend, Lt-General Erskine Crum, Freeland's immediate successor having died less than a month after taking over the command. The force was a very different outfit from that which had been 'loosening its grip' on Belfast just before Christmas. It was now up to nearly 8000 hard-pressed men, and after the deaths of Buckley and Patterson, London graciously condescended to allow yet another battalion to come across. The 3rd Light Infantry had been sent over in the wake of Gunner Curtis' death three weeks before; and now Carrington was sending over still more, and Mr. Chichester-Clark was able to offer yet another pacifier to the Stormont Commons: these soldiers, he proudly explained, would be garrisoned in permanent new bases 'within all the riotous and subversive enclaves'. In other words, all the Catholic areas of town would now get their permanent battalion of British soldiers. The old policy of 'Croppy, lie down' as the Catholics would say was seemingly being re-introduced, with highly trained British soldiers doing a job that Irish history had so often demanded that they do.

But another battalion was not quite what the right-wing men of the party was wanting right then. One can sympathise to some extent with the men we called the 'hard-liners' on the government benches and beyond. They had seen, after all, a Labour government strip away all the political instrumentation with which they had, with some short-term success, subdued the rebellious tendencies of the minority; they had seen a Tory government come to power in London and, while upholding the theoretical right of the Unionists to hold power in their own country, had used their forces with reservation and vacillation to produce a military situation that was deteriorating by the hour. There was no longer any law and order, in the strict sense of the phrase, in many parts of Northern Ireland. The men of the loyalist right first blamed the Socialists for removing their only means of restoring that order, and then blamed the Tories—and their agents at Stormont—for doing nothing to improve matters, with the army under London's command.

Demands of one sort or another circulated from the Unionist right-wingers like sycamore seeds in autumn: one document, which the British Foreign Office observer, Ronnie Burroughs, and the Army Command at Lisburn received, was dignified with the title of a Cabinet document, though its style and presentation —it was a badly typed and hand-corrected list—indicated it was more the work of the dissidents than the Cabinet Office itself. At the end of a long series of fairly routine demands—the restoration of guns to the RUC, the re-establishment of the forces Lord Hunt had recommended should go, and the establishment of curfew and cordon-and-search operations as routine, rather than reaction—came an amazing request: the document demanded that the army begin making punitive raids into Catholic areas after riots that had involved obviously Republican-inspired violence. The request came, in name if not in spirit, from Chichester-Clark: it was obvious then, if not after his fruitless dash to London in January, that the tired old man was soon going to have to be retired.

His end came suddenly and shockingly. Reginald Maudling made a brief visit to Ireland for some pious, pointless pontificating to the Senators and Members of Parliament at Stormont; and his speech, which one Catholic member called, quite rightly, 'a load of platitudinous nonsense', and which John Hume called 'an insult to our intelligence', was followed by renewed Catholic rioting. (In the first edition of the *Guardian* for March 6 I said that 'Mr. Maudling's pious utterings at Stormont. . . were greeted on the Falls Road with a defiant raspberry'; it was quite true, and it was exactly what the rioters were doing: but the sober-suited public relations' man Mr. Maudling trailed behind him telephoned me and complained, formally, about my 'disrespect'; it was not the first time that the sober-suited gentlemen of Whitehall were going to have to complain about disrespect from those of us who reported Ireland. Sometimes their insincere meanderings and their much-vaunted visits seemed every bit as disrespectful to Irishmen, Catholic and Protestant. It was all part of the foreign attitude of Belfast which the Englishman still has such phenomenal difficulty in comprehending.)

The mood in the city that week was low indeed, and it was, technically, a bad moment for me to slip away home. But I had personal affairs to attend to besides Ireland, and late on the night of Wednesday, March 10, I was kneeling on the floor of our house in Newcastle tacking some new curtain material for our slow-motion removal. The telephone shrilled: it was 11.15 p.m., and it was Harry Whewell, the news editor, ringing me from home. 'I'm sorry to bother you', he said, as nice and polite as always, 'but they've just found the bodies of three young soldiers out near the Belfast airport. They were shot in the back of the head, I think. You'd better get back as quickly as you can. I'm terribly sorry . . .'

Once I had phoned the airlines and made the necessary reservations and packed ready for the morning's first flight out, I said to my wife, who was still on the floor tacking the curtains: 'That must be it—Chichester-Clark just can't survive that. He's finished now, poor sod.'

The enormity of the crime had, at that time in Ireland's troubled history, few equals. John and Joseph McCaig, aged 18 and 17, and their friend Dougald McCaughy, had been soldiers in the 1st Battalion, Royal Highland Fusiliers—a battalion that had only recently taken over guarding responsibility for the area that included the lower Shankill Road and the violent little bastion of Unity Flats. The three men, all of 7 Platoon in B Company, had put on mufti and had gone 'walking out' as the expression quaintly has it, that Wednesday night. They had gone first to the crowded and smoky and warmly pleasant city centre haven of Mooney's Bar, for the start of a good session of hard drinking. Somewhere along the line—perhaps in Mooney's, or perhaps in the cosier little nook of Kelly's Bar, three hundred yards away up

Bank Street—they were joined by a group of freelance Provisionals—a group with pistols and a fanatic dislike of soldiers, but significantly, without orders from their superiors.

The trio of youngsters should have been back at their camp at Girdwood Park at 6.30 p.m.—they had been granted an extra two hours' walking-out time because, as their CO put it, 'we hadn't expected any real trouble that afternoon, and these three were pretty reliable boys'. But their meeting with the Provisionals was a fateful encounter; somehow, on some pretext, the soldiers were lured away from the beckoning of their barrack gates and persuaded to have a few more drinks and, so the speculation goes, a look at a lass or two. Whatever the temptation, the three were taken up to Squire's Hill, a remote and beautiful spot up in the shadow of the Divis transmitter, and close to the spot where I had gazed at my first view of the sprawling city. The men were hopelessly drunk: they could scarcely have known what was going to happen when they were forced to kneel down in the hedgerow, and stubby black revolvers were pressed hard into the back of their close-cropped necks. The gunmen nearly blew their heads off— 'they were horribly injured—horribly,' their CO commented the next morning. 'This was a terrible crime.'

Ulster and the whole outside world agreed. Bernadette Devlin, who returned the next day from a five-week lecture tour of the United States, was shocked into a white-faced silence: for weeks afterwards the spot where the three cheerful, goodlooking young boys had been found was marked with a spray of spring flowers; the phrase 'the three Scottish soldiers' became as familiar an expression of the Ulster tragedy as Bloody Sunday and McGurk's Bar were to become in later months.

The Ministry of Defence immediately recalled all the soldiers serving in Ireland who were under 18 years old, and announced they would never be sent back. Scotland Yard detectives flew into Belfast in droves: and an unknown, fat, grizzled redneck from the Belfast shipyards, a man named William Hull, announced he would lead a march of his fellow workers through the city centre to mark Protestant anger at the murders.

The march marked the new political reality of Chichester-Clark's position. On the banners the 9500 angry workers carried were fiercely phrased demands for the introduction of internment without trial for suspected IRA men. The deputation that called on the Glengall Street headquarters of the Unionist Party was fully a mile long, and it snarled up Belfast traffic for hours, taking police and soldiers totally by surprise, and causing the right-wing politicians up at Stormont to mouth silently at the prime minister 'I told you so...'

Within a couple of days John Taylor, who had taken a diluted version of Robert Porter's job at the Ministry of Home Affairs, joined the ranks of those demanding internment. He went on the BBC to say he was 'disappointed' with the way the British army was handling some aspects of the situation: the only way to deal with the kind of menace that brought about the killings of the three youngsters was 'to take firmer action'.

Chichester-Clark's position was growing weaker by the hour. London had refused to listen to the Unionist demands for tougher action and for punitive raids on Catholic territory; they were refusing again now to listen to Chichester-Clark's demands for the introduction of a policy of internment. The Whitehall seers objected to internment on both political and military grounds; they accepted, rightly as it turned out, that the re-introduction of the policy would mean killing and rioting on a scale much more massive than ever seen before. And politically, they reasoned that internment would render the province even less likely to respond to reason: overwhelmingly, the Conservatives believed the British army could, given time, over-run the IRA, and reduce the guerilla powers of the body to an 'acceptable norm' as they put it. They would not give in to Chichester-Clark under any circumstances.

But we did not know this at the time. I dashed back home for a day: Chichester-Clark dashed to London on Wednesday, March 17 to plead with Carrington and Heath for the necessary lifebelt. Would he get it nor not? He flew back to Belfast that night saying nothing, and I flew across to Belfast the next morning intending to hear his address to Stormont at 2.30 p.m., when he would announce whether or not London had agreed to his demands.

And then came one of those splendid moments of supreme frustration. Our plane couldn't land in Belfast because of violent crosswinds—we got within a hundred feet of land before zooming off into the skies again—and we were diverted to Dublin. We were at the Dublin airport just before 1 p.m., and Chichester-Clark, more than 120 miles away to the North, was due to speak in a little more than ninety minutes' time. It was an impossible moment.

Mike Nicholson of ITN was caught in the same predicament: the only thing to do, we reasoned, was to hire the fastest car we could—a souped-up sports car which Hertz laid on at a second's notice—and drive like the wind. The rain sheeted down, the crosswinds nearly blew us into a dozen Irish ditches: but at 2.50 p.m. precisely, we roared up to the ramp at Stormont and rushed into the gallery. Chichester-Clark, white-faced and nervous, was still sitting down: question time still had half an hour to run; and we had time to draw breath and listen to what would either be a valedictory or a victory speech.

It was a grim, saddening performance. The prime minister had been able to wrest only one minor concession—1000 more soldiers and a squadron of armoured cars—from the British masters. He was given no new powers to delegate to these soldiers —soldiers which even Sir Harry Tuzo did not want because, as was pointed out at the time, he had nothing for them to do. Tuzo would be in the odd position of having to play the Grand Old Duke of York with his men—marching them up and down, up and down with the simple aim of letting both the Catholics and the Protestants see they were there, and meaning business. The gesture didn't win across the politicians: the speech was the 'non-event of the year' said Bill Craig, one of the authors of the earlier resolution to force the prime minister to resign. Men like Billy Hull, still flushed with the success of the loyalist march through the city, denounced the impending arrival of the 5th Light Regiment, Royal Artillery, the 1st Battalion the Queen's Regiment and the B Squadron of the Royal Scots Greys, as 'totally meaningless'.

And watching Chichester-Clark drone out his pathetic message to a House for which not one single member from any single bench had a single word of support, was painful and unforgettable. He shuffled up to the despatch box like a senile country gentleman, bowed, nervous, fiddling with his papers, unsure of himself and deathly pale. He looked, as I recorded at the time, 'a broken man'.

Westminster realised this the next day; and late on the Friday night despatched a powerful pair—Lord Carrington and Sir Geoffrey Baker, the Chief of the General Staff and the most eminent spokesman for the military mind—out to Belfast on an RAF jet. It was a desperate attempt by the Heath government to try to persuade Clark not to resign—he had already told Number 10 he intended to go, and late on Friday night Heath himself telephoned Chichester-Clark at his flatlet in the Castle, totally amazed that his Ulster landlord had such strong feelings. Clark for his part, never a great wit, reportedly told the British premier—while crunching away at fried chicken his security man had brought from a nearby café—that he had tried repeatedly to impress upon him the strength of his views—'What more could I have done,' he asked 'leapt on the Cabinet table?'

Saturday's visit of the Defence Secretary was under conditions of the most amazing security: it was the first time I had seen civilian Britons carrying sub-machine guns, but for all its drama it produced little either of show or substance. There was plainly nothing anyone could do for the premier now: he had already told the Chief Whip of the party, John Dobson, that he definitely intended to go, and a special meeting of the parliamentary party had been called for Monday morning. Although not even the unkindly titled 'holy trinity' of moderates within the Unionist party—Anne Dickson, Basil McIvor and Robin Bailie—had been able to find words of support for their leader in the Thursday debate, by Friday night there were open expressions of sympathy from all quarters for a man who, it was now being said in Belfast, had been 'stabbed very nastily in the back'.

We all gathered in the cold and dark outside Stormont Castle late on the Saturday night, after the Britons had gone home to more pressing engagements. The lights glowed inside the tiny offices, ministers convened to thrash out the crisis together: a car was called to take Mr. Chichester-Clark to an unspecified destination.

Then an official appeared and invited us inside, and on to the carpets under the oil paintings of Ulster's worthies. The prime minister's statement, typed under a red heading, was handed around: 'I have decided to resign' it said, 'because I can see no other way of bringing home to all concerned the realities of the present constitutional, political and security situation. It would be mis-leading the Northern Ireland community,' he added, in a reference to the nagging cancer of lawlessness, 'to suggest that we are faced with anything but a long haul. . . .'

And so he had gone, and Ulster had tasted the fifth premier in its fifty years of life. All of them so far had been tagged with the titles of the old noble clans—Craigavon, Andrews, Brooke-borough, O'Neill and, latterly, Chichester-Clark. All these men had been of the British establishment rather than the Irish: all had been army officers or landowners or products of the Eton-and-Oxford network: all, to a greater or lesser extent, had failed in the job of bringing the two communities of their country together.

But Chichester-Clark, unlike the others, had seemed, in that terribly received Stormont speech of the previous Thursday, to have learned something of value from the violence of the months before. His sad words before the despatch box bear repeating: they formed an eloquent summary of the realities facing the little land and its ambitious new leader, Brian Faulkner, who waited eagerly in the wings. Like much wisdom and eloquence in Ulster the speech was to be widely ignored.

There has been a good deal of speculation in recent days, [he said slowly and deliberately] about changes in person-alities. However personalities may change, these facts of which I have spoken will not change. Anyone who comes to this Despatch Box will have to face them just as I have done. And I ask the House to remember too that we do no service to Northern Ireland if we snuff out the present IRA campaign in ways which merely make a resumption at some other time and with increased popular support, inevitable. Our aim is not just to defeat the present vicious conspiracy but *to create conditions in which such men and such activities can never prosper again.*

But the words were lost in the wind that cold, rainy March week: and all we wanted to know, and all the great public wanted to know, was when Brian Faulkner would get the job, and what he would do that his sad old predecessor could never do. Was this, we wondered, a turning point for the better, or for the worse?

7

A Cunning Little Man

It was shortly before noon on Tuesday, March 23, when we learned the official news of the sucession. It seemed as though every reporter who had ever covered Northern Ireland affairs was jammed in under the klieg lights in the Great Hall at Stormont. There was little tension in the air: the result of the small election going on upstairs seemed a certainty: the fact that Bill Craig had entered the race at the last minute would make little difference to the outcome.

A hush suddenly fell on the gossiping hundreds as a shambling, sick-looking John Dobson, the Unionist Party Whip, limped painfully down a few of the stairs and up to a table that had been set up at the base. 'The voting,' he declared in a weak little voice, hardly suiting the occasion, 'was as follows: Mr. William Craig, 4 votes, Mr. Brian Faulkner, 26 votes. Accordingly I declare . . .' and his voice was lost in the mumble of knowledgeable approval.

A few moments later and the winner himself was tripping down the marbles: neat blue suit, whitish hair impeccably trimmed and brushed, the confident demeanour only marginally upset by the ferrety, darting little eyes, Brian Faulkner, perhaps the most sophisticated politician Ulster had known and certainly the first prime minister to sport an Ulster accent, came down to meet the cameras and his first press reception.

There would be no startling changes from the policy of his predecessor; he saw no broad diversions in strategy, but just the occasional fresh tactical move which might be needed he thought, to bring to an end the rash of terrorism in the province. 'I am convinced that what we need on the law and order front are not new principles, but practical results on the ground . . . I

137

will not expect harsh measures or repressive measures . . . no law abiding citizen will have anything to fear from my Administration—but I will be looking for effective measures.'

Afterwards his critics and the sceptics among us placed a few friendly bets on his future. A couple of Catholic politicians thought he might only last a couple of months. Bill Craig, who tended to have a flair for prediction, reckoned Faulkner would last one year: as it happened, he was correct, to within a single day.

But there was little thought of the darkening future during those first days of the Faulkner administration. There was a muted excitement about the immediate task ahead.

By the Thursday night the impression of Faulkner as an adept and cunning little man—'as cunning as a wagon load of monkeys' someone in London had said—had factual reinforcement. His selection of a cabinet was a perfect example of shrewd and delicate tightrope-walking. The balance was to be achieved by the introduction of two curiosities to the camp. From the right came Harry West, the bland, genial countryman from Enniskillen who, until his acceptance into the Faulkner fold as Minister of Agriculture, had been one of those most vehemently opposed to Chichester-Clark; and from the left came David Bleakley, a kindly schoolmaster who had sat in Stormont before as an able and industrious Labour Party member. He was made Minister, appropriately, of Community Relations. Into the middle of the government came Robin Bailie, a young milquetoast who was given Commerce; Joe Burns, a small countryman of little ability who favoured loud suits and bow ties and who was made a junior minister at the Ministry of Health and Social Services; and John Brooke (the son of the then Lord Brookeborough) who was friendly and delightfully indiscreet, became the party's Chief Whip.

We all had our particular interests in Faulkner's chosen team: my own was the curious remark made by Harry West, the High Priest of Arch-Loyalism, who was asked, a little while after his photograph was taken, precisely why he had joined the Faulkner cabinet, if, as reported, it was not planning to plough a significantly different furrow from the one Chichester-Clark had been ploughing only a few days before. 'Well, lads,' he told us all darkly, 'we must look to the future. I have had assurances from the Prime Minister that I can tell you about and certain others that I cannot tell you about.' That phrase '. . . and certain others that I cannot tell you about' haunted us. What 'assurances' could they be? Could Faulkner have been thinking, as early as March, of internment? We would learn soon enough.

At first, Brian Faulkner was to enjoy a reasonably sweet honeymoon. Not that he had been a stranger to the intimate by-ways of the country he now led: it was just that for a few precious weeks Faulkner was given time to savour his new-found power: his real masters in London would have time to evaluate him from across the Irish Sea; and his enemies, both on the right and in the Catholic ghettoes, would have an opportunity to study the man they would shortly have to engage in battle. Most politicians enjoy a theoretical and traditional honeymoon period of one hundred days: Faulkner's lasted for one hundred and six days—until the afternoon of July 7—which may say something about his appearance of durability.

During the honeymoon there was pleasure to be taken, and there were tokens to be exchanged, by all of us.

The pleasures, I suspect, were mainly mine. I went on holiday for a week, to a lonely little cottage way up on the very Westernmost tip of Wester Ross, and spent a peaceful week with the wife and children I so rarely saw, watching sheep and tossing stones into the Atlantic and reading old holiday books and spending endless hours collecting shells and watching the birds curling in the downdrafts. Before I left I gave the news desk in Manchester the strictest instructions I could muster: no one, but no one, was to get in touch with me unless the Irish army itself marched in to relieve the Falls.

It was my own undoing. After a week of total peace I happened into the only phone box on the peninsula and out of pure curiosity telephoned the office. 'Thank God you've called,' they said, 'we've been looking for you everywhere. You must ring the Editor as soon as you possibly can. It's very urgent indeed.'

Was it the Irish army, I wondered, and studied my battered BEA timetable. I duly telephoned. It was not the Irish army. It was Bernadette Devlin, in London, with her astonishing allegations about my account of Barney Watt's killing two months before—would I mind coming back to Manchester as soon as ever I could to allow the paper to give Miss Devlin the answer she so obviously deserved. We packed and left Scotland—we had planned to leave anyway—and drove rapidly through the gloaming and back to work. A reporter, I assured my gloomy wife loftily, had to live for the unpredictable. Wouldn't accountancy —or geology, even, for which I actually had a training of sorts— be much more cosy a life?

Once the Devlin row was disposed of, I went back to Ireland for a while. Things did seem a little easier under the new man. I took a day off to go up to Portrush, on the coast, with the RUC's Special Patrol Group—the riot squad of old—to look for drugs among the holidaymakers. 'It's a great change from Peter's Hill,' said one of the men, who I had come to know well from the midnight vigils we both of us used to keep below Unity Flats. 'The big difference out here is that the yobbos are so much easier to arrest.' The real difference being, I ventured, that out here it was the yobbos who were stoned. He grinned faintly: Ulster jokes were a coming thing in those days. It was being said that the steadiest job in the city at the time was rear-gunner on an Andersonstown milk float. It occurred to me many times more that an Ulsterman—unlike an American or a Japanese who had gone through similar protracted periods of urban turmoil—had a magical facility for making light of his troubles, and turning a riot into a comedy with absurd ease. Perhaps that was another of the more refreshing aspects of covering this 'bloody country'.

Eastertime came, with all its Republican marches: the Provisional IRA and the Official IRA were to be distinguished from that Easter on by the manner in which they wore their paper lilies for the celebrations: the Officials stuck theirs on their lapels with adhesive, while the Provisionals, displaying even then some tangible degree of violence, jabbed a pin through paper and cloth to achieve the same, though more secure, result. From that Easter on the Officials came to be known as the 'stickies' or the 'sticky-backs': the Provisionals, who only weeks before we had been calling the 'Green IRA'—to distinguish them from the 'Red' or Marx-aligned Officials—were known for a short while as the 'pinnies', but that didn't last.

There was an ugly incident that Easter which underlined, for me, the ultra-sensitive role the press was now playing in Ulster. Easter Tuesday is traditionally set aside for the Junior Orangemen to march. In 1970 their return home led to a serious riot that effectively marked the moment when the Catholics and the British army fell out with each other: in 1971 there was a single shooting by an incompetent East Belfast Provisional which very nearly sparked off a massive battle. The Juniors were marching their colourful way along the Newtownards Road. Troops were out in strength near the Catholic Short Strand but not, it turned out, in sufficient strength. From behind the thin line of policemen and Scottish soldiers—Highland Fusiliers, the same battalion which had lost the young trio in early March—a group of Catholics waved, for a few brief moments, the white, green and gold of the Republican tricolour. The inevitable disturbance gave the gun-man time to perform his dirty work. Within five seconds he had fired off four or five rifle shots into the crowd: four people fell to the ground, including one, a 13-year-old Protestant boy, Tommy Martin, who had been hit, and hurt quite badly, in both legs.

At the time of the incident I was a mile away, outside the Unity Flats, where more than two thousand Orangemen had gathered to shout abuse at the Catholics who lived above. The soldiers guarding the Flats were—even though separated by the river Lagan and the mile of Belfast streets—the very same bat-talion that was then policing East Belfast. And as I knew the CO well, he told me outright what he had heard over his radio net: that a Protestant child had been shot and injured beside the Short Strand.

Below me were hundreds upon hundreds of ugly-minded Loyalists, in as mean a mood as one can conjure up on a mild Spring afternoon. The thought struck me vividly at that very moment: all I had to do was to go into the edge of that crowd and put the word around that a young boy—one of their young boys —had been shot by the IRA across the river. The shouting would have turned to rioting within five minutes, the guns would be out before dark, and the Highlanders would be hard-pressed to keep Unity Flats intact . . . all I had to do was pass the word across twenty feet of open air. It was a strange feeling of power— the power of rumour and of instant reporting, and an instant realisation of the effects these two forms of communication would have upon a city and a people who lived daily in such a highly charged atmosphere.

Naturally enough, I kept quiet. But what if I had been working for the BBC, and had reported the shooting; and what if one of the Loyalists in that crowd had had a transistor set? I began to have doubts, from that moment on, about the precise role the press—and particularly the broadcasters—were playing in Ireland. Would not this have been the ideal case for some kind of self-censorship, I wondered? Did we always have to report everything we saw, as we saw it, warts and all?

John Brooke, then newly elevated to cabinet position, said later he had argued at length with the BBC about the possibility of editors using some degree of self-censorship in their dissemination of news of violence in Northern Ireland. He claimed he won verbal promises for a 'one hour' self-imposed delay which news editors could impose if they thought that by reporting incidents the moment they heard them, further violence might result— Easter Tuesday being a prime example. One hour's delay might well have avoided further bloodshed: yet to impose such a delay would be seen by many—including me, I suspect, had I the fortune to work for the BBC—as the thin end of a highly dangerous wedge. An hour's delay might well evolve into deliberate non-reporting of news; non-reporting of news might eventually mean that some events would be chosen, on a purely subjective basis, to be reported, while others would be shelved. And while no one pretends that editing is anything but a subjective business, there must be constraints, in a political crisis of as grave importance as Northern Ireland to keep that subjectivity to a minimum. The

imposition of the 'one hour' rule which John Brooke so very
nearly urged upon the BBC in 1971 would have placed an intolerable weight on the shoulders of the already heavily overburdened
editing staff at the BBC. It might have worked for a short while,
and, in truth, it might have had some dampening effect on some
of the more spontaneous eruptions on the streets. But in the long
term, I believe—and, thank heaven, the BBC and most of the
responsible newspapers believed as well—self-censorship is a
process that should never be confused with responsibility and self-
discipline.

The status of the reporter in Northern Ireland was to come up
again shortly after the Easter marches, but this time, in a Belfast
courtroom. The case involved an IRA man on whom the police
had been desperately keen to lay their hands since the beginning of
the year. Patrick Leo Martin was the identifiable IRA man
who appeared—darkened in shadow and facing away from the
cameras—on a BBC-Tv current affairs show, Twenty Four
Hours, back in January. The interviewer on that programme was
Bernard Falk, a friendly and impressively keen television reporter.
In early April, shortly after the Scottish soldiers' murders, Martin
was 'lifted' and charged under the Special Powers Act with being
a member of the IRA—and Bernard Falk was subpoena'd to testify
against him.

Not unnaturally, Falk refused to tell the court if he recognised
the man in the dock as Martin—it was professionally improper,
he said, and the question offended the ethics of the trade he practised. Falk's counsel argued—before the two magistrates who,
under Northern Irish law, had to hear cases brought under the
Special Powers legislation—that his client's refusal to answer the
question of whether he recognised the man in the dock was based on
a 'just excuse' over and above his ethical reasons. He could, the
lawyers suggested, be prosecuted back in England for misprision,
in failing to report to the authorities that an offence was likely
to be committed by the man he interviewed. The magistrates
scoffed at that one, reasonably enough: but Falk stood his ground,
determined not to compromise in any way the cardinal ethic of
reporting. The upshot was that he went to prison for four days—

most of the time spent in the Crumlin Road Gaol hospital because he developed a streaming cold in his damp cell; Patrick Leo Martin was freed on bail and later—because Falk could never testify against him—freed altogether. The final irony came later in an IRA court: for accepting the bail from a court which the Provisional IRA vehemently refused to recognise, Martin was booted out of the IRA and went off to live south of the Border. It might have been practically more advantageous for both parties if Falk had agreed to identify Martin in court: there would have been freedom for Falk, gaol and a career of continuing IRA service for Martin. On the other hand, he might well have been shot, had he stayed in the battle up North.

'Today you give the world a new message—a new headline— that says that Ulster is basically a green and pleasant place.' This was to come from the newly elected Lord Mayor of London, Sir Peter Studd, at the opening ceremony of one of the world's most unfortunately timed expressions of public celebration— Ulster '71.

Ever since I had started to come to Northern Ireland the government public relations' men had been attempting to press choice little morsels into my hands, telling of the wonders to come with the opening of Ulster '71. To honour the fiftieth anniversary of the creation of the state, the accumulated artistic expertise and the experience of a multitude of ceremonial specialists was to be focused on a half-mile square waste of grass land down by the river Lagan, on which would be built what the Stormont men termed 'the biggest and best exhibition since the 1951 Festival'. There were rumours that Queen Elizabeth herself might grace the festivities with her presence, since her grandfather had opened the first session of the Northern Ireland Parliament half a century before. But by early spring it became apparent that Her Majesty was not going to be expected to take any of the risks incumbent on her subjects. (Belfast was one of the few places the Queen had ever been received with any display of native hostility—a deranged loyalist woman had hurled a brick at her Rolls-Royce on the previous visit, producing the most photographed dent since the birth of the filmland dimple.)

So Ulster '71, a cardboard and emulsion paint paradise that celebrated a province of dubious vintage and even more doubtful future got, instead of Royalty, Sir Peter Studd. No one was permitted to believe this was in any way a letdown, or that the show itself was anything less than a glorious token of esteem to a grand and historic land; the smiles and the enthusiasm were as radiant as anyone could wish, and the opening day in May, if a little upstaged by a circus of students from Queen's University, was a moment of fun of a sort few of us had seen in the country for a long while back.

The best thing about the opening on May 15 was a dodgem ride. All the reporters piled into little electric cars and chased the entire Ulster cabinet about in a ten-minute mêlée watched with horror by the squadrons of armed security men who had come to watch over Brian Faulkner.

I was in a car with a girl from the *Belfast Telegraph*, and we set on Faulkner's car like the nastiest of schoolchildren. We gave it a few hefty bangs, mainly to no obvious effect, and we assumed all was over when our ten minutes was up, the power was finally cut off and we coasted to a heavy stop behind the leader. But as he stood up to get out, the *Irish Times* came hurtling up behind us, crashed into our car and pushed us all in turn into Faulkner's car, knocking the half-standing premier back down into his hard little seat.

He turned round and glared, half-joking, at me. 'Trust it to be the *Guardian*,' he snarled, 'always knocking us down, aren't you?' 'But it wasn't me . . . it was the *Irish Times*,' I pleaded back. 'Never mind,' he returned, 'you're both just as bad!' He pretended not to mean it, and we pretended we realised he didn't.

Ulster '71, a fair we went to when the evenings were quiet and pleasantly boring in town, was rivalled in its early days, by a Catholic 'happening' known as a fleadh, held in the Falls and organised by a chipper little IRA man, a lecturer at a local technical college, called Des O'Hagan. Working twenty hours daily for a month he engineered a week-end-long programme of

events in the Falls for a total sum of £250—there was swimming
and road racing and song festivals and dancing in the streets, and
plenty of home-made cider to be given out free. By all accounts
it was a singularly effective piece of community entertainment.
Ulster '71 cost the government £750,000, and as a jamboree was
a disaster.

The police had a hand in both events: at the bigger affair they
were on hand 24 hours a day patrolling behind the barbed wire
coil fences, to prevent disturbance and to ensure that everyone
who ventured in enjoyed a peaceful visit; over in the Falls they
raided a small upstairs room and took away a small radio transmitter that had been broadcasting non-stop Gaelic pop music.
Of course, the Catholics were breaking post office regulations by
operating the set: but somehow the decision seemed another
petty example of local politics. A small and self-engineered display of Catholic defiance and enjoyment was stopped: a large,
highly expensive government showcase, which nobody had
wanted and few professed to like, was ruthlessly protected against
disruption. An incident of small moment, maybe, but another
step along the road.

A few days later I was in Manchester, talking by phone from
a house in Burnage, to a friend in Belfast. Suddenly I heard, quite
distinctly, the crump of an explosion echoing along the telephone
wires. 'Christ almighty' he said, 'that was a big one. Upper Falls
I'd say, from the way it sounded—I'd better pop up and have a
look.' With that we said our hurried goodbyes—and he went off
to the wreckage while I sat in the forlorn Manchester suburb,
an hour before first-edition time but three hundred miles from
the blast.

As quickly as the British phone system allowed, I dialled the
number of the Central Citizens Defence Committee on the Falls
Road, about a couple of hundred yards from the Springfield
Road crossing. It took the office a couple of minutes to answer,
but when I did get through, and told them who I was, a friendly
little clerk, who I knew faintly, came, and puffing and panting,

told me what I wanted: 'Jesus that was a big one—the bloody police barracks have gone up and they've carried any number of people off. Listen to this'—and he hung the receiver out of the window so I could hear the racing ambulances and fire engines whining their way up to the still fresh disaster.

I thanked him profusely, redialled the army and then the police. Within half an hour the picture was emerging on the kitchen table. By 9.30 p.m. it was about adequate for the first edition, and so, realising the hoax, I called the news desk. 'Simon Winchester here,' I said, omitting to say exactly where I was, 'there's been a pretty nasty bomb, lots of policemen and possibly even a soldier hurt—I'll do you six hundred words right away if you give me copy. . . .' And so it appeared: 'Soldier dead, many injured, in police station blast', by Simon Winchester, and date-lined, thanks to the deception of the telephone, Belfast.

The Springfield Road bomb, as we later came to call it, was both a terrible tragedy and a moment of supreme heroism. The IRA man who had chosen the barracks as the site for his attack chose to toss the gelignite, hidden in a suit-case, into the front lobby of the station. The IRA's profound disregard for civilian life showed its head that night: inside the lobby, talking to the desk sergeant on duty, was a young Catholic woman and her two small children. There was also a burly sergeant, Michael Willets, of the 3rd Battalion the Parachute Regiment, who was passing the time of day with another policeman when the smoking suit-case fell amidst them all.

Sergeant Willets reacted with incredible, cat-like instinct: he shoved the woman and her children away from the path of the possible blast, doubled himself over another man standing in the lobby and fell to the ground, shouting to everyone else to do the same. The bomb exploded, blowing the thirteen stone sergeant torn and smashed against one of the walls: the man he had crouched over was saved, the woman and her two children lived.

For his heroism Willets was awarded—posthumously—the George Cross. No one, Catholic or Protestant, friend or foe of the army, begrudged his family the award. He was one of the great figures to emerge from the miasma of the time.

A week after the Springfield Road bomb—for which I returned to Ireland—I was back in England and chanced to be in Manchester for a couple of days—and actually went out on a 'straight' reporting job, to Bury, Lancashire, of all places. When I got back from Bury I was called into the Northern Editor's office and asked, right out of the blue, in the manner of the newspaper novel: 'Things look as though they might be quiet in Ireland for a few weeks—how would you like to go to Calcutta?'

And off I went to cover the developing cholera crisis in West Bengal: I stayed for six weeks, touring India from side to side, seeing a thousand corpses, sipping tea with the relics of the Raj at Tollygunge, following the sad refugee processions out of the forests and rice-fields of the country that was soon to be called Bangladesh, dodging the rusty bullets of the Pakistan army and watching the local terrorists—only here they were called 'freedom fighters'—placing gelignite charges in the manner of the Provisionals back home. It was an almost incredible, tragic six weeks. When I got back to Ireland I remember telling Paddy Devlin, the SDLP member at Stormont for the Falls, how Ireland's problems seemed minimal compared with the troubles of India—and I was dismayed when he exploded with rage at my sacrilegious suggestion. That Ulster was a small problem, though a nagging one, I only came to realise after seeing the hundreds of corpses produced by the terrors and the tortures of the Bengal tragedy. Perhaps I was sent to get more of a perspective on the Irish problem: it left me, certainly, with a sense of relief that Britain had still not turned so insular that she would ignore such a distant tragedy; but it leaves me still with the occasional depressed feeling that the British press is becoming ever more unaware—in spite of communications improvements—of the problems of the outside world. The copy-tasters' maxim that a train crash five miles away is worth more space than a war five thousand miles away seemed all the more improper after that trip was over.

Little of consequence happened in Ireland while I was away—or at least what there was failed to excite the newspapers which, for a while, attended to their foreign interests, and to the Test Match. But when I arrived back home, and took off for Ireland almost immediately to watch the Twelfth of July celebrations for the second time, two violent incidents took place, the first of which was to lay down the strategic development of the province for the next year; and the second of which was to help decide the tactics.

The first incident, which was to produce one of the watersheds of Ulster history, was triggered across in Derry on the night of Wednesday, July 7, three days after I arrived back.

Although Derry was a considerably smaller and more remote city than the Ulster capital, the feelings of its people were much the same as their compatriots sixty miles to the east. Derry had been, after all, the crucible of the latest unrest, and the passions of the men and women of the border city were a reflection in miniature of the passions of the land: and while relations between the British army and the Catholic people of Belfast had begun to deteriorate from the Ballymurphy riots of Easter 1971, so the relations between the soldiers and the Derry Catholics had started to worsen from that Easter on. By summer 1972 the two sides hated each other with as much venom on the Foyle as on the Lagan; and so the reports of serious fresh rioting in the Bogside in early July came as little surprise to those of us over in Belfast.

The riots had, in fact, been going on for four solid nights. The local army regiment—the Royal Anglians, ironically the same regiment, though not the same battalion, as that involved in the Clonard rioting of six months before—complained that some sixty gunshots had been directed at them from the Bogside and the Creggan estate on the hill to the north-west—the same hill, incidentally, that led to the composition of the hymn, 'There is a green hill far away, Without a city wall . . .'. (Cecil Alexander, who wrote the hymn in 1848, in between composing 'Once in Royal David's City' and 'All Things Bright and Beautiful' was the wife of the then Bishop of Derry. It was the sight of the lush grassy rise of the Creggan outside the Derry walls that inspired her to pen 'There is a Green Hill'. She saw the Creggan as another Calvary—some devout Irishmen might see an irony in the comparison.)

Shortly after midnight on the morning of Thursday, July 8, an Anglian foot patrol deployed in William Street and began to move carefully down towards the Rossville Flats: suddenly, according to the army, a man emerged from Fahan Street, carrying what the army later insisted was a rifle.

His name was Seamus Cusack, and he was a 28-year-old, one-time welder; he was not known to be connected with any of the wings of the IRA. His family said later he didn't like the British army, but as his interest was in boxing, not guns, there was little he could do about the soldiers.

The appearance of Cusack on the scene that early morning caused one of the Anglians to raise his SLR to his shoulder and shout the requisite number of warnings, telling the man to drop his 'weapon' and surrender. The man, according to the army, did neither. After the three warnings had been delivered, the soldier fired a single shot. It hit Cusack in the thigh, severing his femoral artery and leaving a massive puddle of blood and a foot-wide trail of red across the Bogside paving stones to the place where a car took him to the hospital in Letterkenny, forty miles westwards in Donegal. Seamus Cusack died in hospital shortly afterwards from loss of blood: no one in the car had the wit either to take him to nearby Altnagelvin Hospital in Derry itself, or to apply a tourniquet to his leg. The car must have been swimming in gore.

Almost every time an IRA man is killed there is a protest about the circumstances of his killing: usually the initial protests ('He never touched a gun in his life—he was the most gentle of human beings, wouldn't hurt a fly') evolved into the truth the next day, in the deaths column of the *Irish News*, when one would read: 'Seamus——, aged 19, Lieutenant, 2nd Battalion, Creggan Brigade, IRA, in action against British Forces'. But in some cases —Danny O'Hagan, Barney Watt and now Seamus Cusack, the outcry attendant on the death was such that a presumption of innocence became the overwhelming view.

Cusack almost certainly was not a member of the IRA. He

was said by all his friends and relatives to have been out on the streets that morning only as an interested observer, and to have been shot as he stooped over to pick up a helmet that had fallen from a soldier who had been caught up in the riots. Others said he had tried to pick up a rubber bullet, or its case, or had tried to draw a friend's son away from the dangers of the action. Whatever he was doing, it was a risky venture: and one should probably not be too surprised, given the circumstances of the night, that he was shot at by someone. But his dying became a *cause célèbre*, and, far worse, it was to lead next day to a second, and equally controversial, killing.

Brian Faulkner stood up in the Stormont Commons the next afternoon, well aware of the new troubles across in Derry, to utter what would be the final words of the summer sessions of the Parliament—a prayer that 'out of the evil of Derry there may come some good for the whole community'. Even as he spoke the city was erupting once again, mainly in bitter response to Cusack's killing—or his murder, the local people were calling it.

Just after 3 p.m. on the Thursday, an army scout car that had ventured down into the Bogside was rammed into immobility by a stolen lorry: a heavily armoured Saracen filled with soldiers was sent out to help. The local IRA met it with a hail of petrol bombs and nail bombs in a classic and deadly ambush. At 3.13 p.m a Royal Anglian marksman fired a single shot, killing a 19-year-old unemployed Bogside youth, Desmond Beattie. All that is known for certain about the circumstance of Beattie's killing is that he was near the Saracen armoured car. What the army had to say about him later—and the arrogant manner with which the army press office later treated all inquiring reporters—led to even more anger and hostility than the killing of Cusack during the early morning.

At first the army held that Beattie had been holding a gun, and that the soldier who killed him with a single shot to the chest, had fired at 'a man who fired at him'. At the later inquest the soldier—who was hidden by dark glasses, a turned-up collar and the identification of 'Mr. A'—recounted how Beattie had been holding a 'dark, round object' in one hand and what appeared to be 'flame' in the other—the intended inference being that Beattie was about to light, and throw, a nail bomb. There was no mention at the inquest of a gun, or that 'Mr. A' had fired at Beattie because he had 'fired' at him.

Forensic evidence tended to bear out Beattie's innocence: there were no traces of gelignite on his hands or in his pockets, and none of the lead particles on his hands that would suggest he had fired a gun. The coroner had no choice but to return an open verdict.

The deaths of the two men led to an immediate meeting of the SDLP—not attended by all the party, but certainly those who counted at the time—chaired by the man in whose constituency the tragedy had occurred, John Hume. The decision that was to take root at the weekend meeting had a crucial effect on the fate of the Stormont Government: but it needs to be seen in the light of one small concessionary gesture which Faulkner made to the Ulster Catholics back in June, while I was in India.

The gesture was an extremely modest proposal for power-sharing. On June 22 the prime minister had risen to make the first major address on the Queen's Speech, which had been read as part of the half-century celebrations on the legislative hill. He announced, to the surprise of many who heard, that he proposed to create three new committees to help draft the laws of the province—one to be concerned with social services, a second to have responsibilities for industrial development, and the third for environmental matters. The Opposition—the Catholic Opposition—he proudly announced, would be asked to provide chairmen, with fat salaries, for two of the three new bodies.

To a Unionist mind it was a bold and a radical decision. To liberals on the outside of Ireland it seemed a small but imaginative step. And on the Opposition benches a stunned and overwhelmed group touched their massed forelocks in astonished delight, and took to the record with remarks that ranged from 'We give the plans a guarded welcome' and 'I feel he is right in his approach' to 'It was the best speech since he became prime minister'.

As the Opposition took time to think about the plans the early euphoria began to wear off: by next day Austin Currie, possibly the most sensible of the seven, called the committee plan 'tinkering' and John Hume asked, pertinently, 'should we not be discussing the system itself rather than tinkering with it any further?' Only Ian Paisley, either inherently wise and sceptical, or prodded by the deeply cynical Desmond Boal, attacked the scheme with any fervour. The proposed policies had not been tested by the Ulster people, he charged, and the plan was that of a prime minister who had risen to his position without the mandate of the people. The idea was wrong, he contended, because no one had been asked, and because the committees were unlikely to function properly anyhow. His words, and the claims of 'tinkering' from some of the wiser members of the Opposition benches made many remember that Faulkner was presiding over a country smaller and less important than Yorkshire, which only had a County Council and a Chairman to preside and make policy. A few newspapers in Britain were beginning to take the same position, that Stormont as a system needed total demolition, not a repair to the guttering: the committee scheme was seen by some in those days as a fancy bit of repair work to convince us all that the mansion itself was safe and worthy of preservation.

In the event, the killing of Cusack and Beattie tore down all pretence of repairs: Gerry Fitt demanded an independent, impartial inquiry into the shootings: Lord Balniel, the relevant Minister of Defence for the Army, curtly turned him down next day, preferring the word of a single soldier with an apparently faulty memory to the combined word of a people in the Bogside slum. Gerry Fitt then invoked his ultimate weapon: he turned angrily on his heel and marched his men smartly out of all further legislative dealings with the Stormont Government. In effect— in spite of the fact that the Parliament was in recess—he led the entire Catholic opposition out of Stormont. The withdrawal of the SDLP ended Faulkner's brief honeymoon: it also ended for a long time any semblance of real politics in Northern Ireland. From then on until Westminster took over the government functions of Ulster the following March, political activity was all but finished and all that remained were the deaths, the bombings—and the statistics. The remaining weeks of that summer, until the dread date of August 9, were more a catalogue of misery than anything else.

As every incident shocked us and horrified us and terrified us, the bass continuo rumbled inexorably in the background—internment, internment, internment. It had to come, it was inevitable: the army was against it; Faulkner, unlike his predecessor, was against it too. But it had been formally decided as an instrument of probable policy back in early July, when an IRA bomb had totally wrecked a £2 million Belfast printing plant belonging to the *Daily Mirror*. Ulster life was becoming desperately abnormal—even Watney's Red Barrel was no longer to be found in the province: the brewery said 'unsettling conditions' had forced it to withdraw to more peaceful parts of the kingdom. Then the first signal of the impending damburst came: at dawn on Friday, July 23, hundreds of soldiers burst into hundreds of homes across the province, searching for documents, arms and other concrete evidence against the IRA.

Contingency lists of the men who might be picked up in the event that the Special Powers provisions were ever invoked had been drawn up by a joint Special Branch–Military Intelligence working group at least since Brian Faulkner had been prime minister. It was a list which varied in quality from the superb to the ridiculous—for while the senior, secret command of the Provisional IRA and the leaders of all three Belfast and the single Derry battalions were on it, so, too, were numbers of inoffensive students and young semi-political figures whose only qualification for government dislike was that they had voted against them—or not voted at all—in the last Stormont election. As it happened, nearly all on the list were Catholic. The 'dry-run' of July 23 was conducted by the army to make sure that the addresses on the lists were accurate and up-to-date, and that, where photographs and fingerprints existed, they matched the men for whom the army was looking.

Frank Kitson, the 39 Brigade Commander and most practised

tactician in wars against terrorists, was on holiday when the July raids were carried out. He was highly irritated when he heard of them. Internment, if it ever came about, should be a total surprise. The July raids, he later complained, had warned dozens of top suspects into hiding.

The list which resulted was hardly comprehensive, however. Recruiting into the Provisional IRA did not get under way with any vigour until after the June 1970 riots in East Belfast: it was probably not until the time of Danny O'Hagan's death that the 15-year-olds and the young unemployed of Andersonstown and the Creggan began to join up in any numbers. By the time of the internment operation the Provisionals were some 1200 strong— yet the lists named only the skeleton command as it had been known after Card and McKee and Martin had been put away: the young activists, the men who came to be derisively known as 'The Gunmen and the Bombers in Our Midst', were unknown and unlisted. Reasonably enough, the army and police assumed that the capture of a few would lead to the exposure of the many: what they did not count on was the degree to which interrogation techniques had to be employed in the autumn to win the information they had been unable to supply early in the summer.

One of the more celebrated gaps in their summer knowledge was their ignorance of the identity of the man who took over from Billy McKee as Provisional leader in the city after McKee had been arrested and slammed into prison on a highly suspect gun charge. Their knowledge was skeletal, patchy and often horribly wrong: that they did not know names like Joe Cahill was to lead, in part, to the disaster of the internment operation; skilful work by the reputedly skilful intelligence section within the army HQ at Lisburn could have saved a great deal of the agony, and could have allowed the soldiers to proceed without the aid of torture. As with the Anglian's decision to stay in Clonard in February; as with Freeland's asinine decision to curfew the Falls in July 1970; as with the decision to allow the June 1970 Orange marches to proceed unhindered; so the internment operation was a dis-aster—for reasons that were, perhaps, more rooted in military misjudgement than in almost anything else.

Reginald Maudling went on television on July 31, speaking with some warmth about the possibility of introducing intern-ment—this 'distasteful weapon' General Tuzo called it—and told viewers that if the policy were to be implemented, it would be done swiftly and without forewarning. Yet not only did the army move on July 23, but soldiers raided homes across the country once again on the night of August 1. If this was the army's way of implementing a policy without warning, we wondered, what on earth would happen on the day itself—perhaps, someone joked, they would issue an announcement on the late night news. Whatever the tactical reasons for engineering two dry runs in July and August, they removed a considerable element of surprise from the operation when it finally came—and Kitson's annoy-ance, on purely professional grounds, was understandable.

The decision was finally taken in London on the afternoon of Thursday, August 5, after the full Joint Security Committee had met at Stormont. Brian Faulkner and Harry Tuzo flew to London then to request the final permission to introduce the relevant regulation—Number 12—of the Special Powers Act once again. They won the permission, thrashed out the details, were given some more troops, the date of the 'swoop' itself—Tuesday, August 10, and a code name, Operation Demetrius. Early on that morning, it was decided, some 500 men—mostly Official IRA sympathisers, only a few active weapons-men with the Provision-als—were to be picked up, held, processed and dumped un-ceremoniously in the internment camps.

We were given one early clue about the whereabouts of the main internment centre. Tom Caldwell, the independent Union-ist MP who lived out at a village known as Maze, near Lisburn, had a very attractive student daughter, Hilary, who, among her other interests, was a keen member of the Queen's University Gliding Club. Each weekend during the early summer she had gone out for a spin in her machine from the club's HQ, at a little-used military airfield and truck depot near home, that was known by the name of a hamlet nearby—Long Kesh.

Late in July, Hilary Caldwell told me that the army had sud-denly informed all the glider pilots they would have to stop using the old Long Kesh airfield. No reason was given, but Hilary cleverly pointed out that when she had gone there one weekend she had found the Royal Engineers on the tarmac runways, putting up a set of brand new Nissen huts and surrounding them all with a barrier of fences and barbed wire and searchlights like in pictures of war-time Germany. The army told her, and told us too when we inquired, that the buildings were simply to house army vehicles: some of us suspected, with reason, that what we were seeing growing out on the flats beside the M.1 motorway on the old World War Two runways, was in fact the kingdom's first purpose-built internment camp. We were right.

Military plans for triggering Operation Demetrius got off to a bad start; they were upset, in fact, on the morning of Saturday, August 7, when a soldier in the still half-ruined Springfield Road police barracks shot and killed an innocent passing motorist, who happened to be a Roman Catholic.

Harry Thornton was a 34-year-old welder who was driving his small green van through early morning Belfast with his workmate, Arthur Murphy. They were on their way to a pipeline job at Comber, Co. Down. As the van, an elderly Commer, lurched up to the traffic lights it backfired, loudly and percussively. It was only about 7.30 a.m., not the best of times for terrorist attack; a marksman—a paratrooper from the 2nd battalion—thought that Thornton's car was hiding a gunman, and so, without warning, fired through the back window. The single shot demolished half of Thornton's head, killing him instantly. Murphy was dragged off into the police station, kicking and shouting; a soldier wandered up to the van, licked his finger and drew it down the rear window in a cross. 'That's another down!' he shouted, with obvious glee, and loped off back to the barracks.

Murphy emerged from the police station eight hours later; it was painfully clear he had been savagely beaten by someone inside. So far as anyone has subsequently discovered, neither he, nor the dead Harry Thornton, had been in any way connected with the IRA. It was a total mistake, which the army, with something less than good grace, admitted some months later. But they said nothing at the time.

By the end of the day Belfast was in flames again; by the end of the weekend two soldiers had been shot and wounded, dozens of cars had been taken and burned, the barricades were up once more, and more soldiers were pouring into the city and the province from their bases in England. The August 7 weekend had all the appearance of the weekend of June 27, the year before; Harry Thornton's death had triggered a massive passion.

The effect of the rioting was to advance the internment date by a single day, to its final settled date, now riven into local history, of Monday, August 9, 1971.

Before turning to the operation of August 9, and its immediate aftermath, one death remains to be recorded. It happened while I watched on the late afternoon of Saturday, August 7. It was an unremembered killing—an accidental death, in fact, that had resulted from the riots of the day. It brought home for me the utter despair of Belfast that last weekend: the piece I wrote that day follows and ends the chapter, as the day ended the pre-internment phase of Ulster's recent history.

Frankie Cunningham shouldn't have been with the crowds on the Grosvenor Road yesterday evening. His mother, a wizened, kindly old lady from Raglan Street way, deep in the Lower Falls, had always told him to come home and sit by the fire whenever there was trouble about, and there was no shortage of trouble around the Grosvenor Road yesterday around teatime.

But he was there, in the middle of the crowd, a small, 13-year-old boy, looking just like all the others milling around. And because of his disobedience, Frankie Cunningham is now lying half-dead in the Intensive Care Unit in the thirties'-gothic Children's Hospital up the road. His leg is badly broken, his arm is smashed out of shape, and his head and the right side of his face are bloody pulp. He has been in deep coma ever since he was knocked down by a furiously speeding car in the middle of the riot. He will possibly live, but he will never look the cheerful, impish child he was at the time most other children of his age in more peaceful quarters of this land were watching Pink Panther on television.

Frankie's accident—and it was no more and no less than that—was one of those tragic parentheses that invariably interrupts the smooth and steadily unrolling pattern of a Belfast riot. It was the kind of tragedy that simply had to happen to someone in the crowd, and it was no particular fault of Frankie's that the shadow fell on him that day.

All afternoon a dignified group of middle-aged Catholic women had been strung across the Springfield Road opposite the police barracks. A few feet away a hushed, kneeling congregation prayed or intoned a haunting litany beside a small wreath that marked the spot where Harry Thornton had been shot dead earlier in the day. That spot, the women said, was Holy Ground: no car, no lorry will pass the spot for a full day, in memory of the dead man, father of six, a labourer from South Armagh. And so, each time a car approached the line from up the Springfield Road—a road which leads down from the soft green hills of Divis and the Antrim fields, the knot of women raised a big black flag up high, waved their arms, and the car would swing away down a side street.

But at exactly six-fifteen yesterday a silver grey Ford Cortina, driven by a middle-aged man and with a woman and two children sitting in the passenger seats, refused to stop before the human barrier. He edged past the women, who yelled and jeered and threw sticks at him, and finally escaped into the remaining hundred yards of clear road before he came to the junction of the Springfield Road and the Falls.

Here, though, there was an enormous crowd. A moment earlier they had been hurling clouds of half-bricks, bottles, old iron gratings, pick-axe heads or just plain abuse at a platoon of soldiers on the Falls. But now, in a momentary lull, the mobs were smashing up the traffic lights, tearing out the paving stones, building small piles of ammunition against the next time the soldiers made a sortie. Frankie Cunningham was in the crowd somewhere, in his dirty blue jeans, his rough brown jerkin and heavy, muddy boots.

The Cortina slithered to a halt at the fringe of the crowd. With a whoop of delight a dozen youths raced up to it, hammering on the roof, kicking the doors, rocking the whole machine from side to side. Inside the woman and her children were frantic with terror, their mouths open in a soundless scream. The driver was white-faced and horrified, not knowing what to do. But then the crowd ahead thinned, and he saw and took his chance. He pressed his accelerator flat to the floor. The car leaped in the air and lurched down the hill faster and faster towards the safety of the city centre.

It was then that Frankie, 14 next week, stepped out in front of the car. There was a thick dull crack, and his body sailed up in the air, a full six feet above the glass- and brick-littered street. Round and round his little limp body whirled in a terrifying slow motion, cartwheeling past his friends still holding their bricks and bottles beside them. It seemed a full five seconds before Frankie hit the ground, and even then he bounced, once, twice, three times before coming to a rest, bleeding horribly in the gutter. A cloud of reddish dust hung in the silent air for a few seconds. Then another car hurtled off in pursuit of the Cortina, and the crowd, as one, rushed across to the tiny battered body in the dirty gutter.

What Mrs. Cunningham will do when her boy comes home, if he comes home—the matron at the hospital today was far from sure about his prospects—goodness only knows. Her home is too insanitary, too damp and cramped to house a convalescing boy. Her husband is unemployed, and has been for years. There is no money for prescriptions or Lucozade or a television for the child if he does come back. No room for comfort, no peace or rest.

But Mrs. Cunningham didn't blame the driver. 'He was right to have kept on moving—he would have been lynched if he had got out of his car. Our people were in an awful bad mood last night.'

The man who followed the Cortina was less charitable though. He caught up with the driver, pulled him out of the car, and, according to a soldier today, 'gave him a hell of a whipping, right in front of his family too.'

The police say the man made a full statement, but no civilian witnesses turned up until nearly three hours after the accident.

But this was hardly surprising. For all last night the police station was under heavy siege. Machine guns were barking, the gas was smoking across Belfast. Frankie Cunningham's pain, and his mother's ghastly problem, became a tiny part of another night of violence. Two lines in this morning's papers, a simple tragedy without drama, without meaning, to be filed away and forgotten.

Frankie Cunningham never did go home. He died in hospital of multiple injuries some weeks later: his death was not even to be dignified in the statistical analysis of those killed in the Troubles. He was the last person to die before internment—the twenty-ninth to die violently that year. The next to die were casualties of war.

8

' . . . to take away our sons . . . '

The telephone by my bed in the Royal Avenue Hotel rang harshly a few minutes before five on the morning of August 9. On the other end was a hotel waiter who lived in a decaying little house in Andersonstown.

'Listen,' he yelled down at me, 'get out of your bed. It's started. It's begun, I tell you. Get up, man, they've started lifting people by the dozen. It's internment, it's begun!'

'Are you quite sure this is it, Sammy?' I pleaded, not much wanting to get up from a sleep that had begun only about three hours before. 'What makes you think this is it?'

'You just get up and look out of your window—you'll see whether it's true or not,' he replied, and slammed down the phone.

I got up and dressed quickly, rushed out of my room and past the few sleepy night porters who were cleaning up the rooms for the next day's custom. 'What's the rush?' they demanded. 'I don't know,' I returned, 'but it sounds like internment.'

It was clear enough once I had gone fifty yards from the hotel entrance. Fifty yards up Royal Avenue, past the splendour of Tate's Medical Hall and the tatty façade of the Ulster Club, was the High Street, which looked out to the east of the city. I peered down towards the river—and sure enough, past the drunken lean of the Town Hall clock, rose three giant columns of smoke. Something was burning fiercely over there, and at that time in the morning it just had to be the result of big trouble. Sammy seemed to be right.

The city, as I came to realise within half an hour, was in total, terrifying turmoil—indeed every Catholic area of the country, from the hamlets in County Tyrone to the Bogside and the

Creggan and the Shankill in Armagh and the Nationalist slums in Portadown and Lisburn was—and had been since 4.15 that morning—the scene of fighting and bitterness Ireland had not witnessed for half a century.

Operation Demetrius, as the internment lift was known by the army, had been ordered for Tuesday morning at 4.15: the riots brought it forward by a day. Frank Kitson, the brigadier in command of most of Belfast, had been given a list by the RUC only the previous Thursday morning. 'We would be pleased if you would detain, for the purposes of questioning, the following three hundred . . .' the list was headed; and it was signed 'Graham Shillington, Chief Constable, Royal Ulster Constabulary.' Nearly 250 addresses were appended, and Kitson, and his brigade commander colleagues across the six counties, had to detail an arrest squad of three men to move to every single address and pick up the wanted men. They didn't always have a picture of the man, or in some cases, even his age: the age-old practice in Ireland of naming son after father led that morning to innumerable cases of Catholic fury, as sick and elderly men, or crippled sons were dragged away in mistaken substitute for their like-named relatives. That the lists had been drawn up by the police with a lack both of knowledge and care was only compounded by the chilling officiousness with which some of the arrests were carried out by the soldiers.

The Catholics were well-prepared for the internment raids. In some cases, IRA men had already gone to ground, warned off by the two rehearsal raids of the month before. Others managed to escape—one in Armagh jumped out of the back window of his house as the army came knocking at the front: the soldiers had come at 4.15 a.m. to win the element of surprise—but with only three men per squad, they were hard put to recover if in fact their arrival was anticipated.

In Belfast, well-orchestrated trouble erupted within fifteen minutes of the Land-Rovers and armoured cars roaring into the streets—the famous 'Armoured cars and tanks and guns' which, as the song has it 'came to take away our sons' on that chill late summer morning. As I stood in the cold at 5.15, watching the black coils of smoke wind upwards into the fine eggshell blue morning sky, I could hear from the west a distant cacophony, a metallic rattling, faintly musical, drifting in the gentle wind. It was the Belfast bin-lid warning—an urban alarm signal of the crisis North.

Up close it was a huge sound. Women, young girls, small boys in dressing gowns and housecoats or hastily pulled on jeans and sweaters knelt in their hundreds on the corners of Catholic side-streets, holding in one hand the metal lid of their dustbin, and crashing it again and again on the concrete flags below. The sound which echoed and reverberated through the houses, warning anyone who was still asleep to be up and away from the soldiers, went on for well over an hour: whistles screeched warnings from one ghetto to another in a desperate attempt to keep the IRA one step ahead of the raiding parties. And as the soldiers went, under hails of bottles and stones and the occasional rattle of gunfire, so giant barricades went up, cars were overturned, lamp standards were twisted over, piles of rubble were assembled and half a city and one third of a country prepared for battle.

The bulk of Operation Demetrius was over by breakfast time: most of the wanted men were being herded into processing centres in the Girdwood Park army camp in Belfast, the Magilligan camp twenty miles north of Derry city, and at Ballkinler camp in County Down. While this was going on the city was gearing up for the beginning of a wave of killing and destruction that would take many long months to still.

Up in Andersonstown, where I spent as much of the day as I could, the entire area was in the firm control of the IRA. Until that time the only guns I had seen were furtively displayed in midnight meetings with mysterious men: here, in the summer sunlight and smoke of August 9, IRA men were walking around openly with high-powered rifles and machine guns as though they were hurley sticks. Republican platoons were deployed down the Falls Road, heavily armed with rifles and pistols, to capture any lorries foolish enough to be in the area, and drive them back to the barricades. British soldiers made repeated runs towards the barricades to try to put an end to this display of high-powered independence—and it was here that the killing began.

The first man to die that day was, as it happened, a well-known and long-wanted IRA man, Patrick McAdorey, a 25-year-old sniper from the Ardoyne. He was shot dead by a soldier as he crouched, with his rifle, behind a garden wall in Jamaica Street, and he was sent up to the Holy Cross Monastery to lie in state, guarded by unarmed volunteers, for several hours. Patrick McAdorey may well have deserved to die in battle—but he was also desperately wanted by the army for previous alleged crimes. In particular, McAdorey was reckoned by British intelligence men to have played a part in the shooting of the three Scottish soldiers five months before—some soldiers maintain still that he actually pulled the trigger of one of the weapons involved. He was almost certainly on the internment lists; and since there was the view, expressed by some senior soldiers and policemen that while internment was simply one means of removing a dangerous man from society, killing him in battle was another, it remains a possibility that he was killed deliberately, in a retaliatory act. We shall never know.

In all ten people died during that first, terrifying day. Two of the dead were soldiers, seven were Ulstermen, one an Ulster-woman. And most have been forgotten, in the tide of events that so swiftly followed in Demetrius's wake. Who will remember, for instance, William Atwell, a Protestant from Bangor, who was killed that morning by a nail bomb thrown at him as he patrolled the roof of a factory. Mr. Atwell left a widow and two children: he was noncombatant in the true sense of the word—just another nameless, innocent tragedy, like Frankie Cunningham two days before. Later in the year the killing of innocents was to be coldly dismissed as one of the 'regrettable consequences of an urban guerilla war'.

The remainder of the day was marked by more shooting and burning—burning most of all. More than 100 houses were set ablaze in Belfast, and more went up in flames in Newry and Strabane and over in Derry. In Belfast the huge fires that had been set in Short Strand—the columns of smoke I had watched through early morning eyes at dawn—raged all day: four warehouses and an entire bus depot were utterly consumed. By mid afternoon there was an uneasy lull, punctuated only by the distant thud of small explosions; the air, though, was filled with a sour smell of burning rubber, petrol fumes and cordite. In the centre of town, shops were opened and a few people managed to carry on as normal. But there were no bus services operating, and such people as were in the town had a haunted, frightened look, as though what they were doing was not quite proper in the middle of war.

We had learned the details of the internment order shortly after 11 a.m., when the Stormont pressmen summoned us all to gather in a city centre office building to get fresh printed copies of the fateful statement. It was a stirring moment: up there in the calm of a seventh floor office we mumbled our thanks to the clerks who gave us the red and white government press statements that confirmed what we had all thought (for repeated inquiries at both Stormont and police and army headquarters told us nothing specific. Only the BBC, who had been given a hint at 5.30 a.m. in exchange for a case of champagne, felt *sure* it was internment).

Brian Faulkner, acting in his capacity as Minister of Home Affairs, explained his action, and his reason. 'I have had to conclude that the ordinary law cannot deal comprehensively or quickly enough with such ruthless viciousness,' he said, referring to the IRA's excesses of the previous few weeks. 'I have therefore decided to exercise where necessary the powers of detention and internment vested in me as Minister of Home Affairs. Accordingly a number of men have been arrested by the security forces at various places in Northern Ireland this morning. . . .'

Ironically, Brian Faulkner was one of the few cabinet men who had persistently voted against the reintroduction of internment—even though it was he who had operated it back in the 1956 IRA campaign when, as a very junior politician, he was the responsible minister. James Chichester-Clark had been in favour during his term of office—but London had refused to permit it. Cabinet men like John Taylor and Roy Bradford were in favour; but

Faulkner, until the very last moment, counted himself a foe of the policy. Once he had introduced it, however, he became one of the measure's staunchest supporters: he must have realised it was a point of no return.

The rioting spread and worsened over the next two days, and by the night of Wednesday, twenty-three people had been killed and seven thousand Catholics had fled across the border to refugee camps in the Irish Republic. Cynics in the North would later point to the fact that most returned, dissatisfied with their lot in the camps, within a few days—and it did seem a little hyperbolic to refer to most of the crowds who streamed by train and bus and car southwards as refugees. They were leaving by choice; they were leaving for what most of them must have known was a short while only; and their leaving was, for the IRA, superb publicity. Nevertheless there was a sudden and grotesque wave of intimidation that built up over the succeeding days—a wave that led to one of the most significant population shifts ever to have taken place inside a single city. But the immediate reaction was a mixture of panic, fear and, it must be said, manipulated hysteria.

Tuesday saw some of the most tragic burnings in Belfast, when over two hundred houses—mostly Protestant homes that sat beside Catholic terraces from which, it was claimed, gunfire was raging continually—were destroyed by fire. There was a terrible fascination for most of the reporters who went up to Farringdon Gardens that night: row upon row of houses were blazing, totally out of control. Smoke was billowing down the streets. Gunmen scuttled for cover from lamp post to lamp post. Soldiers, crouching flat on the glass-strewn pavements, fired sporadically into the darkness. Figures moved in and out of the blazing houses, snatching what they could from the wreckage. Lorries, piled high with belongings, lurched away from the area to the safety of friends. Cameras clicked away. Men and women dashed to and fro, there were screams, buildings collapsed in showers of spark and tongues of fire. The noise was continual, deafening—banging, screaming, shooting, explosions, shouts, cries, orders, radio messages, crashes and all the time the fierce crackling, sizzling sound of the flames. It was a dreadful, satanic night—and a time when many of us thought that the very fabric of civilised life was coming away at the edges, and some sort of Armageddon was upon us all.

Mrs. Sarah Worthington died in the Farringdon Gardens area on internment night: she was a Protestant and she had been killed (the first woman to die in the Ulster troubles) by a single shot from a 'terrorist sniper'. Or at least, that is what the police said.

Much of the fear and burning that night came as an indirect result of such police reports, to the effect that 'terrorist snipers' were at work in the neighbouring streets—and that one of them had killed a perfectly innocent, fifty-year-old woman. The Protestants who only rented the cramped, aging terrace homes—would remove all they owned, in frightened hysteria and, determined no Catholics would take their houses, smash open the gas pipes and toss a match behind them as they shut the front door.

Ever since the dispute over the February killing of Barney Watt, I had tried to be reasonably circumspect in reporting unexplained deaths. In the post-internment report I noted Mrs. Worthington's death by writing: 'A woman from the Valsheda Park area was found shot by a military patrol . . .'—grammatically ambiguous, but, as it happened, right on both counts. For three months later, at Mrs. Worthington's inquest in Belfast, we learned the truth about her killing. It was not a 'terrorist' who had killed her, but a British soldier—an unidentified Green Howard 'Private A' who told an inquest he had gone into the area to look for snipers. He had been startled by a sudden movement and, the inquest was told on November 4, 'his military instinct took over and he fired from the hip.' He shot and killed Mrs. Worthington; according to her son, Cecil, the same Green Howard then refused to allow him in the house to see if his mother was all right. He saw her body lying inside, near the kitchen door.

The point of this account is twofold: first, it is clear that the Green Howards, 39 Brigade and army and police headquarters must have known Mrs. Worthington had died—albeit accidentally, there being no evidence to suggest that Private A shot for any other than instinctive (though not professionally cool) reasons—and yet they all conspired to lie to the press, saying her killer was a 'terrorist'. Second, the effect of their lie may have been to precipitate more killing and more destruction—specifically the burning of many of the 240 houses in the area the next night. It is the kind of mistake, deliberate, politically inspired or not, which added to the army's often justifiably poor record in Northern Ireland—a mistake which tended to tarnish an internment operation that could have operated more smoothly and which might have been accomplished with far less loss of life.

The men scooped up in Operation Demetrius were to have a miserable time while the faceless civil servants and police 'processed' them, like so much cheese, in the three camps dotted across the country. The law stated they could be held for only 48 hours without charge or trial—and although some Stormont officials were less than punctilious in their observance of this regulation, the police and prison officials due to receive the hapless crew believed in following it scrupulously. And so, in places like Girdwood Park in Belfast, where 185 sleepy, dishevelled, partly dressed men had been herded in the dawn hours of the Monday, vast contingents of policemen and Special Branchmen interrogated each and every individual, matched him against his photograph or his fingerprints or his suspected crimes. Providing enough was found to match him, a detention order, duly signed by the prime minister himself, was served on each man, and he was committed to his prison and, eventually in many cases, to his eventual internment.

Of the original 185 in Girdwood, some 117 were to be served with the detention papers. Those who were not detainable were released, there and then. But for the others, precisely 48 hours after the arresting swoops, a hole was knocked in the brick wall that conveniently separated Girdwood from the massive Crumlin Road gaol, and the first detainees of a decade were herded into their cells in a specially prepared wing. Some would stay there to be released—like an innocent Belfast printer whose pretty English wife would come to cry on the *Guardian*'s collective shoulders during his two week imprisonment—and some would go on to be interned for good. And later in the year long helicopter caravans would swoop down into the Crumlin exercise grounds and remove batches of manacled men out to the newly completed Long Kesh camp. Others would go to a prison ship in Belfast harbour; still others would go, once Long Kesh was filled, to a second camp in County Derry.

But not all were to begin their imprisonment exactly 48 hours after their arrest. Twelve men, the army's dozen prime suspects, were flown off somewhere else as soon as their two days were up: they were flown off, away from their colleagues, as from all outside scrutiny, to be subjected to what the army was to call 'interrogation in depth'. Their appalling, inhuman treatment began to leak into the papers—and was totally exposed in the *Sunday Times*—in the middle of August. It was ill-treatment on a scale and of a degree hitherto unimagined by most civilised inhabitants of the British Isles; it caused the establishment of both a Tribunal of Inquiry and a Committee of Privy Councillors; it remains one of the most shameful blots in the history of British treatment of Irishmen; and it gave still further impetus to the downfall of the Northern Ireland government eight months later.

Twelve men—including such well-known IRA figures as Kevin Hannaway and Francis McGuigan—were flown off to the Interrogation Centre at 4.15 that Wednesday morning, while their colleagues were preparing to shuffle through the hole in the Crumlin gaol wall. They all wore thick black bags over their heads as they were loaded into the Wessex helicopter, brought down from the RAF camp at Aldergrove; they were taken away to what must have been six days of total hell.

It was commonly thought for some long while that the men were taken to a specially constructed interrogation centre inside Palace Barracks in Holywood. In fact, that heavily guarded building was built considerably later in the month, and was used to process men arrested after the initial operation. The first dozen subjects were actually all flown down to an isolated and well-guarded part of the Weekend Training Camp at Ballykinler, County Down, part of which was also being used as a holding centre for men arrested in Armagh and Down during the previous two days. Ballykinler was to be, until its horrors were made public, the Irish interrogation centre for the British army.

At Ballykinler the men were handed over, not to policemen or soldiers or Stormont civil servants, but to highly trained Englishmen who worked for the Ministry of Defence in the branch commonly known as MI5. (In fact the specially instructed interrogators were temporarily assigned to another classification, MI12—but to all intents and purposes they worked under the command of the Director of Intelligence in Northern Ireland, David Eastwood, himself a member of MI5.)

The complaints which eleven of these men subsequently made, and which the Compton Commission subsequently substantiated, made the British sound little different from the Greek Colonels, the South Vietnamese during Operation Phoenix, or the KGB. The Irishmen were forced to wear hoods over their heads at all times when they were in the centre, unless they were being interrogated, or unless they were alone in a room. They were held in rooms or cubicles and subjected to continuous hissing noise—sounds which eleven described as varying from the scream of hissing steam to loud drilling or the whirring of helicopter blades. The noise which interrogators later described as an 'electronic mush', and which was 'neutral' in that no music or speech was allowed to intrude, was designed to prevent the inmates talking to one another and from overhearing any other sounds which might have hindered their questioning. This, at least, is what the interrogators said. But after a few hours of it, the victims later said they felt they were going mad. The sound, which cut them off from all other noise, and the bag, which kept them from all sight, left them so totally alone and so totally at the mercy of their captors as to demoralise them utterly. The techniques undoubtedly 'softened' them up, so that the subsequent interrogation became easier and more fruitful: but they remain, in the view of most civilised people—and in the view of the Geneva Convention and the authors of the Compton report—examples of gross illtreatment.

The question of whether ill-treatment is justified in dealing with men belonging to an organisation as callous with life as the IRA remains subject to passionate debate: and of the three privy councillors who later reported on the techniques, two upheld the use of the British style of interrogation in depth and one, Lord Gardiner, rejected them as 'illegal, not morally justifiable and alien to the traditions of what I still believe to be the greatest democracy in the world.'

Hooding and hissing were not the only means by which the twelve men at Ballykinler were 'softened up'. Compton established they had been telling the truth when they charged that interrogators had kept them standing up facing a wall, their hands placed flat on the bricks above them, their legs spread apart, for hours and hours upon end. One man, James Auld, was kept in this position for nearly *two days* (43 hours), and others were kept there for periods of 40 hours, 30 hours, 29 hours and so on down to 9 hours. In each case guards forced them to stand continuously in this paralysingly difficult position for 4 to 6 hours at a time, and they were hit with batons if they ever wavered.

And in addition to this, few of the men were allowed any sleep at all for the first two or three days they were at Ballykinler, and their food was severely restricted to nothing more than bread and water for the same period. They had arrived at the centre, it should be remembered, at 6.30 on the morning of the 11th; they were given bread and water by their guards at 12.30 p.m. and every 6 hours on until the 15th; only then were they given normal food and allowed to sleep.

For two or three days, then, the men whom the army and police believed to be senior officers in the IRA, men who would lead them, under close and persistent questioning to other and more dangerous members of the irritatingly persistent little army, were kept awake, with totally inadequate food, were kept standing in agony up against a wall, were beaten, hooded and subjected to the most appalling of electronically induced noises: none of their family knew where they were; the fact that they were at Ballykinler, and not in the Crumlin Road gaol was totally illegal; their captors faceless, frightening Britons, the procedures to which they were subjected considerably more severe than those to which captured Germans or Malays or Adenis had been subject in previous conflicts. It was another sorry chapter in the dealings of the British in Ireland; and, thankfully, many British realised it. By mid-November, interrogation-in-depth was formally ended by government fiat. An appalled Irish public reeled bitterly from the disclosures of what Britons had done to suspected guerillas; an equally appalled British public saw fit to put its policy into its past, and to ask for an assurance that it would never be used in its name again.

The raids, the questioning, the brutality, the interrogation and the immediate aftermath of internment remain the most memorable aspects of the operation that took place that August 9. All that, however, was in the short term. The important thing, once the fateful step was taken, was simply, as we asked in our account on the morning of August 10, 'will this resurrected policy succeed?'

More than any other single measure introduced in these Ulster troubles, the internment operation proved a dismal and deadly failure. Its consequences were forecast, in part, by an army that had reluctantly applied the new instrument of policy. The morning after it happened I appalled the army establishment by publishing part of the text of an interview I had with the army GOC, Lt-General Harry Tuzo. I had always managed to get on well with Tuzo, although the relationship remained, it seemed, one of barely concealed hostility for most of his stay in the province. After all, the relationship between pressmen and senior army officers was seen in very different lights by both sides—the press wanted to win total information, and the army wanted to dispense carefully measured and useful amounts of selected material for the entirely respectable aim of winning the publicity battle. Propaganda is an essential part of a guerilla war: and any reporter who thought his interviews with Harry Tuzo or Sean MacStiofain were a reflection on his brilliance as a journalist displayed a total naïveté: both men gave interviews only if they felt their propaganda was going to be printed. They assumed, then, that the reporter to whom they talked was more gullible than brilliant, and often—too often— they were perfectly right.

This particular interview was not, however, to be conducted in the time-honoured fashion. The army had a standing rule for interviews with men of Tuzo's dimensions—no names were ever to be used in print. The opinions expressed were to be attributed to 'senior officers', and occasionally were forbidden to be attributed at all. These were the ground rules on which the army assumed I had been granted the first post-internment interview with the man who oversaw the military aspects of Demetrius. They were very angry indeed when I broke them, though it was only, I claimed, to put the truth on the record. I had given no one my word I would necessarily abide by the army rules—and no honest reporter, in circumstances like these, should.

What Tuzo told me that afternoon as I sat in the sunny comfort of his office was not, in retrospect, very sensational. He sounded gloomy with the way things were going in the city, although cheered that most of the wanted men—not the men *he* had necessarily wanted, he stressed, but men the Northern Ireland government had seen as political enemies—had been roped in during the first few hours of the operation. The operation he had masterminded had worked reasonably smoothly, he felt; his feelings for the future, though, were more grim than he could remember. Internment did not mean the end of the IRA, he said; the killing, he felt, would go on.

And that is how it appeared in the next morning's *Guardian*. 'Killing Will Go On, Says Tuzo' was the headline. The opinion had not been wasted on simply a 'senior officer': it had been placed squarely on the shoulders of the man who uttered the words. Tuzo was portrayed as a concerned and far from confident man, an officer clearly less than happy with even having to operate the 'distasteful policy'. In short, the interview told the truth—but a truth which was both personally embarrassing to Tuzo and partly demoralising for the army. But it was the truth—and to have written otherwise would have been, for me, a suppression of a significant fact. I would have been knowingly used as a carrier of propaganda.

The row that ensued went on for days. Signals went out to army units across the country to the effect that I—like a colleague on *The Times* more than a year later—was to be regarded with something bordering on contempt by all other press officers. I was told not to come up to Lisburn again for some long while. It was suggested that I write—and in fact I did later write—a letter of apology to the general. I felt like a naughty schoolboy; and I was being punished with the one weapon the army could use with effect against me—the denial of information. Happily the affair lasted only a short while, although some of the stuffier souls at Lisburn continued to handle me with a long stick because I had failed to observe one of the cardinal rules of relations between the uniformed and civilian branches of society. The incident marked, I think, the first serious breakdown in relations between the *Guardian* and the army: relations were to become worse, by degrees, over the months to come.

General Tuzo was perfectly correct in his gloomy assessment of the scene. The IRA became stronger, not weaker. The killing rate increased dramatically. The number of bombs planted during the winter went up to a rate of some four every single day. Millions upon millions of pounds worth of property was damaged, and millions upon millions of pounds of taxpayers' money was used to repay the victims. The army began to get more and more disenchanted with its lot in Ireland, and for the first time the recruiting rate—which had accelerated in the early days of the Ulster conflict, when soldiering in Ireland seemed the kind of 'man's life' that appealed to bored English working men—actually began to fall. As more and more local newspapers in England and Scotland and Wales began to print photographs of the burial of local soldiers, as more and more widows gave sobbing interviews to small-town reporters about the futile cause for which their husbands had each died, so the British mood for military disengagement began to displace the excitement that had once characterised the public view of the mainland.

Some of the killing was pathetically tragic, some was unbelievably brutal, some still the product of near-heroic gunfights. British soldiers changed their views about the guerilla army: some began to say openly that the men fought in the Falls and the

Creggan did have an element of courage and determination un-recognised before: others, appalled by the cowardice of their bombing and the casual manner of their sniping and the use of women and children as shields began to regard the IRA men as little better than animals. But courageous or bestial, the British did begin to admit a grudging respect for MacStiofain's men: it was an army that was going to take some rubbing out, they all agreed on that.

Violence of unimaginable proportions grew and grew that autumn, until by the end of 1971 so many had been killed and injured that all vestiges of normal life that Ireland had once known had disintegrated. For while the violence of the post-internment period had increased beyond all fears (Faulkner said later he had been 'stunned' by the first wave of killings), the political life of the province, ailing since July, stilled to the weakest of pulses. The kind of breakdown that had been forecast when the SDLP announced its withdrawal from Stormont in the wake of the Cusack and Beattie killings became a stark reality.

Within two days of internment's introduction Jack Lynch, the diminutive Irish prime minister, called for the abolition of Stormont—he claimed a right to call for its abolition because, of course, his government had never accepted the fact of the 1921 partition, and he regarded himself as having a perfect right to demand changes in all of the thirty-two counties of the island. Lynch's demand was not to be met for some months; but the spirit of his demand was met within a week as, one by one, the columns that had held up the state for the previous fifty years began to crumble away.

Gerry Fitt, the insufferably cheerful leader of the SDLP, took only until the weekend to declare the beginning of a fully fledged programme of civil disobedience: no rents were to be paid on the Catholic housing estates; no electricity or gas bills were to be paid, except for one in every street, so that the authorities could not cut off utilities to entire communities at a time in re-taliation; Catholics were to boycott all committees and councils on which they sat; any Catholic mayors or council leaders or civil servants were to leave their jobs and withdraw their support from the state. And by the thousands they did just as Fitt asked; rent bills of hundreds of unpaid thousands of pounds began to accumulate on the official slates; the gas and electricity concerns began, after only a short while, to feel the pinch from the non-paying masses.

In Derry, thirty prominent Catholics withdrew from their public offices to protest against the policy: General Tuzo went across by helicopter to talk to them, in a visit more designed to show the army had no fear to let its generals visit the maiden city than to achieve a stunning political success. And it palpably failed in cooling the Catholic temper: by the same evening prominent Catholics in Coalisland had decided to withdraw their labour too.

By Wednesday Gerry Fitt was over in New York, asking U Thant to send United Nations observers across to witness the brutality of the occupying forces; and by Thursday Harold Wilson was beginning to realise the political capital that could be made at Westminster out of the evident discomfiture of the Conservative government with internment.

Thursday, August 26, marked a significant development in Westminster's collective attitude to Ireland: Harold Wilson's scathing criticism of the internment policy (he was later to refer, with magnificent truth, to the internment camps as 'recruiting sergeants' for the IRA) was the first crack in what had hitherto been proudly regarded as a 'bipartisan approach' in London to Irish affairs. In truth it was bipartisan simply because neither party had the faintest idea what to do with Ireland, and the policies that were shared were policies of ignorance. The Wilson speech of August 26 marked, however, the beginning of political debate and, eventually, the construction of a policy born out of that debate which might never have emerged in the traditional London moods of insouciance and ennui. To that extent the Labour leader's attack on internment started a welcome political debate in Britain just at the time it had ended, uselessly, in Ireland.

Reginald Maudling once again displayed his abject lack of understanding of what he had once supposedly called 'this bloody awful country' by proposing—at the same time as his government was being accused by Catholics of torture and inhumanity—round table talks on Ulster's future. Wisely, his offer was ignored by all concerned. And a famous round of tripartite talks held at Chequers in mid-September with Mr. Heath, Mr. Faulkner and Mr. Lynch taking part produced no more than a series of fatuously optimistic editorials in the serious newspapers on the English side of the Irish Sea. *Private Eye* put it more succinctly—Brian Faulkner, the journal suggested in one of the most incisive comments to have come out of the Ulster crisis, had gone to Chequers merely to act as an interpreter. Ted Heath, the cartoonist suggested couldn't understand a single word—apart from 'Bejasus!'—that the Irish prime minister said. Faulkner would provide the translation.

On September 26 one of the sadder resignations from the Stormont cabinet was announced: David Bleakley, whom Faulkner had appointed from the Northern Ireland Labour Party to be Minister of Community Relations, told reporters he could no longer serve in a Unionist government, especially one that had introduced a policy of detention without trial. His resignation was as token as his appointment: he had been given the job purely as a balancing act, to take the sting out of the appointment of Harry West to the Ministry of Agriculture: he left it, a day before his term was constitutionally bound to expire, simply to say to the world that he, a simple, decent and honest Protestant to whom the attitudes of Orangemen were as abhorrent as to the more sensible of Englishmen and Irishmen, was appalled at the way things were going in his country.

A month later to the day Brian Faulkner tried again. Where a moderate socialist had failed, a Roman Catholic, Faulkner thought, might succeed. So, to more trumpeting from the leader-writers in London, an elderly, perfectly charming—but somewhat less than effective—Roman Catholic, Dr. Gerard Newe, was given a job in the Stormont cabinet.

He was, it is true, the first such ever to have penetrated the sanctum sanctorum of loyalist supremacy in Ulster, and the announcement of his appointment so that 'the point of view of the religious minority in Northern Ireland is adequately taken into account by the Government' did have a ring of history to it. But

Mr. Faulkner might as well have appointed Norman St. John Stevas or William Rees-Mogg to the job: G. B. Newe, as all Ulstermen seemed to know him, was about as far removed from the problems of his fellow religionists as he was from the problems of Tristan da Cunha. And in the perspective offered by the downfall of the Stormont government, the appointment of such a man—however pleasant and decent a person he was in himself—indicated the absolute starvation inside the Unionist machine for anything that passed as a radical idea. The appointment took in Mr. Bleakley though, a month after his resignation: the appointment of G. B. Newe was, he said, the 'best news Northern Ireland had had in its lifetime'. It was the kind of remark to prompt news editors to note his name again, but it was not remotely realistic. G. B. Newe was just another nail to be hammered into the Unionist coffin.

Another strand began to weave itself during the post-internment days—a steady, silent and utterly sinister rise of Protestant passions, and the growth and organisation of more and more secret Protestant armies.

The Loyalists of the Shankill had, by and large, been remarkably tolerant in the three years of violence that preceded internment. They had rioted, and they had bombed and they had killed: but in all conscience one would never say that their total reaction to the steady destruction of their society's bastions, the steady apparent weakening of their government, the debility and ambivalence of Westminster and the callous brutality of their extremist opponents was wholly unreasonable.

Many of us used to remark regularly on the astonishing capacity the Loyalists had for muting their understandable rage: and as we knew the Protestants had little time for the English press, we said it as often as we could on the radio and television, in an effort to persuade the Shankill men that there was some external recognisance of their plight and their position. The Loyalists felt a deserted people, let down, humiliated, alone: small wonder they began to organise late in 1971, and channel their feelings of subdued bitterness along the traditional Ulster veins. The only wonder was that they had restrained themselves from doing it before.

The first real signs of Protestant militancy appeared in the days leading up to the famous, and utterly useless 'tripartite talks' at Chequers: men like Bill Craig and John Taylor and the working men from which their political strength was drawn began to complain loudly of the possibility of a 'sell-out'; they had little faith in Brian Faulkner's ability to avoid any unacceptable compromise; and they began to march and drill in preparation for protest.

Billy Hull was one of their leaders—the slightly ridiculous little fat man, with a body like Oliver Hardy and a face as wrinkled as Auden and a truculent and uncompromising manner, who had headed the march that followed the murder of the Highland Fusiliers. He welded the Protestant working men into the Loyalist Association of Workers—the acronym LAW was a conveniently happy coincidence—and in the early days of September those under his command rallied and raved in vast numbers under the old Ulster flag of the Red Hand. (This had its origins in one of the older folk-tales told in Ireland. Two Scottish clan-giants were swimming across to lay claim to the Northern shores of the island they could see across the waves. The giant who was losing the race—bitterly aware that the entire country would pass to the giant whose hand touched dry land first—stopped swimming, pulled out his dagger and chopped off his right hand. He hurled it over the waves ahead of him with a mighty swing of his good arm. His bloody hand—the symbol of Ulstermen the world over—landed just on the beach, giving the actual loser claim to all of Ulster as his own.)

The LAW demands were extreme. Whenever I went to see Billy Hull in his tiny, memento-crammed parlour house in Conway Street, his flagpole always rich with red and white, his walls jammed solid with faded Daguerrotypes of Ulster heroes and British monarchs, he would say how rubber bullets should be replaced by lead bullets; how there was no need for any political solution, only a military solution; how all Irish goods—Kerry-gold butter, Guinness, Cadbury's chocolate (which had the un-fortunate plight of being British, but made under licence in the Republic) should be boycotted; how all Irish money (for Dublin's coinage was allowed to circulate freely in all Ulster's shops) was to be refused, or overstamped with loyalist symbols; and that while he and all his kindred spirits were 'British to the core' he would not hesitate to take on the British if ever they tried to force Protestant Ulstermen into any association with the Republic of the South.

This message was repeated time and time again at huge, mightily impressive rallies held in the fields and parks around Belfast. Ian Paisley fell in with Bill Craig for another of their brief flirtations, the Loyalists began to look like achieving another brief period of unity in the face of such probable disaster. After one of the rallies, held within earshot of the internees in their uncom-fortable temporary home on board the old submarine supply ship *Maidstone*, an unarmed police inspector commented dourly to me, after hearing the cheers and the shouts of an assembled 20,000 angry men: 'They'll have to give us our guns back now, they'll just have to.' By October most policemen were carrying sidearms: by the end of the year many were carrying Sterling sub-machine guns. The Hunt recommendations that had disarmed them two years before might never have been written: all the damage and bit-terness and death that they caused had come, precisely, to nothing.

Entwined in the demands for police guns and boycotts of Kerry-gold came new and more worrying threats from the Protestant side, for the establishment of a so-called 'third force' to protect the country against the ravages of the IRA in the way the B Specials had, until Hunt recommended their abolition. The first such force—although its leaders said, correctly, it was unarmed—was Ian Paisley's Civilian Defence Corps, announced in early September. And by the turn of the year reporters were being taken out to Lisburn and Downpatrick and Armagh by enthu-siastic young Loyalists to be shown casefuls of brand new rifles and clips of newly oiled ammunition. The Civilian Defence Corps may not have meant very much: the Protestant vigilantes who were granted limited recognition by the Faulkner government in December may not have been a massive offensive force; but both did represent the beginning of the structure of the new loyalist army. That the structure and the guns were there provided us all, as Christmas came in 1971, with a profound sense of unease over what might happen in 1972. The phrase 'civil war' came more and more easily to our lips that winter.

Just before Christmas I had my first major interview with the leading men of the IRA. It took a great deal of setting-up, and it very nearly proved fatal. But it added importantly to an assessment of the mood and the ability of that little army four months after the internment policy had begun to inflict what the establishment was proudly calling 'a mortal wound' on it: without a doubt, I was able to conclude, its mood, its ability and its confidence were all extremely good.

The details of how the meeting was set up are familiar to any journalist working in Ireland at the time—the furtive meetings in bars with men on the periphery of the organisation, the brief, encoded telephone calls, the mysterious instructions, the blindfolded journeys in dirty cars, the worry that all might fall through —the mixture was to be repeated again and again with extremists on both sides. In the end agreement was reached, and on a bright Sunday morning in late December I motored south to Dundalk, my contact in the car beside me, to meet some of the masters of the Provisionals.

It was, by any standards, a civilised meeting. We gathered in the bar of one of Dundalk's larger hotels—appropriately called The Imperial—and adjourned, after the first introductions, for lunch. While we ate asparagus soup, roast chicken and apple pie and drank cans of lager—the IRA men who had alcohol-sensitive trigger fingers stayed with orange squash—we talked in some detail of the losses that had been inflicted by the British army and the RUC, of the recruiting rate, of the new weapons, of the strategy for 1972. 'The army believe they'll have us on the run by March,' said one of the officers. They were claiming that the level of violence would soon reduce to manageable proportions. That is just pathetic, said an IRA man. 'We can and we will step up the campaign as and when we like. Recruits are coming in all the time. Only one of our major arms dumps has been found (it was in East Belfast, in the Short Strand). Our staff organisation has been hit, but it is still intact, and it is functioning well.'

Above all, the morale of the men was evidently higher than ever before. 'The British haven't hit us nearly as hard as even we expected. Internment has done us far less damage than we might have thought.'

They spoke of the rocket-launchers recently acquired; they spoke of new automatic weapons and explosives that were on order and flowing in by sea and by air; they spoke of the enormous numbers of young men and women who would join Na Fianna Eirann and Cuman na mBan to help the main fighting body of the guerilla group—lining up to assist in what they still romantically called the freedom struggle.

And the conversation went on, in considerable detail, through most of the afternoon. But all of a sudden the mood of the meeting began to change. At about 4 p.m. there was a telephone call, and the hotel receptionist beckoned to one of the men at our table —the most senior IRA officer there—to take a personal call from Dublin. He spoke softly for five minutes, looking back at me and at my Belfast contact with increasing suspicion. He called another of his brother officers across to him once he had replaced the receiver: others joined him in a huddle, looking back at me, now sitting quite alone at one side of the room. I began to worry, and to perspire.

Finally two of the men disappeared, and the three senior officers came up to wish me well, to thank me for my interest and to hope they had been of some use. I left for the car, aware that the two who had disappeared were waiting by their own car outside the hotel: and I fancied they gave me a curiously sinister leer as I choked out a cheery goodbye.

My contact was kept behind with the officers for a few minutes, and then ran out to join me, looking pale and sick. 'Quick, drive north as fast as you can,' he yelled as he climbed into the car. 'Those boys think you're a soldier!'

The telephone call had come, I was to hear later, from Sean

MacStiofain himself. Had you got a Simon Winchester there, he had asked his junior officer. They had, the officer returned. Well, MacStiofain apparently said, one of our intelligence men in Belfast says he's an army contact, and he came down to spy. Get rid of him, any way you want.

I drove like a man possessed, waiting for the black Cortina that had been parked outside the hotel to draw alongside and force us to halt. We chatted as coolly as we could, listening to a cinema programme on the BBC, as we sped towards the border. By 4.30 p.m. we were at the bomb-blasted Killeen customs post; we were in Newry ten minutes later and on our way to Banbridge and safe country half an hour after that. No Cortina had appeared: I was, so far as I knew, now quite safe. And by six I was back in the hotel—by then I had changed to the Europa—and was filing my story for the Monday paper. It had been, in newspaper terms, a rewarding sort of day. But I was still perspiring a little as I read out my story.

Looking back on the incident from a couple of days later, the impression I remember most was thinking how very bad IRA intelligence-gathering must be. I was no soldier, nor was I a spy. I was British, of course, which might give cause for suspicion; and it was fairly well known that I had little enough sympathy for the conduct of the IRA's 'freedom fight'. But for anyone to supply the Chief of Staff in Dublin with the certain information that I was an army agent seemed to me to display something of the lack of skill or true intelligence of the leaders of the movement. Perhaps I should have appended it to my story. The IRA was in a 'confident mood' as the paper's headline read—but by all accounts the mood was not reinforced with the knowledge needed for its proper application.

The year ended more violently than it had begun, with a massive display of early December violence giving way to a Christmas ceasefire, a few protest marches and then a resumption of the destruction. Ted Heath came on a whirlwind visit to boost the soldiers' spirits before the holiday. I was away for Christmas itself, but came back to hear a year-end litany as unremittingly horrifying as usual: a soldier was wounded in the Grosvenor Road on the Monday after Christmas Day; two policemen were hurt in Derry and a youth was found tarred and feathered in the Short Strand next morning; a soldier, a member of the 22nd Light Air Defence Regiment, was shot dead in Derry on the 29th, and riots exploded in the Bogside. There was bombing and shooting across in Belfast. On the 30th, John McCabe, an old IRA bomb expert, died in Dublin while working on a weapon for the North; Housing Executive files were burned by the IRA in Derry, and the Official IRA—which had killed an aging and harmless Stormont Senator earlier in the winter for no good reason at all, set fire to the home of the Stormont speaker, Major Ivan Neill. And on the final day of the year, a massive explosion blew off the back of one of Belfast's remaining cinemas, the Classic, and wrecked a temperance hotel next door.

In all possible ways, 1971 was a terrible year for Ireland. Politics had died an unnatural death, bigotry, hatred, fear and desperation had gripped an entire people. Some 300 men were held without trial in the internment camp at Long Kesh and on the *Maidstone*; half a country was held without trial in homes and businesses, afraid for the bombing and the shooting that went on nightly. 173 people had died, 48 of them soldiers, 11 police, 114 civilians. There had been 1460 bomb explosions, thousands of shooting incidents, hundreds of arrests. In 1970, the number of deaths had been 25, nearly all civilians, no soldiers. It seemed as though no time could be worse, and that a climax had been reached and an improvement was inevitably around the corner. Perhaps it was: but between the year end and the beginning of the better times were to come two immensely traumatic incidents— Bloody Sunday, and the fall of the Stormont government. Better times would come eventually, but the times immediately ahead in 1972 were to be worse still than they had ever been. Nearly five hundred people were waiting to be killed in the twelve months ahead.

9

Murders Most Foul

'The IRA is beginning to lose the war' read the headline above one of the front-page stories in the *Belfast Telegraph* of January 1, 1972. What followed was not the divination of a knowledgeable newspaper, but the promise of a Conservative Home Secretary, sending an optimistic message to his beleaguered colleague, Brian Faulkner, at the beginning of the New Year. The year, he hoped, might see the end of Ulster's violence, the ending of internment and the beginnings of community power-sharing: what it was to see, in effect, was the precise opposite. Violence grew to a scale never before contemplated; a new internment camp had to be opened because of the crush at Long Kesh; Ulster's government disappeared altogether, to be replaced by the constant bogey buried in London's locker—Direct Rule.

What led to direct rule was a gruesome amalgam of tragedy, injustice and horror. What finally provoked the decision, taken in London in March, was half an hour of violence in Londonderry on the final Sunday of January; and what happened on that fateful afternoon had its own birth three weeks before.

Since mid-September most of the men held under the Special Powers Act—and the numbers were climbing into the six hundreds at the beginning of 1972—were being taken to the purpose-built Internment Centre at Long Kesh, five miles outside Lisburn. The Kesh, as it was known, was a desolate, barbarous place in the best of weathers. Two tall perimeter fences surrounded a huddle of shiny Nissen huts built in small 'cages' divided from each other by barbed wire: in the summery days Long Kesh was grim—in the wet driving rains of an Ulster winter it was a grisly fortress. From the outside it looked like the archetype of the concentration camp—high wire fences, gun emplacements on stilts at each corner, searchlights kept switched on all day and night, dogs pacing the perimeter wire with armed sentries, armoured cars cruising the grassy country lanes nearby.

Once inside the huge main gate of iron and corrugated aluminium, there was a quarter-mile walk, past dog cages and barracks and hangars and armoured car ports and dreary office huts to a second and even bigger gate, well out of public view. In case anyone was in doubt, there was a massive yellow notice board on this fine mesh wire gate: H.M. Internment Centre, Long Kesh, it read. No one, except for guards—unarmed prison service officers, recruited especially from England at rather more than the rate at Crumlin Road and Armagh gaol—the internees and a few Red Cross observers and occasional politicians went inside that great main gate. Just as internment itself was a horrendous instrument, so was the camp in which internment had its prime expression: it was a frightening, ugly place. And what was worse, as the Red Cross and others who came to see reported, it was far too crowded.

Thus came the decision that led, ultimately, to Bloody Sunday. A new internment camp was opened at Magilligan Point in County Londonderry, and on Sunday, January 16, round about lunchtime, forty specially selected internees were picked from the hundred or so on board the prison ship *Maidstone* and whisked by RAF Wessex helicopters across to their new home on the wind-swept sands of County Derry. No new men would be accommodated in Long Kesh, the Ministry of Home Affairs said, and the complement on the prison ship would be reduced to more comfortable levels.

In many respects Magilligan was a rather more pleasant place to be interned. It was a wartime army base that had seen very occasional use as barracks for Derry City soldiery, served as a weekend base for Territorials and had last been used as a holding and processing centre for prisoners snatched in the west of Ulster on August 9. There was no collection of all-metal Nissen huts: those at Magilligan were older and more solid, warmer and a little more habitable than the harsh metal constructions at Long

Kesh. But comfort was almost irrelevant in the growing debate about internment. The opening of a new camp, and the transfer of internees with dramatic suddenness that Sunday, merely served to underline the assumption that the policy was in Ulster to stay. One woman I met that week, who had been to see her son in Long Kesh, reported that morale there was still very high: 'People inside just can't believe this madness will go on and on,' she said brightly. 'They think the British will just force Faulkner to stop it—it'll be over in six months.'

The Northern Ireland Civil Rights Association, the energetic movement that operated out of a pair of tatty rooms above a Belfast watchmaker's shop, had already planned a few protest marches that winter to complement the continued boycott of rents and rates and utility bills that made up the non-violent protest against the use of Special Powers. The government, though, had banned all marching in Ulster—and those who did march were booked by the police. It was, in truth, not all that easy to generate the enthusiasm for the massive demonstrations of old: internment, shocking as it was, seemed to stun people for some long months. And for a while such marching as went on was fairly small-scale.

The opening of Magilligan Camp, though, provoked extreme anger among the Catholic people. It was, in many ways, a callously calculated move by the Stormont government: often it was men who lived in Antrim and Armagh and Down who were taken across to the Derry camp, while those who lived in Derry and Fermanagh and Tyrone went across to Long Kesh. It became supremely inconvenient for the visitors: it seemed a cruelly un-neccessary move, and it generated, on January 22, one of the sad-dest of protest demonstrations for some long time.

This time the battle was not on the streets of Ulster, but on one of its beaches. Magilligan Strand is one of those wide, blinding yellow deserted stretches of shore, for which the Northern Irish coast is so justly renowned: it is a haven for bird watchers and walkers and those Irishmen who prefer solitude to society. But on the afternoon of Saturday, January 22, the beach was turned into a battleground.

About 3000 people, mostly from Derry and around, assembled on one of the approach roads to the new camp at around 2 p.m. It was a cold and windy day, with black rain clouds scudding across the bay from the grey Donegal hills. The fields were muddy and wet: the army was out in great strength, though, in all fairness, in an amiable mood. The commander of the 2nd Battalion Royal Green Jackets, who had the guarding responsibility for the camp, offered tea and buns to the protesters if they followed an agreed (though technically illegal) route up to an army barricade near the camp wire: at the barricade, we found later, the troops had set up a huge foam dispenser, the sort used to lay fire protection on runways: it would be used to cover the demonstrators if they caused trouble at the barrier.

In the end the crowd decided not accept the piles of buns and the urns full of tea: they set off, a shambling, straggling trail, across the muddy, soggy lanes that led to the beach, and once on that, turned north towards the camp which stood, as far as the only published pictures had shown, right on the side of the little cliffs of the Derry coast. My wife and small children plodged along amongst them.

The Royal Green Jackets may have been in pleasant attendance at the start and the proposed end of the march: on the beach, however, was an altogether different army unit—the 1st Battalion Parachute Regiment, brought in especially from Holywood Barracks near Belfast, in case of trouble. What the marchers saw after ambling a mile or so along the beach, was a long coil of barbed wire, stretching right out to sea; behind that, about eighty Green Jackets, eighty paratroopers and fifty or so policemen. It was a daunting sight.

When the marchers got to the wire a few stood and gazed across at the soldiery, while others shouted and sang protest songs. But a critical fifty or so tried to run down the barbed wire into the ebbing tide and round the end, which swung aimlessly about fifty yards into the water. Their foray began the battle.

The moment a few men and women had reached the end of the wire a dozen paratroopers opened fire with their gas guns. Volley after volley of rubber bullets flashed and flittered across the sand: a score of demonstraters, hit by the bullets, crumpled up into the water: dozens of others from the main crowd, seeing their plight, rushed into the water to help: and dozens of paratroopers in turn dashed across to stem any further invasion.

For more than half an hour there was bitter hand-to-hand fighting. Police and soldiers lashed out with batons and fists and truncheons and rifles as demonstrators battled with sticks and the few stones they could find on an almost wholly sandy strand. Throughout the shambles soldiers fired volleys of rubber bullets, some of them at point blank range, some into the faces of the protesters. Ivan Cooper and John Hume, the local MPs were there: they said afterwards, as the bleeding and limping men and women made their angry way back to the bus parks, they had neither seen anything comparable before. Cooper had a baton he said he had snatched from a soldier—it had a nail driven through it: all of us saw some soldiers being held back by their colleagues, so angry and out of control had they become. On their way home the demonstrators set fire to a local ballroom: it had belonged to a local man, Robert Noble, who had helped build parts of the new camp. The burning of the Golden Slipper ballroom was the demonstrators' only truly violent act of the day. The remainder of the afternoon had been the brutal act of an arrogant military, which upheld, in as unpleasant a manner as possible, the powers of the Stormont government to lay claim to the beaches and the seas that surrounded the country. Magilligan would be forgotten within a week: the effects of that march, however, were to give rise to a new determination on the part of the Civil Rights movement—a determination that cost thirteen people, and ultimately a government, their lives.

That weekend was in more respects an ugly period: soldiers gassed an overwhelmingly innocent crowd in Newcastle, Co. Down, on the Sunday, and five policemen in the Irish Republic were treated for gassing after they had become snared in an unpleasant incident on the border, where British soldiers tried to disperse a Southern crowd who were filling in a crater made in the road by soldiers to prevent illicit cross-border traffic. In

Lurgan, too, there was rioting and gassing. The people, it appeared, were mobilising again: the army and the police, by all accounts, were playing their rightful roles of the upholders of law in as tough a manner as they could.

The effect of that weekend, and in particular of the scenes on the Magilligan beaches, was to set the civil rights machine into near hysteric motion. At a press conference held on Tuesday afternoon in a back room at the Royal Avenue Hotel, the association leadership unveiled their plans for bringing the crowds back on to the streets: the Official IRA, too, which had lost a good deal of public sympathy in recent weeks for its brutal murder of Senator Barnhill and its burning of the house of Ivan Neill, indicated its support. The high point of the coming rallies, they told us all, packed into that smoky room in the old hotel, would be a march that following Sunday, January 30, from the Bishop's Field in the Creggan Estate in Derry, down through the Bogside to the old Guildhall. Lord Brockway, a socialist life peer, would be the main attraction: Bernadette Devlin, Ivan Cooper and a number of other Republican dignitaries would be there in supporting roles.

The Magilligan violence, the organiser said, had strengthened the resolve of the people against the British army. 'Just as the violence used by the RUC in the march on Duke Street on October 5, 1968, strengthened the determination of people to use their rights peacefully on the streets,' a statement from the Derry CRA said, 'so this latest act of violence by the authorities strengthens the will of the people of Derry to march in peaceful protest on Sunday next.'

Uproar at the announcement was immediate. Ian Paisley condemned the equivocation of the Stormont Government towards previous marches: if they did not stop this one, he said, members of the Londonderry Democratic Unionists would. Brian Faulkner extended the ban on parades for another year, drawing a scathingly accurate retort from his right-wing foe, William Craig, that to do so 'will greatly assist the IRA in their campaign' and would be 'one of the greatest blunders ever made'. Craig forecast that the IRA's plan to move protest on to the streets would provoke a level of violence that could only solidify Catholic feeling against the authorities. He was horribly correct.

Although there was occasional violence for the rest of that week, little could shake the growing public obsession with what might happen in Derry on Sunday. The days wore on: a policeman was shot dead in Belfast; another was captured by the Official IRA in Warrenpoint and released after a day, saying that 'I couldn't have been kidnapped by nicer people'. Bombs went off inside the paratroopers' base at Holywood Barracks, two members of the Unionist Party were expelled for not voting with the government on the question of extending the marching ban, two more policemen were killed in Derry, and in Belfast Protestant leaders, announcing a series of loyalist rallies to be held between then and March, promised that 1972 would be a 'year of decision' during which the loyalist people of the province would 'take their stand'.

But behind all this, sad and unpleasant as it may have been, played the solemn threnody of Londonderry Sunday. Reporters began to move in to the city; political leaders issued lengthy warnings on the radio north and south of the border. A battalion of paratroopers and hundreds of other infantrymen were quietly moved into the city in preparation for the weekend. Derry was gearing up for a showdown, and everybody knew it.

The day before, the Saturday, there was an unpleasant precursor. A protest march had been scheduled from Dungannon across to Coalisland, the six-mile path of the original Civil Rights march in 1968 which had followed Austin Currie's sit-in at Caledon. Normally Saturday was the day off for a daily newspaper reporter: but on that Saturday, partly because the air had the smell of trouble about it, and partly because Bob Chesshyre was planning to go for the *Observer*, I decided to work, and trundle over to Dungannon.

It was a less than pleasant journey: half way along the motorway our car blew up, scattering chunks of metal down a mile-long path of smoke behind us: we had to hitchhike, and were picked up by a reporter from the *People*, who complained to us during the journey that his editors in London were getting rather tired of Ulster. 'People just aren't having affairs over here. There's no sex', he grumbled. 'They don't like it much back at the office.'

We arrived in Dungannon to find, as predicted, the army blocking off the entire town centre, and the straggling crowd of marchers milling around in a soggy field outside town. By tea-time about two hundred of the crowd, prompted by Bernadette Devlin, decided that since the army would be bound to halt any illegal progress on the roads between the towns, they would have to leg it over the countryside. And so for four solid hours, through the cold, the wind and, eventually, the dark, we all battled across the Tyrone pastures, followed by low-swooping helicopters, watched by distant soldiers with fieldglasses, gassed, from long-range launchers and harassed at every road crossing by armoured-car-borne soldiers.

At length, as night was closing in, Bernadette and Austin Currie, a few reporters and the surviving crowd, now down to about sixty, made it to a brick-maker's yard on the outskirts of Coalisland. We were pinned in this yard, crammed with vast piles of red bricks, for the best part of two hours, by two platoons of soldiers in an extremely nasty mood. Nothing would persuade the troops to let us go: if we so much as put our noses around a brick pile, rifles would be aimed squarely at us and invisible soldiers would threaten to shoot. No matter who we were—politicians, publicans or press—the army would not let a soul out of that brick yard. Then it began to rain, and soon the rain turned to wet snow. It was bitterly cold. The soldiers still would not relent. Some of the marchers, tired, cold and wet, huddled inside one of the brick kilns, still warm from the previous day's baking. The gaggle of dishevelled youths looked like a scene from a Dickens novel: outside the scene was just like a country under military occupation. In that brick yard that night it was easy to feel that the military had taken over completely.

Eventually we were allowed to go home—we had to slip through a gap in the paling fence, one every two minutes, so there was no possibility of our joining up into mobs again to wreak havoc in the hushed little town. I got home late that night after a long drive through the slippery snow in a borrowed car. Next morning the hills were covered in white.

I started off for Londonderry at about ten in the morning, after reading the newspapers full of gloomy reports about the imminent dangers of the afternoon. It was a difficult journey. About ten miles out of Belfast, near where the railway crosses the main road at Templepatrick, the Ulster Defence Regiment had set up a road block that had a good three miles of cars backed up on either side. Every single car, every passenger on every bus, every sack on every lorry, was checked and rechecked by men clearly delighted to be delaying Belfastmen on their ways to the western counties. It was an infuriating delay, but reasonable army tactics in the circumstances.

I cleared the Templepatrick block by noon and managed to get through all the others—at Glenshane Pass and on the Altnagelvin side of the city itself, by showing my press card. En route I contented myself with listening to John Taylor being interviewed on the BBC's lunchtime news magazine: he was predicting imminent civil war, and there were predictions of loyalist hard men moving in to the Bogside to rout the heavily armed Provisionals. It all sounded rather tense.

When I got to Derry I parked my car on the quayside at the back of the City Hotel and looked in to see who was about. Only a few reporters had wandered in: television film crews were cleaning their cameras, a few friends were on the phones to their head offices, warning them that tonight's story might be a longish one. The consensus among reporters was that there would be a really big riot development during the day, a riot which would settle down during the night to a long exchange of gunfire, with perhaps the odd casualty on either side. And that was probably all.

This, as we were to learn later, was the basic view taken by the army and police back at headquarters: that after a serious riot, Londonderry would become a deadly battleground, with the IRA and the army fighting it out with their rifles long into the evening. At about 2 p.m. I decided to go up to see the soldiers and to head on towards the marchers, who were assembling up on the Bishop's Field. I found a television reporter friend of mine, and together we ambled up into the Bogside, past the concrete slab and wooden and barbed-wire barricade that had been built at the bottom of William Street, and up to the Rossville Flats.

A few local people I knew told me they did not expect any serious eruption of trouble, aside from some inevitable rioting in William Street. I was promised that the Derry IRA commander had ordered most of the Provisionals' arsenal to be removed from the Bogside 'in case they use the opportunity to search the place'—the 'they' referring to the massed British regiments on the outside. It might be recalled that no policemen had ventured into the Bogside or the Creggan since the previous July, and the army, aside from its daily armoured convoy to relieve the company at the Bligh's Lane post in the centre of the Creggan, did not patrol in an effective way unless there was a specific reason to do so. As Lord Widgery said in his report, 'the Creggan became almost a fortress. Whenever troops appeared there at night, search-lights were switched on and car horns blazed. The terrorists were still firmly in control.' It was because some IRA commanders thought the encircling troops might well use this occasion to break that control that large numbers of weapons were quietly removed to stockpiles in the country. Whether or not that was true, it seemed clear to the Bogsiders themselves that the Civil Rights march would produce only a riot that day; gunfire, if it erupted, would come only much later.

Up at Bishop's Field about six thousand demonstrators had gathered; and towards 2.30 p.m., almost on time, the ragged crocodile, with a flat-topped lorry in the lead, began winding down into the Bogside for the inevitable confrontation.

It was a cold, sunny day, and the marchers were in a cheerful mood. Most reporters walked ahead of the lorry as it trundled its way down the scruffy streets, and looking back the mood seemed almost ebullient, with mothers wheeling prams, children weaving here and there, laughing, joking, playing pranks on the television men and generally adding to an air of a Derry carnival. But as we approached the lower end, and the three army barricades with the lines of helmeted and masked soldiers waiting behind, the sinister signs of trouble began to appear. From behind the lorry about 200 youths, the young boys and girls who appeared each evening at 'Aggro Corner' to pelt some hapless infantry platoon, came slowly forward to the head of the column. The organisers, meanwhile, had long before realized that their planned march to the Guildhall would have to be abandoned, and so, at about 3.20 p.m. the lorry with Bernadette and Lord Brockway aboard, turned right into William Street, to lead the crowd to a meeting at Free Derry corner.

But the youths ahead of the lorry wanted confrontation: and accordingly this small sea of angry Derry youth surged forward, not to the meeting but, breaking away from the main march, towards the three army barricades.

I dashed ahead and up to the barricade on Little James Street. 'Can I get past and watch it from your side?' I asked a soldier, one of a dozen struggling to put on his gas mask behind the barbed wire. 'No, you bastard,' the man said, as his colleagues sealed up the barrier with wire twists, 'you stay there and take what's coming to you.' I said something suitably rude and turned back to the murmuring crowd. The main march, and the lorry, were well away by now, and Miss Devlin and the noble lord well clear of any trouble.

In William Street the press was enormous. Hundreds of men and girls lurched mindlessly down towards the barrier, behind which were a platoon of Green Jackets—the same men who had been involved in the Magilligan Camp disturbance of the previous week—a few police officers, dozens of reporters luckier than I, and a great green Mercedes water cannon.

The crowd reached the knife rests and from where I stood, about fifty feet back, about six feet up the wall of a doorway, I could hear the usual arguments. Some of the marchers wanted to get through: a smooth-voiced Green Jacket officer explained that the march was illegal, and that soldiers would stop any further progress. One elderly man tried to rock the knife rest out of position, but march stewards—who were still among the hooligans—dragged him away. The crowd grew angrier and noisier, spitting, cursing, shrieking at the soldiers. The crush was too severe for action of any sort: the soldiers feared the mob might break through to the concrete and metal by sheer weight of numbers. But then, after about ten minutes some of the mob from the back dashed off to look at the two other barriers in Little James Street and Sackville Street, relieving pressure in William Street sufficiently for the stone-throwers to begin to swing their right arms. So the stones and the bottles began to fly; and within moments the riot guns came smartly up and with the deafening bangs echoing along the tiny lane, a dozen rubber bullets skittled into the mob. The watercannon revved its engine, and a huge splashing, weaving stream of purple liquid hurtled out over us. Riot was joined.

Within five minutes gas was being used by the pound. The water cannon had to be withdrawn for a few moments after an enterprising hooligan had tossed a gas canister under the wheels, choking the cannon drivers: but the gas never stopped for a full twenty minutes. The waste ground filled with a blindly milling mob of choking, crying people—as many reporters as protesters it seemed. Nigel Wade, an old friend from the *Telegraph*, came shuddering over, his coat and his thick black hair dripping with purple, his wet handkerchief clutched to his mouth as he retched hopelessly into the gutters. It was a classic and efficient example of riot control: the Green Jackets had proved themselves excellent and disciplined soldiers: a disturbance was being broken up with brutal efficiency. If this was the worst of the day, I said to Nigel, it wouldn't be all that bad: and anyway, there's nothing like CS gas for clearing the head.

By 3.55 p.m. the riot seemed to be diminishing a little, and so I wandered up the William Street hill a few dozen yards, to get a better view. As I sheltered in the doorway of a taxi company, a single crack of a rifle rang out. 'They're shooting at us,' a woman cried. 'Make sure you put that down, and get it right, you English reporter.' I noted the shot and the time, 4.05 p.m.; and I noted the direction of the shot—it came, it seemed, from behind me, from where, had they been on duty that day, the IRA could have expected to have positioned its snipers.

That was all I heard just then; and along with the television reporter I had met when first going on up to the Bishop's Field, I walked down the slope again, towards the waste ground and the thinning mobs and the banging rubber bullet guns and the drifting gas. At Kells Walk, a row of modern flatlets looking down on the riot, I thought I saw another sinister sign: a crowd that had gathered was being pushed away by a number of youths. They were clearing a way for something—was it, as I noted in my book, for a line of fire?

There was no time to find out. As I walked across to see what was happening now at William Street I saw Kevin McCorry, the organiser of the march—he waved to me: 'Get over to Free Derry corner,' he shouted. 'There's a meeting starting now, tell everyone to go.' My heart sank: CRA meetings were enormously tedious affairs, long-winded and unquotable, like the sermons in the more evangelical churches nearby. But the crowd was drifting in McCorry's direction, and I decided I had better drift as well.

But suddenly a scream went up. 'The soldiers, the soldiers!' someone yelled ahead. I looked around to my left. A line of armoured pigs was speeding towards us: two 3-ton lorries were roaring up; soldiers were jumping out and rushing at us. I did immediately what everyone else on the ground did: I ran forward, as hard and fast as I could.

But then the firing started—ten or a dozen heavy, hard bangs, that two years of street experience taught me were rifle shots, and they seemed to be coming from behind. I dropped flat, tasting the dirty asphalt of the Rossville Flats forecourt, muddying my corduroys as I fell into a glass-strewn puddle. The noise stopped for a second: I was up and on again, heart pounding with fear, breath coming in strained gasps. I got to a line of coal bunkers under the wall of a block of the seven-storey flats. I stopped and looked around, aware of a huge and panicky crowd all around me. In the courtyard the armoured cars were slowing and turning as more and more soldiers—paratroopers, I could be sure from their camouflage jackets and their rounded helmets—jumped out and took up firing positions. And in the middle of the courtyard lay a man, half propped up by the men who had run beside him when he fell. He was badly hurt: a wound in his leg was bleeding heavily,

and blood gushed out on to the asphalt where I had lain myself
only seconds before.

Then I rushed on again and into the crowded stairwell of the
flats, sheltering for a few precious moments while the firing went
on and on. From here I could discern both the hard rifle fire of the
army SLRs and what I thought might have been the sharper
cracks of ·22s and the low steady thudding of a sub-machine gun.
But there was a helicopter chugging overhead as well, and gas
guns were still discharging in the background, and men and women
screamed and glass crashed and voices were raised in hysterical
panic, so it was difficult to be very sure. But gunfire was raging out
in the open, and people, it seemed clear, were being hurt.

I ran on and out of the stairwell, feeling by now terribly alone
and vulnerable as I crossed open space. Paratroopers were
crouched around the far side of Rossville Street and by another
new block of flats at Glenfada Park: beside me, on the west side
of the flats, lay two bodies—one a young boy, dressed in jeans,
the other an older man in a brown coat. At first I had thought
they were sheltering from a rain of rifle fire: I had dropped down,
and a hundred others grouped around a red phone box had
dropped as well. But when the firing stopped again we all got up:
the two on the ground lay still. They were dead.

I moved on back to a vantage point, crawling on all fours, or
walking with my arms deliberately held out wide to show any
watching soldiers I was unarmed. I was wearing a green water-
proof jacket: it might well have looked, through a rifle sight, like
the dress of a Provisional rifleman. I felt very vulnerable indeed.

When I reached Fahan Street East, with the city walls behind
me, but on a slope perhaps twenty feet higher than the soldiers, I
could see more clearly what was happening. The two dead men
lay still where they were; another injured man seemed to lie behind the rubble barricade the locals had built across Rossville
Street some months before. Across near Glenfada Park I saw a
group of ten or so civilians, one a priest, walking eastwards, towards the army, with their hands above their heads. The priest was
holding a white handkerchief. But their gesture seemed to make no
difference, for gunfire blazed out from a group of soldiers in the alley-

ways ahead, and the group fell back, shuffling on their stomachs, to Lisfannon Park and the crumbling houses of the deep Bogside.

A soldier below me suddenly turned my way. He pointed his rifle up and there were two sharp jerks of his arm. 'Christ, he's firing at us!' I yelled to a young boy, who was watching the scene, his mouth agape with horror, beside me. We dropped on to the road and stayed as still as we could for a minute, rolling in to the gutter for extra protection. A small piece of masonry bounced down on to the roadway beside me: I fancied, though I never knew, that bullets had chipped it down, and we had indeed been the targets of the paratrooper down below.

It was all over in less than twenty minutes. By about 4.20, it was clear that firing was now sporadic enough for me to walk down into Rossville Street once more, and I took off, looking desperately for familiar faces. Remnants of the crowd that had been listening to Lord Brockway, and had taken off and fled when the firing started, were coming back to view the carnage. I met up with Nigel Wade again, and with a BBC radio reporter, Tony Fry (who, while surviving Bloody Sunday well enough, was killed in a car crash near Dublin only weeks later). We watched with numbed shock as bleeding men were bundled into a fleet of cars and makeshift ambulances that had been driven into Lecky Road. No one seemed sure how many had been killed: there seemed to be about seven badly injured and perhaps as many as five or six dead, but Bogsiders are rarely conservative in their numerical estimates, and when I left the area, still very shaken and frightened, I thought perhaps four had actually been killed. I had seen two bodies, and about six injured men.

On the way out of the area—we had to go the long way around, down Lecky Road and to the river and back to the hotel through the town—one curious incident occurred. Firing was still going on in sporadic bursts, and at one point we decided to try to climb up a flight of steps that breached the Walls, and leave the dangers through a churchyard. Since it was a Protestant area that we would pass through this way, there would, we thought, be few attendant dangers.

But in the churchyard we were suddenly and startlingly confronted by an armed man: he fired two shots at us, from the hip. He seemed to be carrying a ·22 rifle, and his shots, which missed us by a massive margin, sounded like those from a small sporting rifle. We hurtled into the quiet of the church, where perhaps a dozen weeping men and women were sitting out the dangers, and waited until we felt certain he had gone. Then we dashed out and down the steps into Bogside again, which to us now seemed rather safer, by contrast. The important thing that struck us both was that the gunman who confronted us at 5.15 that night at the Long Tower church was, in all probability, a Protestant. Ian Paisley had warned of possible use of force by his cohorts: and it seemed more than possible that some small loyalist force might become involved in the shooting match. That loyalist gunmen might have been in action that dreadful day—in my account I wrote 'He may have been a short-sighted IRA man, but whoever he was he was firing from a Protestant part of the city'—was never to be considered seriously by those who would later write about that Sunday.

When we arrived back at the hotel, a full moon was rising over a shocked and still numbed city. The William Street barricade was still in place, the cordon still kept tightly around the errant regions of the town. Some soldiers whom we talked to on the way back sounded happy with the way the day had gone: a small group of Royal Borderers, who had been brought in with the paras as reinforcements for the day, asked me if anyone had been hurt. They had heard nothing on their radio net. I told them I thought three or four might be dead, and said how terrible things had been. 'Christ, four dead,' one soldier exclaimed. 'That sounds bad.'

John Chartres, the *Times* reporter who headed his team that day, came from the army post he had remained in and told us he had seen one dead man with nail bombs in his jerkin pockets. This single fact had convinced him that the day's military operation had been, in his words, 'a jolly good show'. I was to remember his phrase for some long while.

It only became evident that what we had seen was to be of historic importance at about seven o'clock. I had already phoned

Harry Whewell on the news desk in Manchester to tell him there was a big front page story in the offing: that perhaps three or four people had been shot dead while paratroopers broke up a civil rights meeting. He was prepared for something pretty big— but not as big as the story finally became.

At about 6.45 p.m. I heard rumours among press men in the hotel that perhaps rather more people had been hurt than we all imagined. Some said it was six: one even thought nine had died. I decided to find out what the Altnagelvin Hospital was saying, and went out into the night to one of the call boxes beside the post office. I dialled the number and was put through, after a wait of perhaps five minutes, to a Mr. Thompson, the hospital secretary. What he said—and I noted it verbatim in my notebook—was ghastly.

'I have seen twelve bodies in here that have all been probably killed by gunfire,' he said. 'There are sixteen people in the wards. Fifteen of these have gunshot wounds and one of them is a woman. There is also a Miss Burke, aged 18, who is seriously ill after being struck by a vehicle. I understand it was an army truck.'

He asked me to wait for a few more minutes while he checked the total once again. 'We think it may be thirteen dead now,' he said. 'Call back in an hour and we'll have the final figure.'

I couldn't believe it. Who was this man, I asked, telling me that thirteen people had died in that twenty minutes of shooting? I asked him his name, demanded to know his position in the hospital so I could verify what he said. He realised my shocked incredulity. 'I promise you I am the secretary here. There is no mistake. It looks like thirteen people have been killed here this afternoon.'

I telephoned Manchester again. Whewell was as disbelieving as I: this was the biggest story of a decade—British soldiers killing thirteen men and youths on a sunny Sunday afternoon just did not seem a credible fact. Peterloo and Spa Fields and the Gordon Riots belonged to another age: the killing of thirteen civilians by soldiers seemed to belong both to another age and to another country.

The day came quickly to be known as Bloody Sunday. The effects of that day were violent in the short term, disproportion-

ately enormous in the long term: for if any single incident has-
tened the death of the Stormont parliament, and ended fifty-one
years of Protestant hegemony, it was the twenty minutes of bloodshed on that sunny, crisp afternoon.

It was long after midnight that I left the saddened city. I drove
home with John Graham of the *Financial Times*, through a brilli-
antly frosty night—a night of total eloquent peace, that contrasted
sharply with the nightmare we had left and the grim days that lay
ahead. The shockwaves began at daybreak. Within hours of the
dawn, Brian Faulkner launched into a forthright attack. Standing
before a hushed gathering, more haggard and determined in
aspect than many of us could recall him, with no trace of the
jaunty huntsman's attitude that had once infuriated the Catholic
opposition, Faulkner spelt out the new situation in its very basics:
we had, he said, reached the bottom line in Ulster politics. What
we heard that day was a clear swathe of political forthrightness
cutting through the tiresome irrelevancies that had characterised
the politics of early power for the previous three years.

It is clear now, as a result of the weekend shootings, that
campaigns are being mounted in Northern Ireland and the
Republic to achieve a United Ireland without the consent of
the Unionist majority. We in the Unionist community will
not tolerate such a proposal. We are more than ready to discuss how the institutions of Northern Ireland may be framed
on a renewed basis of general consent. We are more than
ready to develop the most friendly and co-operative relationship with out neighbours to the South, if and when they
manifest a matching good will. But there it ends.

The Unionist backs were rigidly against the wall now, and they
knew it.

The next day the British Embassy in Dublin was burned to the
ground by a massive crowd of protesters; and IRA men on trial in
Dundalk were set free as a characteristically weak gesture from the
Lynch government to those who were once again to be cast, as
they had been in August 1969, as the defenders of the minority
people. Anything was possible after Bloody Sunday, as an unpre-

cedented hysteria gripped the country: curious and tragic things happened: and little, sad things too—one of the sadder, the sudden resignation of Maurice Hayes, a good friend and a towering figure of reason, from the Community Relations Commission in Belfast. He did so, he said, because of the 'lack of any real sense of urgency' on Stormont's part in engineering a truly radical approach to the troubled nation in the wake of the crisis.

The Westminster government tried to act urgently and expeditiously to right the wrongs of Bloody Sunday by the simplest means possible: it set up a Tribunal of Inquiry 'for inquiring into a definite matter of urgent public importance, namely the events of Sunday 30 January which led to loss of life in connection with the procession in Londonderry that day.' The word Tribunal was a misnomer; the inquiry was to be the work of a single man, Lord Widgery, the Lord Chief Justice, a pillar of the British establishment and, as chance would have it, a former army officer.

Millions of words have been written about the Widgery Tribunal and its report, which was published in mid-April, long after the prime side-effect of the tragedy, the fall of Stormont, had taken place. To an eye-witness the report was in many places enormously good, in others extraordinarily myopic: but Widgery's conclusions were at astonishing variance with his own report; and the manner of the 'leaking' of the document itself was an appalling travesty of honesty, for which both the British press and the British government should feel ashamed.

First, his report. He took as his frame of reference, after some initial dispute with lawyers in Ulster, a remarkably precisely bounded space-time continuum: 'in space . . . the streets of Londonderry in which the shootings and the disturbances took place: in time, the period beginning with the moment when the march first became involved in violence and ending with the deaths of the deceased and the conclusion of the affair:' It is an important limitation, and should be remembered when considering the report's prime conclusion.

After lengthy evidence from civilians, priests, reporters, police officers, doctors, forensic specialists, pathologists and forty soldiers, only five of whom were named, the following facts emerged about the tragedy and its beginnings:

In spite of objection by the Chief RUC Superintendent in Londonderry—who, by chance was a Catholic—a decision was taken 'at higher authority' late in January to allow the Civil Rights march to begin but to 'contain it within the general area of the Bogside'. The Brigade Commander, Brigadier Pat MacLellan, was ordered to draw up a plan for the day, and came up with a scheme for arresting a large number of the rioters who were confidently expected to engage the troops near the barricades. 'An arrest force is to be held centrally behind the check points and launched in a scoop-up operation to arrest as many hooligans and rioters as possible' the plan read in part.

This 'scoop-up' task was allotted to 1 Para, under their commander Lt.-Col. Derek Wilford (who came to be known in parts of Ulster by a highly libellous nickname). The Paras were told to be on hand that afternoon, and to cross the barricades and go into the Bogside on foot 'only . . . on the orders of the Brigade commander.'

Lord Widgery writes, on the basis of press and civilian evidence, that the march began and progressed more or less as I recalled events. He then tells us the army version of the launch of what came to be called the 'scoop-up op' by three companies of 1 Para—the two companies that played a significant role that day, we learned, being C Company and Support Company, the latter being the only group to fire its rifles.

We are asked crucially to believe that Lieutenant-Colonel Wilford acted properly in deploying three companies that day; yet it remains a fact that *no public record* of any such order from the Brigade Commander exists.

The brigade log, which Lord Widgery assures readers was 'a minute to minute record of events and messages, regardless of the method of communication used', indicates that at 3.55 p.m.

the Paras were raring to go in. 'Serial 147, 1555 hrs. from I Para,' it read. 'Would like to deploy subunit [Company] through barricade 14 to pick up yobboes in William Street–Little James Street.'

Fourteen minutes later we learned that the Brigade Commander had indeed issued an order. 'Serial 159, 1609 hrs. from Brigade Major. Orders given to 1 Para at 1607 hrs. for one subunit of 1 Para to do scoop-up op through barrier 14. Not to conduct running battle down Rossville Street.'

But Derek Wilford did not dispatch 'one subunit'—he sent in three. And it appeared he did not totally obey his instructions to keep his penetration down to a minimum and ' not to conduct running battle down Rossville Street'. By 4.15 his men were nearly at the corner of Rossville Street and Lecky Road, as far as you can get: to judge from the use of their rifles, they were indeed conducting a battle, and a running one at that.

Lord Widgery has an easy answer to settle the stomachs of a worried establishment. Serial 159, he says, was 'mistakenly entered' by the log keeper as though it was a response to the request from Wilford in serial 147. But that is a splendidly irrelevant red herring. Serial 159, no matter to what it may have been responding, was the transcript of an order given to Wilford by Brigadier Mac-Lellan, telling Wilford to take one company of his paratroopers and deploy them without going down Rossville Street. The fact remains that the log-keeper records no subsequent alterations to the 1607 order—and yet Wilford sent in three companies, and sent them 200 yards further than we are led to believe he was told. It remains a matter of some controversy as to whether Wilford obeyed orders or exceeded them that day. Regrettably the information on which to base a final judgement is still classified, and Lord Widgery, if he considered it, did not see fit to make it public. It would be unfair to criticise Wilford specifically for his conduct of the 'scoop-up op' without having access to all the relevant information—we do not know, for example, if Wilford was given a briefing by his Brigade Commander that allowed him more latitude and flexibility than the recorded messages suggest. We do not know if General Robert Ford, the Commander

Land Forces, or Brigadier MacLellan made contact with him during the operation, changing his instructions subtly to take account of the changed situation. On the basis of the limited evidence available to the public and the press, it does appear that orders were exceeded by somebody. But Lord Widgery does not appear to agree, and he had access to a great deal more information. The case exhibits, I think, the disservice wrought by the British tradition of secrecy and classification: the public, I feel, has a perfect right to have access to all the facts in a case of such huge tragedy and importance. It is improper for Wilford and his colleagues to have been adjudged and found innocent by their peers: they should have been judged by the peers of their victims or, better still, by a wholly impartial panel. Regrettably, Lord Widgery could not be regarded as wholly impartial, however hard he may have tried.

That being so, the most vital question that remained was—who fired first?

Most of us agreed there had been one shot fired at around 4 p.m.—it turned out to have been from an IRA gun, fired at an army wire-cutting party. It injured no one: but it gave an indication that there were IRA guns in the Bogside that day, despite the assurances given to me earlier, and that they had been used prior to the Paras coming over the wire.

But then evidence varies. I did not hear any shots coming from in front of me as I ran away from the Paras' advance—but there were houses behind me, and so I could have confused army rifle fire with possible Provisional activity. Many observers claimed to have heard machine-gun fire from the flats: I certainly did later, once the first paratroopers' bullets had been discharged. But the fact remains that, in the view of the forensic analysts, very few of the dead were known to be holding weapons at the time of their deaths.

According to Widgery, the hands and clothes of the dead presented evidence that indicated the following:

John Francis Duddy: 'I accept that Duddy was not carrying a bomb or a firearm.'

Patrick Joseph Doherty: 'In the light of all the evidence I conclude that he was not carrying a weapon.'

Hugh Pius Gilmore: 'There is no evidence that he used a weapon.'

Bernard McGuigan: 'The paraffin test . . . constitutes grounds for suspicion that he had been in close proximity to someone who had fired.'

John Pius Young: '. . . the distribution of the [lead] particles seems to me to be more consistent with Young having discharged a firearm.'

Michael McDaid: '. . . I think it more consistent with his having been in close proximity to someone firing.'

William Noel Nash: 'Probably had been firing a pistol.'

Michael Kelly: 'I do not think this [man firing a rifle] was Kelly nor am I satisfied he was throwing a bomb at the time he was shot.'

Kevin McElhinney: 'Lead test inconclusive' though 'I was much impressed with Sergeant K's [the sergeant who shot a "sniper"] evidence.'

James Joseph Wray:

Gerald McKinney:

Gerald Donaghy:

William McKinney: 'The balance of probability suggests at the time when these four men were shot the group of civilians were not acting aggressively and that the shots were fired without justification.' Donaghy, however, was found to have four nail bombs in his jacket of which, in spite of allegations they were planted as damning evidence, Lord Widgery was to say: 'I think that on the balance of probabilities the bombs were in Donaghy's pockets throughout.'

Thus one finds that John Young, William Nash, and possibly Kevin McElhinney had been firing weapons; and that Gerald Donaghy had nail bombs in his pockets. The other nine men were, in Lord Widgery's view, totally innocent of any crime, and they were shot dead by men of 1 Para who had been sent in with questionable authority.

Widgery tells us how no soldiers were hurt in the veritable fusillade of IRA gunfire we were supposed to believe came from the flats: they escaped injury, he said 'by reason of their superior field craft and training'. This training led one paratrooper, Soldier H, to fire '19 ... of 22 shots ... [which are] wholly unaccounted for.' It allowed Lieutenant N to fire three rounds over the heads of a crowd, against all written orders on the Yellow Card that every man learns as his biblical writ for opening fire: the 'training' led to an army round entering a house in Glenfada Park occupied 'by an old couple happily sitting in another room'. 'Training' prompted Soldier S to fire twelve rounds into an alleyway, in Lord Widgery's view 'unjustifiably dangerous for people round about'. And the 'training', finally, allowed a highly elite group of British paratroopers to kill 13 people and wound another 12—a total of 25—with the use of 107 shots, all of them we are told, aimed shots fired from the shoulder. Subtracting Lieutenant N's three shots fired over the heads of an aggressive mob, we are left with the stark fact that the same unit whose superior field craft and training enabled them to escape wholly unharmed from a withering rain of IRA gunfire, allowed them to miss their targets on no fewer than 79 occasions: only one in every four of the shots they fired hit and took effect. Some training.

Lord Widgery came to eleven conclusions. In spite of his personally chosen limitations to the streets of Derry during the twenty minutes of the gunfire, he takes a considerably wider view in his first. 'There would have been no deaths in Londonderry on January 30 if those who organised the illegal march had not thereby created a highly dangerous situation in which a clash between demonstrators and the security forces was almost inevitable.' The conclusion was as spurious as it was irrelevant: there would have been no deaths that day had Northern Ireland not been established in 1921; there would have been no deaths had Catholics been treated with human decency in the years before 1970; there would have been no deaths had Harold Wilson not

ordered in the soldiers in 1969; and there would have been no
protest march, and no deaths, had there been no internment
policy.

Indeed, Lord Widgery qualifies his first conclusion two paragraphs later. 'If the army had persisted in its low-key attitude and
had not launched a large scale operation to arrest hooligans the
day might have passed off without serious incident.'

And further, Brigadier MacLellan may 'have underestimated'
the dangers involved in launching his arrest operation.

But the crucial conclusions, from the army point of view, were
contained in paragraphs seven, eight and eleven. 'There is no
reason to suppose that the soldiers would have opened fire if they
had not been fired upon first. Soldiers who identified armed
gunmen [whatever that might mean] fired upon them in accor-
dance with the standing orders in the Yellow Card. There was no
general breakdown in discipline.'

The report itself was to be issued on the afternoon of
Wednesday, April 19. In fact, the astute press officers of the Ministry of Defence telephoned the Defence Correspondents of the
national newspapers the night before—the Tuesday night—to
'leak', in highly selective terms, the Lord's conclusions to be
published the next day. No mention was made in the 'leak' of
any 'underestimate of the dangers', of any army gunfire that
'bordered on the reckless' as Widgery remarked in Conclusion
Number 8. Those who read their front pages on Wednesday
morning would have had to have been very short-sighted indeed
to have missed the results of the PR work. 'Widgery Clears
Army!' they shrieked in near unison; and a relieved British public
read no more—Bloody Sunday, thanks to the propaganda
merchants and a half dozen lazy hacks, was now a closed book,
with the Irish fully to blame.

The last straw, so far as I was concerned, came next morning.
I was in London, just back from a short holiday, when the report
was issued, and I arrived in the office fully aware of the imminent
publication and the ensuing press conference to be given at the
Ministry of Defence. I asked our Defence Correspondent if I
might accompany him to Whitehall to ask some questions of the

Minister. He told me he would phone the Ministry PR people, to ask. They told him I would not be allowed to come; the spokesman would be speaking only to 'accredited defence correspondents'. I was furious. None of these accredited correspondents had been in Derry on the day in question, save for the elderly Brigadier Thompson of the *Telegraph*, who became something of an Irish joke by admitting in print the next day that he missed the entire story because he was parking his car.

I telephoned the army press office and repeated the question. Would I be allowed to come—I had after all, some degree of interest in the case? No, I would not, I was told rather firmly. And if I came down and tried to get in? 'You would be stopped, sir,' the man replied. I wasn't going to risk a Bloody Wednesday in Whitehall, so I sat glumly in the office, writing a sour missive entitled 'The Hardest Report to Take' which ended with the conclusion that—like the dreadful Hunt report of three years before—'Widgery will produce more lasting trouble than it ever sought to destroy.'

After the shocking afternoon in Derry, the Stormont government was just fifty-four days away from death. The clock had started ticking down on a century of Protestant privilege, and before the spring was on the countryside, London had taken over where Belfast had failed so dismally before.

IO

London Takes Over

A reincarnation of political life—albeit a spurious one—came about in Northern Ireland on the Tuesday following Bloody Sunday. It was a reincarnation of desperation, and it began with a speech from William Craig, whose followers had helped unseat the last two prime ministers. He spoke in Stormont on the first legislative occasion after the tragedy, to tell of a plan to allow parts of his sacred Northern Ireland to be chipped off and allowed to merge with the noisome Republic to the South.

'We must seriously consider now whether to secede these areas of the Bogside and Creggan, Newry and Strabane,' he told a fascinated audience. 'It would not be the first time that a city had been partitioned. It would be interesting to see just how many people would remain in the Catholic areas and how many would come to live in the part of Londonderry that would remain in the North.'

It was the old-style Ulster politics, of course—a snide dig at the chronic want of prosperity and social facilities in the South compared with the North, and a display of scorn at the rebellious behaviour of the minorities of Creggan and Bogside, whose very existence, Craig reasoned, was the reason for the Sunday tragedy. But his speech did indicate to those of us watching from the press gallery above that something was beginning to give in the make-up of Northern Ireland politics. The log-jam, it seemed, was show-ing signs of breaking up. Politics, quiescent for so long during the post-internment months, had been jarred awake once again: change was in the making.

And it would not be long before we got to hear the phrase that was to become, in the making of that change, one of Ulster's most overworked clichés—a shorthand expression of what London was concocting in the wings, the 'political initiative'.

Westminster used its tame political correspondents in London to good effect in trying out various forms of potential initiative. The first, and most important kite to be flown was that which appeared briefly on the pages of the *Sunday Times* on Sunday, February 13. The British idea, only two weeks after the Bloody Sunday incident, was to force on Ulster a crude form of community government—a loyalist prime minister with a Roman Catholic deputy prime minister, the permanent reservation of three or four of the cabinet seats for Catholic politicians, the guaranteed staging of a referendum every dozen years or so to gauge the public mood on partition—and, to mollify further the Catholic population, a rapid softening of the internment policy with the release of hundreds of the more obvious political prisoners, and the continued detention of only those 'known' gunmen. How, the government asked Ulstermen through the paper, would that suit you?

The offer was not made on the most auspicious of occasions. The Protestants, whose militancy had been a growing factor for the past six months or more, were by then beginning to come out into the open in strength: and the night before the *Sunday Times* story appeared, the first rally of a new body, known as Ulster Vanguard, was held out at Lisburn, ten miles from Belfast.

Vanguard was born, officially, on Wednesday, February 9, the day which the Civil Rights Association had lamely designated as 'D' for Disruption Day in further protest at the Derry killings. It was not, in fact, a very disruptive day; a few trees were felled across country roads, causing minor annoyance, and a few small shops were forced to close for the day. But as an exercise in co-ordinated disruption, it was a total failure: it showed, rather pathetically, how very little economic power was held in Ulster by the Catholics, and it made one realise how persuasive was the minority case for turning to deadlier weapons to achieve their social protests. The Protestants always had enough economic power to wield to allow their protesters several options before the need to resort to guns.

With the formation of Vanguard we smelled the cordite of organised protest. Bill Craig, the least charismatic, but the most knowledgeable of loyalist leaders, announced the group's establishment at a mid-morning press conference, held at the same East Belfast hotel as the Alliance Party had used for its launching in April 1970.

Craig had been in the forefront of loyalist unity for some time—effectually since a meeting in October 1971 of a loyalist 'steering committee' in that ardently loyalist of country towns, Portadown. He had been made chairman of this steering committee, charged with the duties of formulating 'policies which will be acceptable to official Unionists around the country'. The loose structure that was set up in Portadown that October grew and became sturdier during the winter: and on February 9 Craig was able to appear before the press with his praetorians—Martin Smyth, the appealing, soft-spoken County Grand Master of the Belfast Orange Order; Billy Hull of the Loyalist Association of Workers; Austin Ardill, an intellectually undistinguished Stormont member from a North Antrim constituency; and two younger members of the loyalist hierarchy whose dependence on Bill Craig was all too evident. We were told, at that short news conference, that Vanguard was not a political party as such, but an 'umbrella of organisations'. This umbrella, presumed to keep the compromising rains of British intent off all stout-hearted Orangemen, would hold a series of rallies: the first would be at Lisburn in February, and the final culmination of Vanguard's rise to power was to be scheduled for March 18, in Ormeau Park in East Belfast. The organisers were sure enough of their support to have chosen a date and a site for what they were already promising as the biggest rally to have been held in Northern Ireland since Carson's days. So the mood of that initial meeting was cocksure and impressive.

The first rally at Lisburn was deeply sinister. It was a clear, warm sunny afternoon when we assembled on a green Irish field—to see arranged before us something Ireland had not seen since the days of 1912—Protestants in their own fighting uniform, the very makings of a loyalist army. There were 500 or more men, some in battledress jackets and jeans, many in berets and wearing insignia of rank in their epaulettes. Craig, who arrived in an ancient car escorted by a motorcycle outrider squad, dismounted in the manner of a latter-day Mussolini to inspect the readiness of his band of tough-faced men. And then he mounted the dais to read the words of the old Ulster Covenant, and to win from the crowd an approving triple shout of agreement, recalling the Nuremberg rallies or the Mosley meetings in London and Liverpool. And the words were as heady as the pictures. 'We are determined, ladies and gentlemen,' the loyalist führer said, 'to preserve our British traditions and our way of life. And God Help Those Who Get In Our Way!'

The rhetoric got headier as the days went on and the rallies became bigger. After a rally at Bangor, on the Down coast, early in March—a rally at which the military lines were longer and more impressive than ever before—Craig went on the radio to admit that Loyalists might now have to kill to achieve their ends. 'It could go as far as killing,' he told an interviewer. 'It could be similar to the situation in the 1920s where Roman Catholics identified in the Republican rebellion could find themselves unwelcome in their places of work and under pressure to leave their homes.'

Brian Faulkner must have recognised his dilemma: he never once criticised Craig personally, but remained content to mouth vaguenesses, as he did at Killinchy in mid-February, about the 'alien' and 'sinister' aspects of the 'comic opera' presented by the rallies. But it was no comic opera. Vanguard was more than that. The ranks who paraded in the chill spring Saturday afternoons were more than a slightly ludicrous Palace Guard. A very real and very dangerous army was forming in the loyalist heartlands, and Vanguard, like Sinn Fein on the Republican side, was simply the political wing of a forceful organisation that had been forming for weeks and weeks under our very noses.

It came eventually to be called the Ulster Defence Association, the UDA. It had had its real birth as far back as August 1971, the month of internment, and at the time when the determination of the Stormont Government might have seemed, to most laymen, to have been at its most impressive. Yet three days after the Operation Demetrius had started, a notice, that must now be construed as indicating the true conception of the UDA, began to circulate in the bars and meeting places of loyalist Belfast and loyalist Derry, and up, eventually, to my room at the hotel. It was scarcely noticed at the time: it deserves to be printed in full today:

Being convinced that the enemies of Faith and Freedom are determined to destroy the State of Northern Ireland, and thereby enslave the people of God, we call on all members of our Loyalist institutions and other responsible citizens, to organise themselves immediately into platoons of twenty, under the command of someone capable of acting as sergeant. Every effort must be made to arm these platoons, with whatever weapons are available. The first duty of each platoon will be to formulate a plan for the defence of its own street or road in co-operation with platoons in adjoining areas. A structure of command is already in existence and the various platoons will eventually be linked in a co-ordinated effort.

This then was the situation when the *Sunday Times* was persuaded to report Westminster's first furtive policy feelers into the minds of Ulster. How, London asked, would you Ulstermen care for a proper community government, with a loyalist leader and a Catholic deputy, with cabinet jobs permanently reserved for Catholics, with proportional representation, perhaps, and with a periodic poll on the issue of the Border?

Bill Craig had led Vanguard for little more than a week by the time he read the message, and his Lisburn rally was held only the day before. 'It is the recipe,' he mouthed down the phone when I called him next morning, 'for civil war. Community government is just not on. Our people will not have it. I am afraid there will be a very violent reaction if anything of that nature were to be imposed.' He was in a better position to warn London than I thought at the time: for although I thought the Lisburn rally impressive and ominous, I did regard it—considering it had been billed as 'the most important rally to be held in Ulster'—just a little small. My own tea-leaves led me to think Craig's warning was less than substantial: to judge from the later scale of loyalist opposition, it was a mistake I would regret.

Harry West, bluff and genial as ever, spoke from County Fermanagh about the plan. He would be happy, he said, to sit next to a Catholic any day—he sat next to Dr. Newe every day at Stormont Castle. But what he would not do was 'to have anyone like John Hume or Gerry Fitt sitting beside me. If Heath wants to impose them on us—and that's the only way he's going to do it, because it will never be accepted—I will definitely resign. I want nothing to do with it.'

Roy Bradford, who liked us to think he had a little imagination, rejected London's proposal as 'messy'. It would, he said, be extremely tricky' for Loyalists and Republicans to sit next to each other and discuss affairs of state. But Bradford somehow indicated by his manner that he would not be wholly averse to talking about the plan with the politicians in London: like Brian Faulkner, Bradford was able to recognise the limits of political reality in Northern Ireland, and would never commit himself to outright rejection of a scheme he might suspect would one day be his only chance for an influential future.

But generally the Loyalists expressed total disapproval of the plan: equally generally, the Catholic side, while affecting a profound lack of interest, warmed to the idea. At last London was beginning to think, they said privately—though at what cost. There was no official comment from the SDLP, which since the winter had been holding semi-comic weekly meetings of the grandly titled Assembly of the Northern Irish Peoples in a dance hall at Dungiven. 'They have flown this kite for us,' Ivan Cooper huffed, 'and we're blowed if we're going to react to it. Let them come to us direct, not via the Sunday papers.' It seemed a fair point.

Inside a week there was, half thanks to London, a significant shift in Ulster's political traditions. Three Stormont MPs, one of them a former Unionist cabinet minister and another an Independent who invariably voted in the Unionist lobby, left their traditional allegiances and joined the fledgling Alliance Party. It was a great night for moderation.

The Alliance party, which had seemed to have been still-born two years before, held an exuberant press conference to announce the switches. Phelim O'Neill was the star; a former Minister of Agriculture under Chichester-Clark, he had been booted out of the Orange Order some years before for attending a Roman Catholic wedding (though ironically owning the land on which sat his local Lodge) and was generally regarded as an aristocrat too interested in the nice complexities of his own life and his farms to be bothered with the sordid rantings of the political bigots he shared a party with.

He had never been thought of as a very notable politician, but his stated reasons for moving across to Alliance were eloquent enough. 'The Unionist Party,' he said, 'is basically a sectarian organisation and so, whether or not they like it, is the SDLP. The only way out of the impasse is to try to get Ulster people to restore to non-sectarian politics. I have made my move *as a signal to London* of the desire of many people here to shake off the old Protestant and Catholic dogmas. I hope they take notice.'

With O'Neill, with Bertie McConnell from Bangor and Tommy Gormley from the country, Alliance became a real political party, endowed with all the rights and privileges of the others at Stormont. In fact, Alliance was to be the third largest sitting party in the Parliament building: the Unionists had 27 members, the Democratic Unionists, headed by Ian Paisley, had 4, Alliance now had 3, the Labour Party had a solitary member and there were a trio of independents. The Catholics—with the exception of Tommy Gormley—were still staying away.

The next week the Parliament sat again: 34 members on the right-hand side, behind Brian Faulkner; 4 members—O'Neill, McConnell, Gormley and the Labour member Vivian Simpson—on the other. A more pathetic symbol of the futility of Ulster politics could scarcely have been found.

And while we waited for London to act, so the violence worsened. By mid-February bombs were exploding at the rate of about four every day: by February 24, less than a month after Bloody Sunday, 106 devices had been exploded across the province. The stunning shock of a mighty explosion is a memorably ghastly event—those of us who lived in the city lived with one, or two or more, each and every day, deafened, nervous, perpetually scared. Factories were closing down: fine old town halls and houses in the lovely country had been totally wrecked; car show-rooms and warehouses were crumbling at the rate of one or two a day. There was serious talk about shutting the cross-border roads into the Republic to halt the massive flow of gelignite into the North. Soldiers went down to place huge concreted spikes into the roadways, but each night they were torn out by enraged farmers, or by local IRA men, or by both; the border stayed open, in spite of the efforts of the army's impressive Operation Ashburton, which blew vast craters in the border lanes. By spring 1972 most were filled in, the spikes were torn out; the flow of gelignite seemed to have diminished little indeed.

Then, on February 25, a Friday, came a crime thus far without precedent in Northern Ireland. There was a serious attempt at a political assassination by the Official IRA.

John Taylor, the young Minister of State for Home Affairs, a prime mover in the internment operation and a stout proponent of border-closing measures, was shot six times as he got into his car near his office in Armagh. There were bullets in his neck, his jaw and his chest: he had not had time to pull out his own gun (each minister had one by then) to fire back at his assailants. He was rushed along the motorway by ambulance, unconscious, bleeding heavily: in Belfast an age-long operation removed most of the lead and left him in critical condition for a night. But then, miraculously, he recovered; within a few weeks he was able to go back to his new and pretty wife, Mary, and to the child she was to bear him just a fortnight later. The crime spoke eloquently of the ineptness of the Official IRA, as well as of the organisation's callous and insane choice of targets. The movement was heavily criticised from all quarters: happily it was one of the last violent acts that particular ragged army was to perform.

But what, oh what, we all began to wonder, was the fabled Initiative to be? The phrase began to sound a hollow joke as early February became late February and late February became early March, and still nothing had been done. One hint of Westminster's fast-crystallising resolve was to be heard in a curious debate in the House of Commons late in February—a debate which came about because, it turned out, the army had been operating quite illegally in Northern Ireland for some long time past.

The uncovering of this embarrassing fact had begun with the post-internment arrests in Derry of two local MPs, John Hume and Ivan Cooper. They were charged on the spot with 'failing to move on command of Her Majesty's forces' a sonorous phrase quite certain to ensure maximum Catholic rage. They had been charged, we read later, under a section of the notorious Special Powers Act—the same Act which authorised the very detention and internment policies at which they were protesting.

Hume and Cooper, who were released on bail after the arrest in early September, appealed their automatic conviction. Their lawyers, it turned out, had found a convenient and mightily embarrassing loop-hole. It appeared in the Government of Ireland Act 1920—the Act that was, in fact if not in name, Ulster's hallowed constitution.

Section 4 (3) of the Act said the following: '[The Parliament of Northern Ireland . . . shall not have the power to make laws in respect of . . .] The navy, the army, the air force . . . or any other naval, military or air force matter . . .' And yet Hume and Cooper had been arrested for a specifically Northern Ireland offence of refusing to move on command of Her Majesty's forces —over which Ulster, the law said, had no powers. The spirit of the law may not have been infringed: the letter, however, most clearly had been, and the Northern Ireland High Court, in a reserved judgement, upheld the appeal on the grounds that in this incident—and by inference in virtually all others—the army had been acting beyond its powers. The internment operation, one might thus argue, had been illegally carried out.

The British government was caught in an acute dilemma: and it responded in a manner as perfidious as its repute. By sitting late into the night and pulling out every Parliamentary stop known, it simply changed the law. A new Act, the Northern Ireland Act (1972) was whistled through the Chambers to legalise military activity carried out in the name of the Northern Ireland government, and to indemnify the army for all its previous operations in the province. Small wonder Bernadette Devlin pithily remarked next day with some justification: 'We have always been taught that in Northern Ireland the courts are supreme. Yesterday's action shows that if ever a Northern Ireland court challenges the Tories, then the Tories just change the law to make sure it never happens again.'

But it was what was said during the debates, both in the Commons and in the Lords, that gave the clue to the way London was thinking.

Mr. Maudling, the Home Secretary, allowed that the new bill raised wider issues about—a new phrase—the 'transfer of responsibility'. 'I know,' he said, 'there are considerable feelings one way or another about the transfer of responsibility for law and order. This is a very big issue indeed and can only be discussed in the broad context of a settlement for Northern Ireland. By passing this Bill tonight we will do nothing to prejudice the argument on that one way or another. . . .'

And later in the night, Lord Hailsham made an even more significant remark. 'I said before, and I repeat,' he told the sleepy peers, 'that I thought events will probably overtake this measure in various ways, some of which I can foresee and some of which I am not sure that I can foresee.' To a close student of late-night parliamentary rhetoric, it seemed more or less clear what was in the minds of the Tories now—a transfer of security powers from Belfast to Westminster, backed up by a threat—if Faulkner were to refuse the package—to bring Stormont to a sudden end, and take over entirely the rule of Ulster from Belfast and give it to London.

Brian Faulkner was to hear the proposal less than a month later, on Wednesday, March 22. As he flew off to his critical meeting in London, he left behind him a country that was battered and sickened but, according to most loyalist spokesmen, defiantly determined not to give in. He left after a weekend rally of Protestants larger than anything seen before; he left after the UDA had begun to march through the streets of Belfast; and he left after the Provisionals had left one of their deadliest bombs of all in a parked car in Belfast—a bomb that killed 6 people, and mutilated 150 others.

In that blast—one of the most vicious planted by the IRA—the killing was horrible: the maiming, too, was grotesque—147 people, many of them office girls and women shoppers, were terribly hurt. Few will forget seeing a young paratrooper—a member of the unit that had operated in Derry two months before—cradling in his arms a pretty teenage girl whose legs had been blown off entirely. Everywhere in Donegal Street, in the very centre of the city, was blood and glass and severed limbs and the stink of death. The timing of the bomb was significant: it gave Brian Faulkner all the power he needed, he might have thought, to persuade Heath to allow him continued control of security and even give him added powers to wield against the guerillas. But Ted Heath, it appears, saw the situation rather differently: if the Donegal Street bomb, the worst planned explosion of the troubles thus far, had convinced him of anything, it was that Brian Faulkner ought no longer to be in charge of the security of his little country. And that was what he was preparing to tell the Stormont team that Wednesday morning as the RAF jet swept up off the Antrim moors and headed east to the capital.

Bill Craig expected the worst. The Ulster loyalist community, he said, as the prime minister prepared to leave, was about to be 'betrayed by a British Government that is about to impose direct rule, covered up by a system of undemocratic committees'. The days of the Union between Great Britain and Northern Ireland, he warned, were coming to an end.

Nevertheless, the remainder of the Loyalists of note in Stormont, nervous as they might have been, stuck solidly behind their leader. At a sober, expectant meeting in the Parliament buildings on the Tuesday afternoon the Unionists had badgered Mr. Faulkner to give them an assurance he would only give his assent to any plan that the British might put forward after he had first consulted them: it goes without saying, Faulkner replied, that the Stormont government would wish to endorse or otherwise whatever might be proposed. He was not, however, going to pledge any more than that—he had, after all, to give the appearance of leadership. You will all, he said, just have to trust me.

Little did Faulkner suspect what Mr. Heath had in store. To those of us who watched Faulkner and John Andrews, the deputy prime minister, waving and smiling outside the dark door of 10 Downing Street early that Wednesday morning, it seemed as though Stormont might well be about to enjoy its finest triumph of a sad year. Then the pair went inside for five long hours of talking, and to get the biggest shock of their political careers.

For a while, according to aides who were at the meeting, the discussions proceeded at a workmanlike pace, with nothing said on either side that was likely to raise any eyebrows. It was an impressive gathering, though—the presence of Reginald Maudling, Lord Carrington, William Whitelaw—then a little-known Lord President of the Council—the Chief of the General Staff, General Sir Michael Carver and the Northern Ireland GOC, Lt.-General Sir Harry Tuzo may well have given Faulkner and his friends a cold shudder down the spine. But the talks, as they began that morning, ranging over the security issues, the military forecasts, and with an up-to-date assessment of the civil disobedience campaign and so on, were perfectly routine.

Then quite without warning, late in the morning, Heath dropped his bombshell. Starting up from a long, thoughtful silence, the British prime minister began, rapidly and decisively, to rattle off the proposal he and his colleagues in London had drawn up. There would be, Heath told the startled Ulstermen, a total take-over of all security affairs in the Province. There would be a total take-over of the courts, the prisons, all the emergency powers, the duties of prosecuting—everything, in short, that mattered. London was to take over the police, the RUC reserve, the prosecutors, the organisation and appointment of magistrates, the direction of public order. It was to Faulkner an appalling, debilitating, almost incredible take-over. The Ulster party was horrified.

Lunch was served at noon, and it lasted until just after two. Then the talks began again, the Briton outlining to the Irishman the precise details of the plan he had announced just three hours before. At around 4 p.m. there was a break in the proceedings: a still-shaken Faulkner withdrew to consult with his colleagues and, by telephone, with his party leaders in Belfast. Mr. Whitelaw went off to the Commons, Mr. Heath worked on other affairs of his troubled state: it was five o'clock before the talks got under way again, and nine before they broke up for the night. Faulkner managed a smile for the television cameras that had been waiting outside the residence all day, and sped off to Northolt and to the waiting RAF plane. He was back in Belfast by midnight, tired and, according to his closest friends, quite shattered.

Next day the premier met his cabinet—a cabinet that included the courageous figure of John Taylor, who only a month before had been half-killed by a hail of assassins' bullets. The meeting was brief and to the point—not much longer, in fact, than a regular Tuesday cabinet: those of us waiting outside for a while thought its brevity augured well for the settlement, and that all would soon be resolved happily.

What happened was that Faulkner rose before his thirteen colleagues and outlined Heath's plan, telling them in no uncertain terms that he would do what they would expect him to do—reject it outright. The thirteen came in at 10.30: by a few minutes after noon they emerged, smiling confidently, refusing all of our questions as we badgered them one by one while they clambered into their official cars. Only one man—Roy Bradford—gave any indication of the way things had gone. 'Do you see a future, Roy?' someone asked him as he wedged himself into his black official Austin. 'It won't be the same anymore,' he said—and then sped off.

Some of the key figures in the cabinet stayed behind for lunch at the Castle, and afterwards Faulkner himself, looking pale, drawn and, so I thought at the time, a little dejected, strolled into the House to read out the business of the day. It seemed appropriate that the sole measure of importance he had to list that afternoon was the scheduled second reading of the Northern Ireland Museums Bill. He listened patiently as Ian Paisley's chief lieutenant, William Beattie, asked four questions about security; and then he went back down to the Castle and picked up the official telephone. Heath had asked him to telephone as soon as the Ulster cabinet had been told—it was only the telling that delayed any Downing Street announcement of the plan on Wednesday night.

What Faulkner had to tell Heath was predictable enough—there was no chance, he said, that either he or any of the Northern Ireland cabinet members could accept the package. In short, the message he gave London that afternoon was: 'No dice.' But Faulkner continued bravely on. He agreed, as he had promised the day before, to fly back to London once again, this time to work out the details of the transfer of power. He agreed, as lesser men would never have done, to stay on in office for as long as London took to pass the necessary legislation. He would do all he possibly could, sour and angry as he might well have felt, to ease Heath's passage at this supremely difficult moment on the political trapeze.

Faulkner and Andrews left again late on Thursday night: they took with them a plane-load of advisers and friends, all of whom were packed in to the Downing Street dining room to sample a final dinner in their honour. It was, by all accounts, a reasonably congenial occasion. The negotiations were, after all, completed. Faulkner had been beaten down, the all-powerful government in

London had pulled the rank that it had always been able to pull. There was nothing more to do, except to lie back and enjoy whatever there was to enjoy.

Across in Belfast we knew little of the situation until Roy Bradford, in a telephone call to the BBC's local political correspondent, Billy Flackes, admitted the worst. Faulkner, he confided in a leak designed to make that evening's 9 p.m. news, was now prepared to resign and take his cabinet with him. That decision, which had been discussed during the brief morning cabinet, had been confirmed shortly before the Ulster group had left the airfield for London. All the officials who remained in Belfast that night, while expressing public coyness, confided in private that Bradford had got the message: and so while Heath and Faulkner were finishing dinner, Ulster knew, at long last, that the initiative had been rejected, that the Stormont government was on the verge of resignation and that, if two and two made four, direct rule was inevitable.

The Ulster party arrived back late that night, saying nothing to newsmen who waited in the cold, but grinning broadly to those reporters still wide enough awake to know a knowing look when they saw one. It was, in a sense, a slightly sad occasion.

Next morning we gathered in the misty gloom beneath the long-stopped Stormont Castle clock. At 11 o'clock, by our watches, a haggard premier came out to deliver his statement: it was exactly as predicted. The Westminster plan, he said, had been to 'appoint a Secretary of State and transfer to Westminster vital and fundamental powers we have exercised for over half a century'—and worse—'even these radical changes were simply to pave the way for further, entirely open-ended discussion with continuing speculation and uncertainty as we have seen it in recent weeks.' It was, his colleagues said later, the thought of 'open-ended discussions' about Ulster's future that worried Faulkner more than any of the other repugnant aspects of the package. For as he rightly said, open-ended discussions would drive the province only further still down the risky path of uncertainty and ignorance, with all the violence and disruption that had attended uncertainty in the past. It was not a risk worth taking, he said, an objection responsible Ulstermen might have thanked him for more profusely than they did.

Faulkner told reporters that during dinner the night before he had presented to Mr. Heath an envelope containing a terse, three-paragraph letter, signed by every single member of his cabinet—as historic a document as any in Ireland's formative years. The most pertinent paragraph was the middle one. It read quite simply:

> We now convey to you formally the unanimous view of the Cabinet of Northern Ireland that such a transfer of powers is not justifiable and [the appointment of an Advisory Commission to help the Secretary of State] is basically undemocratic.

The Faulkner statement at 11 a.m. paralleled a statement made by Mr. Heath in London. Direct rule it was to be: Mr. William Whitelaw would be appointed Secretary of State, an Advisory Commission would be set up, and for one year—and possibly two—the 51-year-old Stormont Parliament would be, in the official language, prorogued.

The reaction was swift. Willie Long, the slightly ludicrous Yorkshire-born Minister of Education, complained how it was 'so tragic that such a great Prime Minister has let us down in this way'. Joe Burns, the bow-tied country boy from County Derry, harrumphed that Heath's action was 'typical of the way Britain placates its enemies and crucifies its friends'. And the ever-cultured John Brooke, son of old Lord Brookeborough, who had been Prime Minister from war-time until the early sixties, went so far as to compare Heath with Hitler and Faulkner with Dr. Schussnigg, the Austrian Chancellor at the time of the Anschluss. 'We will all keep together,' he intoned over the telephone in tones that were meant to sound Churchillian, but sounded more like a complaining county councillor, 'and we will look after the interests of our people.'

Nothing violent happened that night, thank heaven. But the Falls was full of rumours and fears, and the men in Short Strand, where I spent a short while late that evening, were worried sick. Short Strand and its few thousands pinned in by the loyalist masses to the east and the south, were the traditional hostage to Catholic good behaviour: any sell-out, and the Protestants would want to take it out on someone. In Short Strand they feared it might well be them.

The IRA was now in a dilemma. The province's Catholics, by and large, welcomed London's plan. Direct rule seemed to them to restore the equities they had missed for so long; it would ensure that gerrymandering and discrimination and police brutality and all the aspects of their one-party government they so abhorred would gradually melt away. There was no good reason, of course, for anyone believing this; but generally speaking that is the way the Catholic people felt. Chairman Mao would have detected a perceptible cooling of the water in which his fish of revolution swam. The Catholics were in danger, the IRA leaders felt, of needing the gunmen no longer.

So a plan was dreamed up by some of the senior men on the Belfast Brigade staff. In the light of the changed circumstances, they said, they wanted Dublin to order a four-week ceasefire. This would, they thought, indicate to the outside world, and to the Northern Catholics, that the IRA was highly responsive to what they saw as 'reasonable' political moves on the part of the British. Only two weeks before, after all, Sean MacStiofain, the Provisional Chief of Staff, had made a formal offer of a ceasefire to the British: he had asked for a withdrawal of the British forces to their Belfast and Derry barracks, the abolition of Stormont, amnesty for political prisoners and an acknowledgement of the right of the Irish to self-determination. (The British reacted stiffly to the offer, in spite of a patchy three-day truce which MacStiofain organised to show his 'good faith'. And then the 'truce' ended with no fewer than sixteen massive, well-prepared explosions, and the stiffness, borne out of justified scepticism, was proved reasonable.)

This time the brigade staff men who wanted a cease-fire wanted it 'for real', as they said. The leaders of the second and third battalions in Belfast wanted peace; only the commander of the Andersonstown battalion, the first, wanted to continue with the war. Late on Friday evening Seamus Twomey and his senior staff met in a house in Andersonstown to discuss the position: Twomey, sensing the disagreement, travelled down to Dublin to see MacStiofain, leaving the North in an expectant and hopeful mood. He returned on Saturday. The word came back with him: the war would go on. The hopes were dashed. MacStiofain had relented only slightly: in view of the changed circumstances, he said, he would be willing to restrict his killing to soldiers alone: he would run down the bombing campaign and restrict the border murders of policemen and UDR men. But basically the campaign would go on as before.

The militant Protestants displayed their anger at the British scheme as soon as the weekend was over. They did as they had always threatened: they stopped the Province, as they were well able, in its tracks. The tactic which most seriously disrupted normal life was their decision to call every single Loyalist out of the power stations. The result was the almost total loss of electric power in Ulster and the shutdown of most industries that were wholly dependent on electricity.

It was a cold March day when they started their boycott, and most of us huddled by peat fires in the dark and cursed them under our breaths. But it was, in all fairness, a thoroughly responsible demonstration of an understandable rage. No one died as a result of their protest, but every one had time to think why they were protesting. And the bare bones of their situation did seem monstrously unfair: the loyalist community of Northern Ireland had sat back, it seemed so often, while bombs exploded and gunfire raked across the buildings and the fields that were part of the fabric of their little country. They sat back and they took it, with remarkable, praiseworthy stoicism, for eighteen long months and more. Ted Heath made a single trip across to tell them of his admiration for their courage and their patience: and then he rewarded them by taking away their police, their courts, their prisons—and their government. Small wonder the Loyalists were a bitter people that weekend.

And the army didn't help. Part of the package which Tuzo and Carver had worked out at Downing Street was that there would be an immediate change in military policy. We learnt the phrase quickly enough: there was to be the adoption of a 'low profile' in the Catholic areas.

Raids would cease; arrests would be reduced to as few as possible, and then only for specific offences; the practice of patrolling in the Catholic areas, night and day, would cease. But on the other hand, the soldiers divined, there would have to be increased wariness in the Protestant heartlands. All of which had the result, as one turbanned loyalist lady put it to me that Sunday, of making the Protestants feel as though they were Catholics, which is not the most healthy condition for the Loyalists.

'The soldiers used to come down our street in groups of four or five,' she said almost wistfully. 'They never had batons or anything like that. We used to give them tea and they would stand chatting us up when our husbands were out. It was really great—they were grand fellows. But now look what's happened. Down here it is just like the pictures we see of Ballymurphy or the Clonard. Friday night we had *nine* of them come down our street, all in a long line. They all had steel helmets and their plastic visors were down and they were carrying batons and rifles and gas masks. They really looked ready for a fight. I told them they had come to the wrong place.'

It was another of those decisions that made no friends, that made a great number of enemies and that helped destroy such little good will as there remained. The decision to adopt a 'low profile' had the effect of alienating the Protestants and forcing the UDA and all the kindred loyalist gun groups out into the open; it enabled the IRA to regroup and strengthen and widen its areas of influence to the point where most Catholic heartlands became rigid 'no-go areas'; and it led, inexorably, to political pressure for a massive military operation later in the summer. Had the army remained as tough in March as it had tried to be in December then, one can imagine, the no-go problem would not have arisen to the same extent, the UDA would have found the going considerably tougher than it eventually did, and the need for the operation that was called Motorman might not have arisen.

Stormont came to its official end on Tuesday, March 28, the second day of the loyalist walk-out. It was both a melancholy occasion, and an impressive one. Fifty-one years of an historic kind of government had no more to show, it seemed then, than just eighty-four bulky, blue-backed, gold-blocked volumes of the Official Report. The solid silver mace that had watched over all the proceedings—except for the time that one irate member had tossed it across the floor and wounded an opponent on the ankle—was to be locked away in a velveteen-lined box, as though all its watching had come to practically nothing.

Less than twenty-five members turned up for the final meeting. The questions down for answer that day were as pedestrian as any: John McQuade wanted to know how many Southerners had been recruited into the Ulster Youth Employment Service; John Laird wanted to ask something about the internal workings of gelignite sniffers; Josh Caldwell was worrying on about the RUC Reserve. The Committee for the Museums Bill was to sit, and the Births, Marriages and Deaths Amendment Bill, the Fire Services Bill and the Firearms (Protection of the Public Interest) Bill were to be debated. There was also down for debate the attempt by Gerry Fitt to have the Criminal Justice (Temporary Provisions) Act repealed—an attempt that would of course have proved fruitless, but which would have assured opponents of the dreadful law some access to the newspapers—had any one cared to listen.

But none of this was to be. The eight-page order paper that had been printed the week before for March 28 was scrapped: in its place was substituted a single pale blue sheet that said, as protocol demanded, that the Leader of the House should propose 'That this House, at its rising this Day, do adjourn until Tuesday, 18th April, 1972.' The technicality was required by procedure: in fact, the House was to stand adjourned for more than a year, and as one wise old Hansard reporter said to me in the corridors, now echoing dumbly, 'This Parliament is never going to meet again. Maybe some Assembly will sit in the Chamber some day, but it will be nothing like the Parliament we have today.'

The thin blue order paper was handed around in the chamber as the Speaker read out the motion: members who were present signed it, as though it was the menu at their Last Supper. The speaker, Ivan Neill, read out two letters of resignation, one from Desmond Boal, the other from his horny-faced, docker-disciple, John McQuade. Boal was to say he would take part in future, 'in no charade, no matter how elaborate, at the whim of an insensitive and clumsy Westminster. Having therefore no desire to remain a member of a parliament that does not exist, I tender you my resignation.' Few would regret his going. John McQuade, who would leave the dignities and privileges of Parliament for the humble work on the docks from which he had come, said more simply: 'An example has already been given to the country of members who have been prepared to draw their salaries for a representation they refused to perform. [He was speaking of the SDLP, most of whom continued to take their pay, constructing an elaborate argument to justify doing so, while they were boycotting Stormont in protest at internment.] I am not going,' McQuade continued, 'to follow that example.'

Brian Faulkner then rose to make a brief statement on the adjournment debate: the Speaker thanked everyone and was thanked in turn for his pains; and then the Deputy Speaker and Chairman of Ways and Means, a little-known character called Walter Scott, proposed the motion. William Beattie, the Paisley lieutenant (Paisley himself being absent, regrettably—his presence would have given a cheerless affair some sense of occasion) proposed a division: and the votes were cast—20 in favour of adjourning, 4 against. 'At fifteen minutes past five o'clock', the final Hansard reported the event, 'the House adjourned.' Stormont was no more.

Outside, a huge assembly of Loyalists, many waving the Red Hand, none at all carrying the Union Jack, had gathered to hear their leaders. Brian Faulkner joined forces under the columns of the Stormont façade with Bill Craig and William Beattie, normally his arch-rivals, to tell the thousands below him that 'we understand the feelings that have persuaded you to come out here today. We do not only understand those feelings, we share them.' None of the trio was an orator of any standing: only Ian Paisley could have whipped that mob up into an angry frenzy that afternoon and perhaps, since the army was strung fairly thinly around that day (though Lt.-Colonel Derek Wilford was there with 1 Para, keeping a distinctly 'low profile' and turning away whenever he saw the Bloody Sunday press pointing him out) it was just as well he was away.

As it was, once the strange trinity had waved its goodbyes, the mob, said to have been the largest seen in Northern Irish history, drifted quietly and sadly back to homes still chilled and darkened by their brothers' strikes. They must have known their Parliament was finished, and that change of a kind they could scarcely imagine was on its way: but that Tuesday night they seemed to be taking it all in a dogged, resigned sort of way, just as though there was no point in complaining any more.

I I

Arrival and Departure

William Whitelaw arrived in Belfast on the following Saturday. He was, by comparison to those who had gone before, an impressive figure. He seemed very large—Stormont politicians, we suddenly realised then, were all really rather small men, either in physique or in intellect, and usually in both. Whitelaw's size, his warmth, his apparent total competence came across hugely well as he appeared at a brief press conference and then on television to explain to the people of the North his hopes and his fears.

He was a little wooden, a little nervous perhaps; but small wonder—this 54-year-old Scot, a gentleman farmer with lands in Cumberland and a background well rooted in the British establishment, seemed to have all the wrong attributes for dealing with the Ulster people, and must have known it well. The *Belfast Newsletter*, as tiresome as usual, noted that Whitelaw was a Roman Catholic—a member of no less than one of Britain's 'leading Catholic families' it informed its loyal readers. But he wasn't, of course: he was of the same Presbyterian stock as most of the *Newsletter* readers' ancestors, though he was careful, when taxed on the 'irrelevant' question of religion, to point out that he was, in fact, a member of the Church of Scotland, and thus 'technically neutral'.

His nervousness disappeared over the next few weeks, when he came to spend three days of every seven in his office in Stormont Castle, with a small group of able junior ministers—David Howell, Lord Windlesham (who *was* a Roman Catholic) and Paul Channon. As that first sense of unfamiliarity began to evaporate, so the first realisation of the freshness of his approach, the rationality of it all, the end of doctrine and the beginning of

234

common sense, began to shine through. Early in April, for example, he was faced with the question of whether or not to reimpose Mr. Faulkner's ban on marching: his arrival had already angered the Unionists to breaking point—might he not soften the blow a little by permitting them to have their Twelfth once more? His reasoning, as we heard it that April, just before the Republicans were due to hold their traditional Easter parades, was, after two years of doctrinal rhetoric, almost incredible.

'Were I to order the ban relaxed now,' he told us, 'I should be rightly criticised for over-hasty action. Instead, I shall wait for the Easter Weekend to pass and if things are quiet, I plan to meet the organisers of the various traditional marches to see if they think they can march in peace.

'If the organisers say they can, and if I am satisfied with the assurances I am given, then I will consider lifting the ban.' And he went on, in more general tones, but no less refreshing to those of us who listened. 'There is sometimes a rather fine dividing line between what is a march and what is not. Sometimes the law has been broken in a way that seriously aggravates the offence; sometimes the offence, though it has remained an offence, has been mitigated by peaceful behaviour, good humour and a limiting of marching to areas where offence is not given to other people, and a readiness to observe scrupulously the directions given by the police.' One could hug him for his sense. Even the grammar was an improvement.

The Whitelaw touch, that almost magical, ineffably graceful touch that spoke of peace and reconciliation and goodwill and harmony and decency and patience and care, was to win him many friends over the coming weeks. Within days a powerful consortium of former Stormont ministers came to pledge their future allegiance and help to the oyster-eyed, slightly untidy giant of a Scotsman who now held sway where their ancestors had before. Robert Porter, Robert Simpson, Robin Bailie, Roy Bradford, Willie Fitzsimmons and a half-dozen more made it clear they would not stand in his way. Brian Faulkner, who retired to his pleasant little estate in County Down to give affable interviews to visiting journalists, became one of Whitelaw's more helpful spies on the ground. They spoke by telephone at first, however, to avoid notions of over co-operation, which might have been bad publicity for both. Faulkner, on whose side I argued constantly in countless Irish bars, was a community government man from the start. His affinity with Whitelaw was natural.

Roy Bradford criticised the new London mandarins for 'totally alienating the responsible Protestant community' and suggesting that 'the battle of Belfast will not be won on the playing fields of Eton or Winchester'. (Whitelaw was a Wykehamist, Howell an Etonian and Windlesham had his schooling at Ampleforth.) Bradford may have been correct in his latter, snide suggestion; but he was wrong in saying that Whitelaw was alienating the responsible Protestants. It became very clear within a few weeks of his arrival that anyone who was at all responsible, be they Catholic or Protestant, was flying to the one source of responsibility that loomed above them, Willie Whitelaw. It was only the irresponsible who were being alienated—and their alienation became a frightening reality within a matter of only five weeks after the British take-over.

The end of Stormont marked the most profound of all the changes that we had seen in the two years of the troubles. It was the beginning both of an irreversible change in Northern Irish politics; and of a sinister increase and variation in the type of violence. It also meant a change for me: a few days after Stormont had ended I was told that, come autumn, I was to be posted to the United States. I had to accept that I could not expect to see the political changes through to their conclusion.

I was, in many ways, delighted with the new posting. In the two years I had then been in Belfast I had watched and listened to history being made in the streets and the little houses of Ireland, North and South. Now with the arrival of the British politicians, much of what was to change Northern Ireland's future would happen behind rigidly closed doors in fashionable parts of a distant English city, and would only see the light of day when the cabinet papers of the time were published towards the end of the century. History would still be made, but with less drama and less public awareness. It was, I felt, a good time to go.

But in the four more months I stayed on in the province, reporting on the apparent successes and the failures of the new men, so the violence on the streets became both dramatically worse and dramatically different. And so while I would not feel competent to report on any further of the political developments of that summer, two aspects of the continuing troubles, which White-law was to try so hard to resolve, still fell within my purview. I saw them grow and burst, and I would leave Ireland dreaming of them. There was, first, the rise to truly frightening power of the Ulster Defence Association. And there was, second, the renewal in strength of the IRA, and their eventual, though temporary, humiliation by the British through that gigantic effort known as Operation Motorman.

The Protestants began the terror.

John Hume, the generally level-headed Derry politician, had long considered the notion of a massive loyalist uprising as a 'myth' and had demanded on many occasions that the British call the loyalist 'bluff' by taking a radical step they had been hitherto afraid to take because of their fears of loyalist reaction. Generally speaking, the army agreed with Hume, and many times during 1971 I was to ask General Tuzo and his commanders for their assessment of the degree of Protestant-inspired violence, and of the potential for Protestant terrorism. With few exceptions, the word from Lisburn in 1971 was that the Loyalists were un-armed, unskilled and, in plain language, not dangerous at all.

I went to see Tuzo again in mid-March, about a week before the Initiative. His assessment was then very different. 'I hope the politicians in London will give us a day or so's notice before they announce their plans,' he said. 'Frankly, I'm not sure how we will be able to cope if Craig and his chaps don't like what they hear.' Was the myth at last exploded? 'I think that would be fair comment,' Tuzo replied gravely—and he went on to out-line how the army and police were only now beginning to build up their files on the known ultras on the loyalist side. The British were making the same cardinal error as they had in the case of the IRA—they were preparing to fight the enemy only when the enemy had been given time enough to prepare himself and flex his muscles. Tuzo had watched the early Craig rallies with 'deep concern'; he could see another irregular army forming under his very nose, and had neither the orders nor the strength to do anything about it. 'I just hope they give us a bit of notice,' he repeated morosely, as I left his room.

But even so, the army's assessment of the Protestant strength was, it later turned out, still woefully inadequate. What caused Tuzo to suffer palpitations was the evidence of structure in the Protestant community—structure evidently urged in the leaflets we had seen in the Shankill bars in August and accomplished by the time Craig began his Vanguard rallies. And he was also worried by the growth of a number of rowdy Protestant street gangs, known as the Tartans. These groups, fifty to a hundred strong, could be seen after any football match, leading the crowds towards each and every possible confrontation with the Catholics. They wore—boy and girl alike—blue denim tunics and jeans, heavy boots, studded belts and, as evidence of their affiliation, a tartan scarf dangling from a hip pocket. They looked little different from the 'skins' or 'bovver boys' that had afflicted cities on the mainland for the past two years: but their rhetoric was wholly sectarian, their capacity for nuisance of the most severe kind was immense. Nonetheless the army, which had built up fairly full dossiers on the Albert Tartans and the Pass Tartans and the Young Newtons, and the other gangs, still tended to classify their kind as 'politically motivated hooligans'—capable of causing huge disruption and massive bitterness, but not, happily, armed with 'serious' weapons.

That reporters had been taken off to see cases of freshly-made rifles the previous winter did not impress the army; that an actively militant Protestant could be arrested at Aldergrove airport with a sub-machine gun failed to impress them, too. Rumours of gelignite smuggling from Scottish ports began to filter down to street level failed to sway the official impression.

They admitted the capacity for disruption, for rioting, for burning, for tragedy, for the very worst type of hooliganism was vast; and there was, too, they agreed, a formative structure of an army; but there were in the army's view no weapons of consequence, no gelignite in quantity and 'frankly, not much of a will for terrorism on the Protestant side' as one soldier put it. Nonetheless, Tuzo's colleagues did talk of asking for the eventual internment of the gang ring-leaders once they had been identified, and once real trouble had begun.

It was five full weeks after Whitelaw took over in Belfast that the Protestant trouble started. It began, as the troubles themselves had begun in October 1968, in the maiden city of Londonderry.

On the afternoon of Saturday, April 22, there was a small rally of members of the local branch of the Loyalist Association of Workers, outside the Guildhall. A few Catholic youths from the Bogside sauntered down William Street to have a look at their enemy, rarely seen in numbers to the west of the Foyle. By all accounts the Catholics behaved themselves: but suddenly a detachment of the Loyalists, bent on teaching the Bogsiders a lesson, turned and chased after them for a fight. Inevitably, stoning began—the first time for many, many long months that Protestants and Catholics were stoning each other.

It was a vicious fight: police were called in, and one luckless sergeant was hit and removed with a fractured skull. But what was most dangerous of all was that, for the first time in the disturbances so far, the rioting spread eastwards across the river and into the normally sober section of Derry, the Waterside.

All that night there was stoning and barricade-building in the tiny Catholic area of eastern Derry, the Gobnascale estate, and the Protestant Lisnagelvin nearby. There was even some shooting —about ten shots were fired, probably at loyalist vigilantes who were put on duty by the LAW officers after the first rioting started. It was, however, the police who had said where the shots had been directed: no reporters were on the ground to be certain.

Rioting continued through Saturday night and into Sunday; and, by unhappy coincidence there was inter-factional rioting at other places in the province—most notably in Lisburn, where

Protestants from the previously tranquil Old Warren Estate began a night and a day of burning and destruction. Bernadette Devlin and Michael Farrell staged a microscopic demonstration near Long Kesh, and were stoned for their troubles by a mob of Tartan youths. The weekend, while less violent than many, had an unpleasant odour to it. The message from the Protestant camp seemed adeptly spelt out by Martyn Smyth, the dog-collared Orange leader who told a rapturous assembly in Newtownards that there most certainly was a place for arms in their coming struggle. 'I disagree totally with those who tell us we cannot stoop to such a level,' he said. 'The Church of Rome still plans the domination of Ireland, not simply as a Nationalist Ireland but as a Roman Catholic Ireland.' And with the arms the Orangemen might be permitted to carry, Smyth said, this domination of Ireland should be fiercely resisted. Whoever had said Ulster was not the scene of a religious war?

If the weekend of April 22 was bad, the week that followed was worse. On the Wednesday police on the Albertbridge Road battled for several hours with mobs of Tartan youths who had gathered on the fringes of a Vanguard rally. Those of us who had become so used to racing around West Belfast late at night to seek out the truth behind the incidents in the Catholic quarters in the West now had to relearn the geography of the East: the Ministry of Defence 'tribal map' of the city which was published in various editions that year, showing Protestant as pink, Catholics as brown (though orange and green, more suitably, in the later editions) came in handy for finding the trouble zones.

On Thursday the disturbances switched back to the west, with Tartan youths attacking Catholic houses in the Limestone Road. Catholics complained that neither soldiers nor police came to their aid—though many would have hardly blamed them. On Friday we were all back dodging bricks and petrol bombs on the far side of the Lagan once more. Severe rioting, with shooting and more petrol bombing went on all through Saturday and into Sunday, until a combination of an engineer regiment, the Paras and a steady downpour of Belfast's soothing rains put a temporary end to the angry passions.

That weekend saw the 100th British army unit sent to the turbulent province. It also saw the publication of a truly frightening report on the state of the Protestant army—a report which the BBC rightly chose, in view of the weekend incidents, to lead most of its Saturday bulletins. Nigel Wade, the shaggy-maned Australian with whom I had spent so much of Bloody Sunday, had been taken off by a group of Londonderry Loyalists, to see their private army in a barn out in the countryside. He had been enormously impressed. The standards of discipline and drill he reported were fearsome: the training was near superb; the numbers said to be associated with the group—the leaders said 10,000—were unprecedented. And the guns—brand new, freshly oiled, loaded British army rifles—were indisputably real. This, Wade concluded, showed the Protestant militants were no longer a group of 'politically motivated hooligans'; this was a world far removed from the Tartans and from the tedious speechmaking of the old Stormont politicians. This was an army—a well-equipped, well-trained, potentially powerful army that could and should be of immense concern to the Ulster authorities.

In the characteristic way of beaten pressmen, those of us not taken to the barn were somewhat sceptical. The BBC, which does little exclusive reporting of its own, was happy to replay a major story that could safely be attributed to a Fleet Street source. The rest of us had to rely on the reaction of others to the report—and since no one in authority seemed ready to say he believed Wade's story we had to print low-key denials that smacked of sour grapes. In my case I quoted the army as saying that the '10,000-man armed force' was 'that familiar fictional animal'. We could hardly have been more wrong.

On Sunday, May 14, during one of the nastiest nights in recent memory—eight people died in explosions and gunfire in and around Ballymurphy, and it stopped only when paratroopers moved into the area in strength—the first major haul of loyalist guns was found. It wasn't a particularly impressive arsenal—just a few very old Czech Stehr rifles and a couple of thousand rounds of rifle ammunition. But the guns had been fired, and the houses in Springmartin, where they were found, had provided evident cover for a group of gunmen who undoubtedly had contributed to the carnage of Ballymurphy that weekend.

And that night, we at last saw the Ulster Defence Association—representatives of that '10,000-man force' out on the streets. Just before midnight members of the UDA, young men dressed in parkas, jeans, balaclava helmets and dark glasses, gathered in the small triangle of lanes between the Upper Shankill and Crumlin Roads in West Belfast—an area known as Woodvale. They were there to put up barricades of wood and oil drums and 'borrowed' cars, both in order to protest to Mr. Whitelaw about the continued imprisonment of what the community called their 'political' prisoners—meaning, generally, a small number of Protestants put in gaol for attacking Catholics, a crime which the Loyalists said should be regarded as 'political'—and to make formal and noisy objection to the 'no-go' areas of the Bogside and the Creggan. They warned they would go on barricading enclaves at weekly intervals for five more weeks. If Whitelaw had done nothing by then—by mid-June—every part of loyalist Ulster would become, they said, a permanent no-go area.

The members of the UDA looked more than a little ludicrous. Grown men and spotty youths, crammed into jeans three sizes too small for them, wearing sunglasses in the dead of night, keeping up barricades with the tacit understanding of the army at first that there would be no attempted incursion by the forces—it all seemed too pathetic for words, like Toytown gone mad. And in 24 hours, as promised, the tired toy soldiers reinflated the tyres of the cars and lorries, neatly dismantled their barriers and waved in the traffic once more. The protest could hardly have looked and sounded less ominous: yet all of us knew in our bones it was the worst of all the events that had happened since direct rule had begun.

Whitelaw was faced with a grim tally-sheet when he returned that next Monday from his weekend in Scotland. The dead and the wounded and the bombed, he concluded, were one matter; but the erection of Protestant barricades, he told his officials, was something else. For the first time since his arrival, his colleagues in the office painted for us a picture of a dejected and deeply worried man. What, he was clearly wondering, would he do with the UDA next week—and the next, and the next. Should he permit them to build more barricades? Should he have the army tear them down? Should he try and talk them down? Or should he give in to their demands, free their prisoners and move in to the Bogside and the Creggan? It was an agonisingly difficult choice to make.

By Thursday he had decided. The barriers were not to be tolerated, and if they went up again, he ordered General Tuzo, they must come down. So we all waited tensely over the Saturday night to see if the UDA leaders were as good as their word, and if, in fact, a confrontation with the army was inevitable.

At a minute or so to midnight, we learned the worst. Members of the East Belfast UDA were out in force, the police said, in Willowfield, an easily defended enclave between the Woodstock and Castlereagh Roads. They were building barricades just as they had the week before.

A girl from one of the loyalist women's groups, who provided a convenient passport into the by now quite frightening Protestant back-streets, took me across the river. In Willowfield as we walked down the road all the signs pointed to trouble: lorries were being stolen and pushed across the narrow street entrances: half-bricks, 'clod stones', angle iron and bottles were being stockpiled in strategic positions behind the barricades; and hundreds of crudely uniformed men were marching and wheeling, practising karate chops into the cold night air, flourishing their rubber bin lid shields and waving axe handles as clubs. There was a subdued, sombre, but violent note in the antics of the men: it was comedy no longer.

The army stayed away until dawn. At about 4.30 a.m. men of the Royal Horse Artillery and 2 Para moved in at speed, knocking the barriers flat and dealing briefly and roughly with any UDA man who dared to fight. Half a dozen shots were fired—by whom and at whom providing ample controversy for the locals to discuss with us when we came down in the wake of battle—but there was no serious violence. 'I'm beginning to think those Bogsiders were right,' one old loyalist woman told me that morning. 'Those bloody Paras go mad whenever they come onto the streets.' The 'madness' had cost no lives, however; and it rid Belfast of one 'no-go' area, just as Whitelaw would have wanted, within the hour.

But the trouble was not over for the day. Enraged and humiliated, the UDA across the city decided, after a hurried midmorning meeting, to barricade the rest of Belfast. Accordingly, the most efficient of the Belfast UDA, the Woodvale (efficient possibly because their CO was a Londoner, Davie Fogel, who had been an 'excused boots' soldier in his national service days, but was now passionately converted, for no reason we could ever discern, to the country he called 'Ulstah'), was ordered to blockade the Shankill—and by mid-afternoon six massive barriers, many of burned buses, were strung out across the main road, and a fight of what seemed massive proportions was breaking out.

In the rush to set up the new barriers, an innocent man who was tinkering with his car was killed: a telegraph pole, hit by a stolen bus, fell onto him and crushed him to death. The tragedy of the killing, which seemed again so utterly futile, was lost in an evening of fighting with soldiers and police. And then that ended at midnight when the UDA, after holding talks with the army that finally dignified them as a negotiating force, ordered their barricades removed. The army worked side by side with the ragged reactionaries until the task was done.

I went along to see the UDA leadership the next day. First, after a long and frustrating series of telephone calls, I was told to drive to a house in Rosewood Street, off the Crumlin Road. A tall and lugubrious man with an old and dusty face that belied his youth, met me there, and ushered me, after frisking me first and demanding a complicated series of identifications, into his sitting room, where I spent an agreeable half hour chatting to his young daughter. Finally, as he peered through his window at the terraced house opposite, he announced that the UDA council meeting was over for the week: I could go and see whoever it was that lived in the house. He wouldn't say who it was; his daughter, though, told me his name was 'Jim'—she thought his second name was 'Anderson'.

Across the road lived two tired-looking men—one was indeed called Anderson, was the owner of the house, and of a large and unfriendly Alsatian dog; he sat back, talking only occasionally, and nodding with what was meant to be sage agreement. The other man was a fierce, red-headed and voluble individual called Tommy Herron, who gave a vague indication of what we could expect next.

Another small enclave would be sealed again in one week's time, Herron said. There were arms inside the organisation—indeed he had one in a holster there that moment—but they would hesitate to use them. The army, however, 'should not interfere with next week's peaceful gesture' or—and the implication was heavy—there would be trouble.

It had scarcely been a meeting with the romantic, cunning forces of rebellion. Anderson and Herron were little better than common thugs—no improvement at all on the Twomeys and the Adamses they sought to destroy on the other side. Anderson, it seemed, was almost wholly stupid: Herron was a braggart, a ruthless, unstable man with just enough faint charisma and powerful friends to assure him of support in his movement. They did not appear clever enough or imaginative enough, we thought, to run their band of men efficiently for very long—remembering of course, that an illegal army can have all the guns and all the men it needs, but is quite worthless unless it has imagination and flair in its organisation, and a goal upon which all its leaders agree and with which all its members concur.

During the next few weeks, helped partly by a visit to a loyalist hero, Gusty Spence, in Crumlin Road gaol, and partly by a couple of sympathetic articles I wrote about loyalist prisoners, I made some few friends within the UDA, and was able to see their small 'clubs' and something of their training and the court-rooms and their 'romper room' where they punished their wrongdoers. Only one man impressed me at all—a jockey-sized officer in the Woodvale UDA called Ernie Elliot. 'Duke' Elliot had lived in West Belfast all his life. He had gone to schoolboy parties with Tony Doherty, the Catholic from Ardoyne who went on to become one of the more flamboyant and more brutal members of the Provisionals. Elliot had been an early member of the Civil Rights Association, and had joined in anti-discrimination marches. And yet here he was, a half-colonel in the UDA, working with Davie Fogel to build barricades just like those in the Bogside—but as a protest at the Catholic barriers and as a deliberate taunt to the British army. How could he justify it?

Elliot and Fogel—who was also no fool—told reporters in some detail of their feelings, of their hopes for reaching eventual detente with the Catholics, and of the possibilities of working with the Catholic Ex-Servicemen's Association and with NICRA to improve the lot of the working men on both sides of the peace line. But they always made us swear not to publish their feelings while the trouble continued—the men 'up there', Elliot used to say, jerking his fingers towards the Crumlin Road homes of Herron and Anderson—were not very sympathetic.

Elliot, however, was not to last long in the UDA. Later that year, long after I had gone, he was found dead, shot in the head. He had been killed by rival members of his own organisation whose desire for improving relations with the Catholics was rather less. Fogel, too, had quit the UDA and had fled to London. And Tommy Herron, a man I was never to like, was killed a year later, also probably by his own people. It was a turbulent world.

My own relations with the UDA fluctuated. In early June, after another weekend of barricade-building—the army by now had decided to leave the Protestants alone, aware of the destructive potential of any confrontation—I phoned Herron at home, and he gave me the information that he, Anderson and another officer would be going to Stormont next morning to see Mr. Whitelaw—the first-ever meeting between the secretary of state and the new army. I duly reported the news in the paper.

Next day I was told in no uncertain terms that I had 'betrayed a UDA confidence' and that I would be 'punished'. I was telephoned late that evening and asked to come down to stand 'trial'. I demurred politely, though I fancy my voice was trembling. For the next several days, anonymous phone calls and abusive, threatening letters became the order of the day. Everyone in Ireland seemed to know of my disgrace—porters in hotels would recognise me and mutter darkly of my coming 'trouble'; other reporters would come back from meetings with the UDA, warning of my imminent 'beating' and saying that if they were me they'd get out while the going was still good, and other helpful advice.

In early July came the most massive of all confrontations between the UDA and the army, over the question of the barricades. Both sides met, en masse, in Ainsworth Avenue, off the Shankill Road. On one side were five thousand UDA men, all masked, all armed with clubs, all looking and sounding very ugly indeed. On the other side, behind a row of barbed wire, were three companies of soldiers and about twenty-five reporters —I was there, but I had to lurk behind an armoured pig for most of the time as Tommy Herron and his cronies had the annoying habit of trying to rush at me and drag me into the crowd to receive some rough justice at their hands.

General Ford, and the newly appointed 39 Brigade Commander, a taciturn former Argyll commander, Brigadier Sandy Boswell, negotiated the peace with Herron and Anderson, Fogel, Elliot and a few others. Fogel, who was still 'on my side' in my dispute, winked broadly: the others waved their fists. That evening seemed far more personally menacing than a threat to the peace and stability of Northern Ireland. In the end, happily, both Ulster and I escaped total destruction. The talks between Herron and Ford ended with a compromise (Ford said later he had 'no doubt' his forces would have 'had to kill a lot of people' to avoid being over-run in any confrontation); and relations between Herron and I suddenly improved enormously. By August I was taking tea with him and his friends in the lounge of the Europa, and shaking hands like old friends. It was curious to hear later on that he had been shot.

It would be ungallant indeed to pretend I was the only member of the family who entertained occasional fears about survival. My

wife, Judy, went on two successive Wednesdays to the local
post office, to be held up at gunpoint on both occasions. The first
time was when the till was raided by a pair of pistol-toting men
from Andersonstown. The second time a week later the army was
planning to catch any raiders by waiting and watching from an
adjoining house. My wife went into the post office, two youths
with machine-guns rushed in behind and pushed her against the
wall and poured the contents of the till into a pillowcase. The
army saw it all from their house, but couldn't get out because
their door was jammed. They finally broke through as the Provisional raiding car roared off, and pumped a magazine-full of
bullets in through the rear window, hitting one of the IRA men
in the back. Judy, stoical as ever, lay flat on the floor as the
soldiers raced about, pumping out lead and cursing the sticking
door.

During the months until the UDA showdown, the IRA
had been by turns active and quiescent. There had been an
amazing orgy of bombing that had reduced lovely old town
centres like Derry to a total shambles. There had been encourag-
ing peace moves from the community—half a dozen Bogside
women stole the hearts of the country by coming across to
Belfast to see Mr. Whitelaw to explain their plans for a peace
movement in the ravaged city. (One of the women, Mrs. Mary
Barr, said she was 'a little scared' when she had gone into the
sitting-room at the Castle to see him, but thought later he was
'a real gentleman'.) And there were hopeful signs in Belfast,
too, where an ecumenical movement of housewives, Women
Together, attempted to rally the ladies of the city to stand up
against the IRA.

Although neither of these movements got anywhere on their
own, they did lead the Provisionals to offer, twice, to stage a
ceasefire. The first time they offered—on June 13—Whitelaw
refused to meet to discuss their peace plan. But the second time—
and the SDLP leaders, the independent MP Tom Caldwell, a
senior Stormont civil servant and a Dublin TD had all acted on

this occasion as intermediaries between the IRA and Mr. Whitelaw
—a deal was settled. There were no pre-conditions, like the ending
of internment or the withdrawal of troops to barracks. The intermediaries had had their way—John Hume and Paddy Devlin
had flown to see Whitelaw in London on June 15, and had told
MacStiofain and David O'Connell, who they saw later in Donegal,
of British agreement to respond to an unconditional ceasefire,
and that Whitelaw might actually see the IRA men in person.
And so the IRA announced from Dublin on June 22, an indefinite,
unconditional ceasefire. It would begin on June 26, a minute after
midnight. The British, Whitelaw said, would 'obviously recipro-
cate'. It looked as though there might be an historic peace. I
even got out my files and wrote a 1500-word retrospective on the
two-year campaign which had begun—so I calculated—with the
killing of the policemen in Crossmaglen in 1970 and which would
finish, once and for all, on June 26, 1972. But I was very, very
wrong.

Six people died in IRA-related killings over the last weekend
before the truce: Monday, the final day of war, was in many
ways the fiercest of the entire campaign, with precise and
efficient sharpshooting continuing until a soldier was shot dead
less than two minutes before midnight. But came twelve
and there was, in fact, a blessed peace. Soldiers travelled into
Catholic areas without their flak jackets and, in some cases, without their guns. Policemen were issued with memoranda telling
them to halt arrests under the Special Powers Act. The tension of
the last months evaporated like fine perfume and people came
down into the towns to shop, some barriers came down and the
atmosphere lightened with every day that passed. Only the
UDA confrontation upset matters: the UDA were quick to
realise that this had the prime effect of persuading people, especially those outside, to blame the militant Protestants for 'stirring things up' when at long last there seemed a chance for peace.
So for a while even the UDA went on short time.

Sadly, it was to be only a very brief peace. The IRA men
went to London by RAF jet to see the British ministers—a meeting that seemed, at the time, to have historic significance, but

which, in the event, served only to reinforce Protestant mistrust of Mr. Whitelaw. And, on Friday, July 7, came the beginning of the end with an event that came to be known as 'Lenadoon'.

Lenadoon Avenue is marked on the tribal maps of West Belfast as containing the homes of both Protestants and Roman Catholics. It lies on the western side of Andersonstown, in an area where gentility tries hard to mix with the ugliness of the IRA's prime training ground—and where, in many cases, gentility succeeds. On Friday, July 7, however, the residents of Horn Drive, which is at the lower, Protestant end of Lenadoon Avenue, were horrified to learn that the Central Citizens Defence Committee was planning to move some sixteen Catholic families into empty houses there, houses which had been vacated by Protestants earlier in the summer. Since the Protestants had gone largely as a result of intimidation, there were reasonable grounds for apprehension among those remaining. The CCDC decided to go ahead, nonetheless.

Next morning the Public Protection Agency, the CCDC, the army, the police and local Catholic and Protestant leaders met to discuss the plan. A UDA spokesman warned that any Catholics who took up residence would be burned out—it was no threat, he said, but a statement of fact. The Catholics protested that the government had agreed to let them have the houses— they had nowhere else to go, they pleaded. The army commander said that since tempers were so obviously inflamed he would have to 'review the situation' and his permission would be needed before any rehousing could begin. A decision was postponed for 24 hours, with the Provisional IRA threatening to rehouse the Catholic families themselves if the army did nothing about it.

Came the Sunday afternoon, and a lorry loaded with furniture began to wind its way down the hill of Lenadoon Avenue towards the houses in Horn Drive. It was the Catholic caravan beginning. At the bottom of the hill was an army barricade, behind which were a platoon or two of soldiers, the press and a handful of members of the UDA. The army commander had vetoed the move. So a thousand Catholics preceded the van and, once down the hill, tried to force it past the troops. There were ugly scenes at the knife-rests, with soldiers and Catholics fighting hand to hand, with Seamus Twomey, the IRA commander, arguing bitterly with the army officer and warning him of 'the consequences' of his action. Gas was fired; rubber bullets began to whine through the air. The tension grew and grew until finally, in mid-afternoon, Twomey told the army commander that in his view, as chief of the Belfast Brigade, the British had 'violated the truce'.

Twomey retreated up the hill: there were warning whistles, and the IRA opened up with rifles and automatics. The British—and the reporters—retreated to defensive positions and, after some initial army confusion, perhaps understandable, the soldiers were given orders to fire back.

Within the hour the Provisional Sinn Fein headquarters in Dublin issued a brief announcement: the ceasefire was over. It had lasted for just thirteen days. That the IRA hard men like Twomey had not wanted it at all was borne out by the sudden explosion of two bombs in Belfast, only hours after the announcement of the resumption of war. Some men in the organisation, it was clear, had planned a new battle from the very beginning. All cynicism about the IRA had been amply borne out by the events at Lenadoon and after.

Mr. Whitelaw was now, after this latest disaster, under truly enormous pressure to avert the civil war which everyone seemed to think, was now terribly near. The UDA, he had discovered, was a huge and dangerous animal, with real teeth and sharp intentions. The IRA had enjoyed thirteen days regrouping and rearming. Hundreds of men had been released from Long Kesh as gestures of conciliation—and many of them were back in their old jobs in the movement once again. Should he upset the Catholics and raid the strongholds? Should he confront the UDA and risk massive loss of life? Should he do nothing at all? The turning point of mid-July was, in retrospect, the most anguishing of all.

He had no need to look for an answer. One came, horribly, quickly, ruthlessly, twelve days later on the afternoon of Friday, July 21, since generally known as Ulster's Bloody Friday. Simon

Hoggart and I, both in the city at the time, wrote a long account of the most brutal of all bombing assaults, some of which follows:

At least eleven people, including two soldiers, a little girl and a young messenger boy were killed, and nearly 100 civilians were taken to hospital with injuries in Belfast yesterday, during one hour of concentrated bomb attacks which were seemingly deliberately aimed at civilians. Last night the Belfast Brigade of the Provisional IRA accepted responsibility for all the explosions.

After 2.45 p.m., when the bombings began, and for much of the afternoon, Belfast was reduced to chaos and panic. Girls and men wept openly, hugging each other for safety in the main streets as plumes of smoke rose around them and dull thuds echoed from wall to wall.

It was impossible for anyone to feel perfectly safe. As each bomb exploded there were cries of terror from people who thought they had found sanctuary but in fact were just as exposed as before.

Thousands streamed out of the stricken city immediately after the attacks and huge traffic jams built up. All bus services were cancelled and on some roads hitch-hikers frantically trying to get away lined the pavements.

Those who watched television that night will probably never forget what they saw: amidst the smoking ruins of the Oxford Street bus station, one of the civilian targets which the IRA had chosen for their demonstration of power, they saw a man—or rather, a heavy, bloody chunk of dirty meat—being shovelled, hacked and carefully shovelled, into a polythene bag, by a tearful soldier. That Belfast was a place where men had to be lifted up with shovels must have seemed a dreadful, degrading fact to anyone who watched. Those of us who saw the event itself—even those of us who had nurtured an occasional friendship for some IRA men—were appalled by the carnage. Gerry O'Hare, the IRA's chief press man, and a contact I liked and had some sympathy for, wept openly himself that day, as he confronted

Twomey, the hatchet-faced bookie who had organised the affair. 'What the hell am I going to tell them now,' O'Hare cried at the commander. 'Do you really want me to say that all of the bombs had warnings?' Yes, Twomey said, tell them there were warnings. And that was what O'Hare said when he phoned later that evening. 'The Belfast Brigade,' he said, before I shouted at him to stop being so pompous, 'gave warnings before every bomb. . . .' and his voice trailed away in shame. 'You just can't say that, Gerry!' I said. 'This is over the top. You can't go on making excuses. This was deliberate, wasn't it—admit it, he planned it to kill civilians, didn't he? Didn't he?' There was a mumbling and silence from the other end. 'I can't say,' the wretched youth replied, 'I'm sorry, I truly am,' he mumbled, before putting down the phone.

The British response was quick and dramatic. Seven major army units were flown into Northern Ireland within a week— bringing the force levels to some 21,000 men, higher than at any time since the beginning of the century. The motorways began to hum with armoured convoys that rushed to and fro between Belfast and Londonderry. Army helicopters blackened the skies from dawn to dusk. Generals conferred in Ireland and in London. Ministers met for long hours at a time. Officials were unusually tight-lipped. And then, at 9.30 p.m. on Sunday, July 30, White-law issued a statement from Stormont Castle.

There would, he said, be 'substantial activity by the security forces in various parts of Northern Ireland during the night'. People, he warned, should stay off the streets. The message, he stressed, was merely precautionary and it was not indicative of 'any immediate move by the troops'. But as we looked out of our windows to see the long columns of dark-green armoured cars pushing through the dusk, we knew it could not be long before that 'substantial activity' would begin.

It was called Operation Motorman, and it was the biggest and certainly most impressive operation by British forces since Suez, sixteen years before. It resulted in the total demolition of the barricades surrounding the IRA no-go areas, and the establishment of a powerful British presence in all the regions in which the Provisionals had previously held sway for so very long.

It started, as had the war, in Derry. For the first time in Ulster history, the British came in tanks. Huge Centurions, weighing 50 tons apiece, were unloaded at the dead of night from the destroyer HMS *Fearless*, which had steamed into Lough Foyle in the evening. Their cannons reversed, their bulldozer attachments firmly down in front and their inscription 'Royal Engineers' touched up with fresh white paint, the Centurions roared and smoked through the sleepy city and up to the Bogside barriers. There was virtually no resistance: within three hours the operation, which had begun at 4 a.m., was over. Two men—one an IRA rifleman and the other a petrol bomber, according to troops —were shot dead in the advance. But by 7 a.m. all the barriers were down and the tanks clanked back to the docks. Bulldozers— huge green engineers' bulldozers—rumbled in from assault craft out in the river to finish the task: a few IRA booby traps were dismantled; most of the loyalist barriers were brought down; an antique Browning machine gun, once owned by the Official IRA, and a Boyes anti-tank rifle, were found. Five Derrymen were held for questioning.

Across in the capital eleven battalions, including marines, paratroops, artillery, cavalry and tractor-equipped engineers moved in to what the army nicely termed the 'troubled areas' at dawn. Within seven hours, with some occasional good-natured help from the citizens (some of whom, now feeling a little safer from the IRA's intimidation, even painted out IRA slogans on the walls), the operation was over. The whole of Northern Ireland, it could be safely reported, was clear of Catholic barricades. And the UDA, who now had what they had wanted for so long, agreed to remove the few barriers they had standing. The month of August could begin with not a single barricade in existence, and with the fair smell of hope, at long last, in the Ulster air.

There was more killing, of course—much of it in the form of 'knock in the night' assassination that had begun in January 1971 and had slowly risen to become the major cause of violent death in the later part of 1972 and 1973. The Protestants—the UDA, the UVF and smaller more vicious groups, could be credited with most of the assassinations: the IRA, who conducted interrogations and court hearings with depressing frequency, and had a rough and violent honour code and punishment list, were responsible for many; and the special reaction forces of the army, who carried out secret intelligence operations, could possibly have been responsible for three or four. But assassination became a common way of death only after I had left—it was a new chapter to be reported by new men.

There were occasional protests, too, about Motorman and its uncomfortable after-effects—the occupation of Belfast schools, for instance, and the army's use of a Gaelic football ground as a camp. But these were essentially minor matters, for what really happened in the wake of the Operation was a steady, dramatic and blissful decline in the number of explosions in the province. The IRA ceasefire had produced a rapid and temporary lightening of the public mood: Motorman, steadied and maintained the public cheer. It was, for me, an appropriate time to depart.

I left, finally, on Saturday, September 9—two years and six months since I had been sent for that 'short weekend'. There was a small party in the Europa on Friday night, as I said my sorry farewells to dozens of friends. Much of the day I was on the telephone, talking to men who would not talk to each other—in fact, men who would have killed each other as soon as talk to each other—wishing them good-bye and good luck, and being wished the same in return. Then next morning, deathly early, I loaded my car and my belongings into the British Rail ship in Donegal Quay, waved a fond farewell to two friends who had motored down to see me off, and watched sadly as the boat moved carelessly off down the Lagan and into the lough and past the skyline I had come to know—and love—so very, very well.

The boat, it turned out, was filled to the bulwarks with Orangemen, off to England for a two-week spree. One of them, a red-headed man of about thirty, came across to me as I was leaning into the breeze, gazing at the fading city.

'You're Simon Winchester,' he said, with the accent and approach moving me to wonder if I was going to leave not just Belfast, but the boat as well. I confessed that I was. 'Well, I just wanted to say that I heard you were leaving us. I didn't agree with all that you said, but I thought you were fair. Really I did. You said a lot of things I didn't like, but me and the boys,' he gestured over to a grinning pair of men across the deck, 'we thought that on the whole, you were pretty fair.'

And so it was with an exquisite mixture of pleasure and sadness that as the city faded to a smudge on the horizon I turned and went below to sleep out the journey. Ahead lay the M.6 motorway and, eventually, Washington.